Th

MW00465168

The Moonlit Path

Reflections on the Dark Feminine

FREDERICK GUSTAFSON, EDITOR

NICOLAS-HAYS
Berwick, ME

First published in 2003 by
NICOLAS-HAYS, INC.
P. O. Box 1126
Berwick, ME 03901-1126
www.nicolashays.com

Distributed to the trade by
Red Wheel/Weiser, LLC
P. O. Box 612
York Beach, ME 03910-0612
www.redwheelweiser.com

Library of Congress Cataloging-in-Publication Data
The moonlit path : reflections on the dark feminine / Frederick Gustafson, editor.
p. cm.
Includes bibliographical references and index.
ISBN 0-89254-064-8 (alk. paper)
1. Goddesses. 2. Mary, Blessed Virgin, Saint—Symbolism.
3. Femininity—Religious aspects. 4. Liminality—Religious aspects.
5. Black—Religious aspects. I. Gustafson, Fred.
BL473.5.M68 2003
291.2'114—dc21
2003005094

VG

Cover and text design by Kathryn Sky-Peck
Typeset in 9.5/13 Sabon

PRINTED IN THE UNITED STATES OF AMERICA

09	08	07	06	05	04	03
7	6	5	4	3	2	1

The paper used in this publication meets the minimum requirements of the
American National Standard for Information Sciences—Permanence of Paper
for Printed Library Materials Z39.48–1992 (R1997).

CONTENTS

Illustrations

Acknowledgments

Grateful acknowledgment is made to the following people and organizations:

Liguori Publications for permission to reprint excerpts from *A Human Search: Bede Griffiths Reflects on His Life* by John Swindells, copyright © 1997, Liguori Publications.

Georges Borchardt, Inc., for Editions du Seuil for permission to reprint excerpts from *Hymn of the Universe* by Pierre Teilhard de Chardin. English translation copyright © 1965 by William Collins Sons & Co., Ltd., London and New York: Harper & Row, Inc. Originally published in French as *L'Hymn de L'Univers*, copyright © 1961, Editions du Seuil.

Riverhead Books, a division of Penguin Putnam, Inc., for permission to reprint "Raise Up Those Held Down" from *The Bond Between Women* by China Galland, copyright © 1996, China Galland.

Thomas Kinsella for permission to reprint "Dark One" from *The Tain*, copyright © 1970, Thomas Kinsella.

Farrar, Straus and Giroux, LLC, for permission to reprint excerpts of "To Sadness/II" from *Fully Empowered* by Pablo Neruda. Translation copyright © 1975, Alastair Reid.

Laura DuBois for permission to use her photo of the Techno Cosmic Mass in honor of the Black Madonna.

Janet McKenzie for permission to reprint her painting "Jesus of the People," copyright © 1999.

The image of The Black Madonna of Einsiedeln, Plate 3, between pages 110 and 111, comes from Eberle Qualitätskarte Nr. 2.346, Verlag Beat Eberle, Einsiedeln.

liminal
barely perceptible

Preface

Murray Stein

Murray Stein, Ph.D., is a diplomate Jungian analyst and member of the Chicago Society of Jungian Analysts. He is the author of several books including *Midlife: A Jungian Perspective* (Spring, 1983), *Jung's Treatment of Christianity* (Chiron, 1985), *Practicing Wholeness* (Chiron, 1996), and is the editor of *Jung's Challenge to Contemporary Religion* (Chiron, 1990). He is currently president of the International Association of Analytical Psychology. He practices in Wilmette, Illinois.

As we enter further into the new millennium, it seems wise to reflect on the Dark Feminine. Since caution is a good part of valor, we would be remiss to plunge ahead without at least taking a respectful glance in the direction of the "other side" of the Great Goddess who is increasingly finding expression in our personal and collective lives.

Patriarchal rigidity is crumbling throughout the world. To be sure, there are regressive attempts to restore the hegemony of the Father in every possible fashion—social, cultural, religious. But history is not with the fundamentalists of patriarchal patterns. What this struggle implies is that with the resurgence of the feminine there will come a vast mixture of dynamic interactions between masculine and feminine thrusts and tendencies. Turbulence is the hallmark of this phase of transformation in the underpinnings of social and cultural forms. Liminality is upon us. The Dark Feminine will show her face in many combinations of image and emotion within the personal and collective spheres of life.

The essays in this volume comprise an attempt to begin naming and charting the transformation that is underway in our time with respect to the re-emergence of the feminine after several thousands of years spent in the shadows. It is not that the Dark Feminine is a product of

masculine hegemony and dominance during this period, however. This
aspect belongs to the archetype of the feminine itself; it is a part of the
inherent polarity within the pattern. It would be a strategic error, therefore, to suppose that accommodation on the part of patriarchal structures would ameliorate or subdue the negative force ("negative," that
is, depending upon one's point of view) of the Dark Feminine. The
larger reality is that the dark side of the feminine must enter into a
dialectical dance with the bright side and work in the direction of an
integration of these opposites within the feminine itself. This is the
internal struggle within the feminine *per se*. Beyond that, there is the
masculine-feminine dynamic, which is still in the earliest phases of entry
into a further dialogue.

What can the individual do in the face of such massive changes
transpiring within the collective, which today is truly universal and
global? We need to realize that this moment of historical transformation is also taking place deeply within each of us individually. The
Dark Feminine is as much "in there" as she is outside of our psyches
and in the world around us. In fact, it is precisely at the point of contact between psyche and world that the Dark Feminine has its home,
so that when we find this factor within us we are also engaged in the
politics of the world. As without, so within. The transformation takes
place personally as well as collectively, and here we can truly affirm
that the personal is political. Many of the essays in this volume speak
to this point.

It is a truism that those who have made contact with the Dark
Feminine within, through dream work and the inner work of active
imagination, are prepared to meet the Dark Feminine in the world.
Only a fool would be fearless in the face of the Dark Feminine, but
deep previous acquaintance with the inner feminine is the best possible
antidote to panic when this aspect is confronted in collective milieus.
This is not only due to a greater familiarity with the face and force of
Her mystery, but more because inner work transforms the dark by
bringing it into contact with individual consciousness. A glimmer of
light in the darkness promises the dawn of a new day.

Can we foresee today a personal psychology and a collective culture where the fully integrated polarity of the feminine—dark and light
contained in a single form—stands on an equal plane with the fully
integrated polarity of the masculine? For this we have to look out sev-

eral generations (at least) into the future. Most predictions of the future feature technology—new flying machines, miracle medicines, time travel, etc. Cultural prognostication is more rare. Although all predictions of futures end up far from the mark, it does not hurt to imagine them. The images generated may have a guiding function. Culturally and psychologically, then, let's imagine a future world in which a quaternity would define the boundaries of the human soul: Light and Dark Feminine in constant interplay with light and dark masculine energies, creating, re-creating, interacting in a dynamic balance of forces. With respect to the individual, this would amount to free and open communication between conscious and unconscious aspects of the psyche, a life not without stress and suffering to be sure, but one of growing awareness and steady movement toward wholeness. On the cultural level—covering social, economic, artistic, and religious dimensions—it would mean intelligent tolerance for paradox, tough-minded respect for important differences, and compassion for the alien other in our midst. If this is utopian, so be it. At least it is not without recognition of the dark. It is a goal worth striving toward. This volume is a contribution in this direction.

Introduction

Fred Gustafson

Fred Gustafson, D. Min., is a senior analyst with the Chicago Society of Jungian Analysts and a graduate of the C. G. Jung Institute of Zurich. He is a clergy member of the Evangelical Lutheran Church in America and in full-time private practice as an analytical psychologist and pastoral counselor. He is the author of *The Black Madonna* (Sigo Press, 1990), *Dancing Between Two Worlds: Jung and the Native American Soul* (Paulist Press, 1997), and contributing author of *Betwixt and Between: Patterns of Masculine and Feminine Initiation* (Open Court Press, 1987).

During the 20th century, the Western world experienced an increased awareness of the feminine archetype—of the damage its centuries-long suppression has created, as well as the psychological and spiritual liberation the feminine has brought and promises yet to bring in the 21st century. This liberation most obviously affected women, but on a broader scale it has challenged the attitudes and ways of doing business for all people and throughout the varied institutions and structures of our entire culture. Women are claiming more presence and respect in the business world, men are more in touch with their feminine side, and a deeper ecological awareness is steadily increasing.

Yet, hidden in this awakening is a shadowy concern. It exists in our very notions of what the feminine archetype is. In our efforts to "bring the feminine back," we can just as easily err in assuming the feminine principle is now being adequately integrated. What we are only now beginning to become conscious of is the side of the feminine archetype that cannot, nor does it even necessarily desire to, fit into the existing cultural structures. That other side has best been described as the Dark Feminine.

In the last quarter of the 20th century, writings dealing with this shadowy side began to emerge, and readers were seeing names like

Lilith, Kali, the Black Madonna, Morrigan, Guadalupe, and Tara. Here are reflections of the darker side of the feminine that are not so easily contained in cultural perspectives, psychological theories, or religious dogmas. With the return of the feminine and the gains this brought for everyone comes the opportunity to journey more deeply into Her darker side and bring to the light of consciousness—personally and collectively—what promises to be a deeper and more passionate and compassionate awareness of ourselves as human beings set in the context of a great cosmic story.

About three years prior to the publication of this book, a woman client of mine who had read a great deal of the literature on the Dark Feminine and who was quite psychological in her view of life, asked a question during one of our sessions that had an edge of frustration to it: "Just what is the Black Madonna about, anyway?" My answer was quite spontaneous without much forethought: "Everything that is not white." What more was she really asking, and what was I really trying to say? Her question and my answer became the template for this book.

In putting together the many authors who contributed to this work, I presented this story and asked them to try to answer her question and unpack what was behind my answer. Both the question and answer were broad enough to give room for thoughts, experiences, dreams, and personal imaginings of the Dark Feminine. I wanted a broad representation and I wanted men to get involved in this discussion. Fortunately, I feel the strong material in this book accomplishes both objectives. Here, you will get perspectives from Irish, Jewish, Hispanic, American Indian, Christian, and Hindu contexts. You will also find a wide range of personal experiences and theological and psychological viewpoints. I have included a chapter from the writings of Pierre Teilhard de Chardin in which he describes a mystical experience of his confrontation with matter in the form of a woman, as well as one by Father Bede Griffiths describing his experience of the Black Madonna after his stroke when he was in his eighties.

So what do hydrothermal vents, Kali, and the destruction of the World Trade Center Towers in New York have in common? What does the seductive Lilith of the Jewish tradition share with the seemingly benign character of the Black Madonna of Einsiedeln? And, what does it all mean for us personally and collectively for our times, anyway? Why do we, and should we, care?

This work is an attempt to do a walk around, to circumambulate the theme for the purpose of drawing closer to it. It is obviously not exhaustive. In fact, I hope that the diversity of presentations found here will stimulate the far-reaching dimensions of what the Dark Feminine is about and cultivate further discussions.

We now live in a time when manifestations of the archetypal feminine confront us at every turn. Reconsiderations in how we educate, how we do our economics, how we use the environment, do our politics, conduct business, live, and die are all being challenged. What we mean by the Dark Feminine is playing a major role behind all of them. In the last analysis, each individual will have to answer for him or herself how the missing feminine is trying to be played out in his or her life. Finally, I encourage you to answer for yourself just what the Dark Feminine in particular means, and what relevance it has for your psychic evolution and for that of your own culture.

The Dark Mother, the Dark Earth, and the Loss of Native Soul

Fred Gustafson

Since 1984 Fred Gustafson has been active in the ceremonial life and culture of the Lakota Brule Sioux on the Rosebud Sioux Reservation in South Dakota. This chapter is adapted from a symposium titled "Restoring the Temple: A Celebration of the Feminine Spirit," given at the C. G. Jung Institute in Chicago, Illinois, April 27, 1996.

In 1972, my wife and I visited a small village in central Switzerland known as Einsiedeln, which has a Benedictine monastery that contains in its interior a chapel dedicated to a Black Madonna. Within this chapel is a statue of Mary holding the Christ child. Both are black. I remember how it struck me then as a curiosity, interesting, something I had never seen before. But since we had just arrived in this country where I was soon to begin a course of study that I knew would last several years, what concerned me most was getting settled and figuring out how to support my wife and two small children. So the visit to the Black Madonna of Einsiedeln was dampened by a case of survival anxiety and an eagerness to get going with my life. Consequently, I did not think much more about it. Then, about a year later, someone recommended I read a book titled *Myths and Symbols in Indian Art and Civilization* by Heinrich Zimmer. It was here I first read about Kali of India in a way that deeply touched me. He writes:

> To us of the West, brought up under the shadow of the Gothic Cathedral, where the benign figure of the Blessed Mother, immaculate, is uncontaminated by the darker principle . . . India's Mother, eternal India's horrific-beautiful, caressing-

murdering . . . symbolization of the totality of the world cre-
ating-destroying eating-eaten one, seems more than difficult
to love. Yet, we can discover if we will pause, something that
will speak to us of a wonder beyond beauty and ugliness, a
peace balancing the terms of birth and death.[1]

It was a short jump from reading this to remembering my visit to
Einsiedeln. What about Her, I wondered? Fifty kilometers down the
road from Zurich was another black goddess right here in the
Western world. She, too, is black, though hardly horrific and murdering on first appearances anyway; but was she not of the same
archetypal constellation? Indeed, she was, I concluded. I spent the
next two years working on this, or rather, letting it work on me.
What came into focus was that the Black Madonna of Einsiedeln,
along with her some 475 counterparts, is a compensatory psychic
figure for our times. She is an expression of the need for psychic-
spiritual wholeness in an age and culture that has far over-valued the
place of reason and the need for causal explanation. She represents
the unofficial acceptance of the fickle nature of life, doing just what
She pleases but always with a wisdom that is beyond our reason and
with a goal beyond our vision. She carries an aspect of life that is not
only important but also essential for a full perspective on the rhythm
with which life moves. Not to know that rhythm—the process of
birth, life, and death—would doom anyone to naiveté and sentimen-
tality, and to a world of undernourished piety. If you have ever seen
a picture of Kali, you know there is nothing sentimental or naive
about Her. So to talk of reclaiming the feminine in our time is not
enough. We must also reclaim the Dark Feminine. Whether speaking
theologically of God or psychologically of the Self, the issue of
psycho-spiritual wholeness is identical. In either case, the Black
Madonna, or the archetype She represents, is key.

After finishing my studies, I returned to the United States and, as
time went by, began asking myself, "Where is She here?" There were
no indigenous icons here of a black goddess that were not replicas of
some other place in the world. Though Our Lady of Guadalupe in

[1] Heinrich Zimmer, *Myths and Symbols in Indian Art and Civilization*, Joseph Campbell, ed.
Bollingen Series VI (New York: Pantheon Books, 1946) p. 215.

Mexico is considered the "Patroness of All the Americas," she is mostly a national emblem for Mexico itself.

Strangely, though, and to my surprise and delight, I did find one outstanding piece of artwork that stands at the entrance/exit area of the San Francisco International Airport. It is titled "Peace" and is by the Italian artist Beniamino Bufano. The viewer cannot avoid noticing that the obvious shape of this piece of art is a missile that has been changed to represent the garment of a very black, goddess-like figure who holds in the folds of her dress a ceramic representation of St. Francis. Here was the structure of war now converted to the image of peace.

Just as Bufano's statue has the Dark Feminine embracing St. Francis who was so very close to the land so, too, in a parallel manner, the Dark Feminine on this continent is first and foremost the land itself that also desires to embrace us. The Dark Feminine land of North America has been in an undifferentiated form for us, collectively, over the last 500 years. For a differentiated relationship to the dark earth to develop, we must face issues about how we treat this land, the Earth in general, and the earth we are made of, attitudes we have toward those who seem to carry earth for us, and what our spiritual attitude toward matter itself is. The Western spiritual system has not been very receptive toward matter, a fact for which we have paid dearly.

For the most part, matter has been seen as dead, without life, waiting to be used in whatever way we can. It is easier this way, for then we can place ourselves outside the complex web of inter-relationships that the Earth as our Mother provides. To the indigenous mind, the Earth is a living Mother that holds us all in unity. To see Her as dead disembodies our spirituality and places humankind at the center of the universe, which leads to an anthropocentric view of life. This is to say that all of life takes on value only by how it is seen in relationship and benefit to humankind. We will forever war to determine whose anthropocentric view is most valid. Meanwhile, the Earth and all its inhabitants suffer.

It is easy for the modern mind to pretend a distance from nature and hold to this anthropocentric point of view and the distorted spirituality that goes with it. But no spirituality of any worth is disconnected from the Earth. We will pay some price, at some level—both within ourselves and in the body of the Earth, itself—for turning our backs on this reality. About this Jung says:

The Platonic freedom of the spirit does not make a whole judgment possible; it wrenches the light half of the picture away from the dark half. This freedom is to a large extent a phenomenon of civilization, the lofty preoccupation of that fortunate Athenian whose lot it was not to be born a slave. We can only rise above nature if somebody else carries the weight of the earth for us. . . . The dark weight of the earth must enter into the picture of the whole.[2]

It is presumed in Western cultures that matter is evil or, at best, somewhere between evil and good, thus requiring others—usually minority groups, indigenous peoples, and our own dis-eased bodies—to carry the dark weight of the earth for us. Those who carry this weight have taken a blow in our attempts to keep the idea of matter incarnate from our theological and psychological doorsteps. This is easier to see theologically from the perspective of our two thousand year history, but psychologically this split is still true in our times. For the most part, modern psychology sees psyche as confined to the limits of ego with its personalized history and adaptational problems. There is little recognition of one's personal soul being related to a world soul or having or needing a relationship to the earth. Western psychology has not yet embraced the idea that most of our psychotherapeutic ills are the direct consequences of being separated from a living environment conceived as home.

Matter is the Dark Mother that has been rejected. Matter, *Mater*, Mother. Matter is living, a fact that is consistent with the discoveries of modern physics. With this view, all of matter is in motion, vital with energy, and part of a system of force fields that link any given aspect of matter with the entire cosmos, challenging the mind to open itself to a vast understanding of inclusiveness and unity. The notion of incarnation must include these two principles so that the entire cosmic landscape can be seen as one ecosystem providing the mind and the imagination with a chance to see this wonder in a tiny particle of matter and to see matter in the fullness of this wonder.

It was no accident that with the rise of the patriarchy, not only the feminine side of life would go into decline and hiding but any connection

2 C. G. Jung, "A Psychological Approach to the Dogma of the Trinity," (1942/1948), in *Psychology and Religion: West and East*, *The Collected Works of C. G. Jung*, vol. 2, Bollingen Series XX (Princeton: Princeton University Press, 1958/1969), § 264.

to our indigenous past would be held down or cut off along with those peoples who hold to this way of life. Since "indigenous" means "to be born from within" (Greek, *genes*, meaning "one born," and *indu*, meaning "within"), to loose our connection to this past means to lose any sense of our Earth as the womb and home that brought us into being. Meanwhile, matter, in a sense, becomes a forgotten "relative." The stage is set for a non-incarnational view that strips soul from the Earth. And so we wonder why we despair and why violence is so easy! How we view the notion of incarnation is a most important issue for the Western world, and it moves beyond solely Christian definitions. It is an issue for everyone insofar as we need to re-think, re-imagine and re-claim a living relationship to a living Earth. It is also important because whatever view we take determines how we will place ourselves in the creative structure and what value we give to creation and ourselves as part of it. It is important because it determines the limits of how sacred or unholy we believe matter to be, how at home in the Earth we feel, and how ethically committed we are to healing the suffering of the Earth.

If the land is living, and if we truly know it to be so, we would treat Her carefully, responsibly, and compassionately. If the Earth were like our Mother, if this is more than a New Age sentiment or fantasy, then we would never treat Her as we do. As one very spiritually tired man told me years ago, "If I could only let myself do what I needed to do, I would get down and hug the earth."

I believe there is sadness in the land today. Collectively, we are weeping, though I believe it is unconscious. I believe this collective grief is the dominant unexpressed feeling of our modern Western world, though one would not think so from looking at the surface and the nightly news. My belief is based on the idea that we cannot do violence to another person or people without simultaneously doing violence to ourselves. It is based on the idea that we have been terribly separated from any serious notion of the Earth as a living Mother and Grandmother and, like any child, we grieve that loss. And finally, because a living connection has been lost with the Earth as Mother, we have also lost connection to our indigenous soul that is born from the Earth, itself, and knows how to live upon Her and honors Her laws. In  other words, we grieve for the loss of the feminine, for Her darkness expressed in the soil we have rejected as unholy, and for having our own native soul severed from Her body that has nurtured and given us definition for four billion years. This is beyond gender, race, or age. We are all under this yoke. For this we grieve. If there is to be any restoration of the Earth and ourselves as part of it, we must deal with our grief.

The sadness of which I speak may best be understood by two of my own dreams:

> I saw as though I were a bird looking down on the earth, a town as it might have been a century ago. At the same time, I saw an Indian on a horse who had fought a war in this town. I wondered what he wondered. He was on the edge of the community, and I wondered if he were now a statue or landmark. He seemed sad.

From the perspective of a bird, we can understand history, sort the pieces, and extract perhaps a new morality based on the lessons of the past. But at the moment of our living, we are not birds, we are humans playing our parts, doing what we know and not always so wisely. From the privileged position of time, we can have a spiritual overview of yesterday's collision of two cultures. The town here is the stereotypic community on the North American soil and represents the routine mainstream of American life that had its roots of origin in the need to tame the wilderness and conquer its native dwellers. The American Indian was the spiritual custodian of the Earth, who stood in the way of Western expansion that demanded land ownership by the common person who, in turn, supported the notion of free enterprise. The dominant culture wanted to accomplish its "manifest destiny" at any price. Even a superficial reading of the history of this process leaves us keenly aware of how bloody and dishonorable it was, disrupting the land and illegally seizing the properties of thousands of peoples who were then relocated on forced marches to lands unknown to them. Wiping out vast herds of buffalo, bringing the indigenous people to near starvation and violating promises and treaties were further transgressions.[3]

---

[3] It is estimated that originally between 50,000,000 and 75,000,000 buffalo roamed the Great Plains from Canada to Mexico. By 1896, there were 256 left, not counting some 600 in various places in Canada. The American Indian's sacred vision of the buffalo was as female; they were the Mother, the provider of all of life. With the near annihilation of the Mother, a severe blow was dealt to the feminine principle of this land and has been coded into our history in a way that most of us discount. It seems so long ago. Yet in 1994, outside the small community of Janesville, Wisconsin, a white female buffalo calf was born. It was the first in several decades and totally unexpected. It drew thousands of pilgrims and curiosity seekers, most of whom were non-Indian.

All of this was not so long ago. To those in the dominant position, it does not seem to matter, for it is as though these occurrences are lost, forgotten, faded in time, and have no consequence today. But feelings do not die on the battlefield or with the passing away of the veterans of those battles. I remember a conference I attended in 1983 on Native American Spirituality during which a white clergyman and a Santee Sioux were talking at the dinner table one evening. As they shared their stories, the clergyman said his great-grandfather had fought against the Sioux during the New Ulm uprising in Minnesota in 1862. The Santee then responded to his new friend by telling him that his great-grandfather had also fought in that same battle and had been hung along with 37 others in Mankato, Minnesota, for participating in that war. It was the largest legal mass hanging in U.S. history. Now, here they were, 121 years later, trying to make connections across time. It was certainly not so long ago for these two men. There are peoples today on reservations throughout the Americas who had grandparents or great-grandparents or known distant relatives who died in such battles and massacres.

So now we can be as a bird and take flight and try to see from a higher perspective what happened, and how we are all affected by this history. The Indian in my dream is sad and is on the edge of the town as a mere landmark. He was not included in the emergence of American consciousness. For this, everyone has paid a price. That Indian on the edges of the present social structures is that fundamental, indigenous, "native being" in everyone's soul, without whom we are all less than human.

The second dream I had occurred in the early fall of 1990 about four months before the centennial memorial of the Massacre of Wounded Knee to be held on December 29, 1990 at Wounded Knee, South Dakota:

> I was talking with a man who knew nothing about the Massacre of Wounded Knee on December 29, 1890. What I shared was nearly accurate to what I had indeed heard about in waking life. I stated that Chief Big Foot brought his band of Minneconjous to Wounded Knee and gave himself up to the Federal troops. Such surrender was expected as a result of the fear developing in local white settlers over the Ghost Dance that was spreading throughout the Plains. I went on to

say that Big Foot and his people turned over their weapons as ordered. No one really knew how the shooting started. An estimated 250 native men, women, and children were gunned down. At this point, I began to cry. I went on to say that on a nearby hill, Hotchkiss guns opened fire. I wept hard and said that I did not realize I had such feeling in me for this event. I related that some wounded crawled to the ravines and died there. I wept harder and said the final tragedy was that the wounded Indians eventually were taken to a church in Pine Ridge for medical treatment because the local hospital was filled with wounded federal troops. Christmas decorations were still up with a Christmas banner that read "Peace on Earth Good Will Toward Men." I wept and wept.

My dream of Wounded Knee shook me with a clarity few dreams do. It was a dream that took me to a place of too many deaths. Yet, it was a dream absent of guilt and blame. Rather, it spoke to a deeper awareness of the profound grief lying deep in the American psyche as it is related to the tragic and failed relationship between the dominant culture and the Native American communities.

At one level, as Carl Jung said, the conqueror takes on the attributes of the conquered. Immigrants and their descendants are in search of a home and are affected by the character of the land and its ancestors. But, on another level, the attitudes and actions one takes toward this land and its original inhabitants affect not only them but also oneself. In other words, what we have done to someone else, we have also done to ourselves.

December 29, 1990 marked the centennial year of the Massacre of Wounded Knee. This event itself has become a metaphor for what has happened to all of us. It was not only the final *coup de grace* of the original way of American Indian life; it also portrayed the attitudes of 500 years of American Indian/non-Indian relationships. It reflected the dominant culture's broken relationship to the Earth as a Mother and toward those who were closest to Her in their way of life and spiritual attitude. Here was lived out the misunderstandings, the hatred and fear of the unknown, the failed promises, and the indiscriminate killings. If this event were treated like a collective dream, then what is before us is not just a violation against the actual Indian who dwelled upon the American soil, but is also a violation against that same figure who lives in the collective psyche, that indigenous, Earth-connected side of every person of every nation and religion that is the source of soul and all spiritual attainments. The violence known at Wounded Knee is not just against the Indian but also against the Indigenous One who lives within us all, and from whom we have been cut off. The Indian can take on a symbolic reflection of oneself as an essential person. To kill or repress that side leads to soulless indifference, a condition that seems to afflict our land today. Even the mass burial at Wounded Knee continues the metaphor of how we as a nation have indiscriminately and without regard buried our love and respect for the land, our interconnections to one another and all life, and what it basically means to be a human being, that is, one who is from the *humus*, or soil. Here, the feminine spirit was defaced one more time. With reference to Dee Brown, author of the book *Bury My Heart at Wounded Knee*, it is safe to say that the non-Indian heart was also buried at Wounded Knee.

We are a guilt/blame society. We go out of our way to avoid, minimize, or deny our complicity. We concentrate our attention on it in such a way that it leaves us consciously immobile and unconsciously resentful. It is true that reparations need to be made for the violations done. Wrongs need to be righted and justice restored. We do need to experience that kind of healing guilt that can bring transformation of consciousness, individually and collectively. But even more fundamental and restorative than guilt is the recognition of grief, the condition of seeing, admitting, and weeping! Sadness certainly can acknowledge the guilt, but moves on to the loss behind it. Blame includes one part of the population, guilt another. Grief includes everyone. It is the common element we all share and that can join us in the mutual task of finding our way back home to the Earth. What is unique about my dream was the overwhelming presence of weeping and sadness and the absence of guilt and blame.

The spiritual hunger for and fascination with indigenous peoples today reflects this need to reconnect to the Ancient One, the Ancestral Elder, the aboriginal within us. For us to forget such roots can result in sentimentalizing the remaining, active six hundred million indigenous peoples of the world and thus avoid the responsibility that also belongs to the rest of us. What is critical for our times is that we of the modern, technological world remember that we are also indigenous peoples at some forgotten place within ourselves and have a living, indigenous past with a sense of intimately belonging to the Earth. "Indigenous" really refers to an attitude and a way of life that respects the unity of all things and the according relationship to the Earth. The Dark Feminine face of the sacred has no problem accepting this.

The return of the feminine divine is something we all wait and long for, even those who resist Her coming. Men also carry sadness for the lost feminine, if only unconsciously. In India, it was partly Kali, in Switzerland it was the Black Madonna of Einsiedeln. Here, in North America, the feminine divine is seen in the land itself, in the indigenous peoples close to Her and in our own struggle to reclaim native soul. She is reflected in our long historical struggle over 500 years to become conscious of Her repression and cry for consciousness.

Twenty years after my first viewing of the Black Madonna of Einsiedeln, my wife and I and a few close friends were able to revisit that sacred shrine. When I stood before Her this time, I knew a lot had changed. For me She was neither a Catholic nor even a Christian phenomenon. She was an icon of the mystery of life and death that defies definition and speaks to the deepest layers of the human soul. She was no longer a curiosity. I was no longer a tourist. Now I was a pilgrim.

At the Threshold of Psycho-Genesis/
The Mournful Face of God

Cedrus N. Monte

Cedrus N. Monte, Ph.D., is a diplomate Jungian analyst, graduate of the C. G. Jung Institute, Zurich. Her research into synchronicity and the creative process is published in the anthology, *Images, Meanings and Connections: Essays in Memory of Susan R. Bach* (Daimon Verlag, 1999), and was funded by the Susan Bach Foundation. Her most recent research, *Project Soul Dance: Accessing the Unconscious through Movement*, is also funded by the Susan Bach Foundation, and is an inquiry into the relationship between psyche and soma through the study of *Butoh*, a Japanese dance form.

The secret is that only that which can destroy
itself is truly alive.
—C. G. JUNG[1]

For some of us, if not for all, meaning in life periodically finds its way through a piercing and deadly darkness. Hopelessness and despair can descend like a toxic cloud, even in the midst of a joy-filled life, a life of spiritual discipline and intent, and dedication and commitment to conscious growth. Dark moments can strike like a sudden, rending eruption from mysterious and subterranean places. Without warning, the crust of a forever-healing wound, or an old, insidious trauma is torn open unexpectedly, and we bleed again. We feel that we have entered into the abyss, body and soul. In the darkest of these times, nothing—no word, no prayer, no loving gesture, no therapeutic intervention—reaches the mark. Everything is lost, crumbled, and gray, pointless, our life hopelessly flapping in the maw of a terrifying yet welcome annihilation.

---

[1] C. G. Jung, *Psychology and Alchemy, The Collected Works of C. G. Jung*, vol. 12, R. F. C. Hull, trans., Bollingen Series XX (Princeton: Princeton University Press, 1968), § 93.

How do we find our way through these darkest of spaces? Jettisoning a way out is impossibly dangerous, a too-heroic feat for this tenuous and precarious state of being. Remaining at this threshold of pain feels intolerable. And yet, given the grace of enough psychic ground, by staying with the intolerable dissonance, we can once again restore our faith and experience the rare jewel of equanimity. Here, at an unfathomable but fecund threshold, something can change, something new can come forth.

The Paradox

Faith that arises at points of near-unbearable suffering is a faith born by sustaining absolute paradox. Those who endured the Holocaust and the devastating events of the Third Reich have been able to communicate the profound meaning and acceptance of this paradox and provide us with unprecedented teachings. Innocent suffering in the Holocaust, as in Christ's innocent suffering, has helped to redeem humanity's ignorance and lack of true compassion. The unparalleled gift of such understanding shows us how to survive trauma of inexpressible dimension. In testimony of this, Dietrich Bonhoeffer writes:

> We cannot be honest without recognizing that we must live in the world "as if God did not exist." And so we recognize this—before God. God himself compels us to this recognition. So our coming of age leads us to a genuine recognition of our situation before God. God lets us know that we must live as those who get along without God. The God who is with us is the God who forsakes us. . . . The God who lets us live in the world without the working hypothesis of God is the God before whom we eternally stand. Before and with God we live without God.[2]

Others have also offered insights, quickening to paradox as a means toward spiritual and psychic regeneration. Robert Sardello at the School of Spiritual Psychology suggests that the explosion of the first atomic bomb traumatized our consciousness as a planetary people. Considering this situation, Sardello reflects:

---

[2] Dietrich Bonhoeffer, *Letters and Papers from Prison* (New York: Macmillan, 1981), pp. 145-146.

The explosion of the Hiroshima bomb in 1945 opened the crust of the earth and created an entry into the Underworld for all of humanity. The anxiety provoked by this event—a mythic occurrence—has profoundly disturbed ordinary consciousness. It has completely separated human beings from past spiritual meaning and brought unresolvable unrest, leading to indifference and to a preoccupation with comfort. That is to say, since this event, ordinary consciousness has lost its meaning.
What is the soul's response? It is the quality of stillness. The soul becomes completely quiet, for it has entered into the realm of death. . . . there to begin the task of learning how to be awake and fully conscious. It is a test. The aim of this test is to find whether the force of love, no longer arising from attachment to things in the day-world, can be born out of the soul itself. In other words, can love arise where there is nothing to love?[3]

According to Sardello, our task in facing the threat of total annihilation is to find a way to regenerate our world, both inner and outer, psychic and physical, through the power of love born not of existential security but of the inescapable presence of annihilation. Here, as well as in the example of Holocaust survivors, the presence of a lethal, traumatizing condition prompts and demands the emergence of an even greater vivifying force. A traumatic condition begs a bio-psychic genesis, an instinctive and spiritual arising of new life.

Finding new life through the profound acceptance of death is the paradoxical solution. In paradox, we stand at the threshold of life's resurgence. Holding fast the divergent reigns of painful dissonance, we enter realms of deeper healing.

Paradox Site One: Hydrothermal Vents

In 1991, a crew of marine biologists had the unprecedented opportunity to witness the birth of a deep-sea hydrothermal vent. Hydrothermal vents, originally discovered in 1977 in their advanced state of development, are one of the most toxic environments on the

---

3 Robert Sardello, "Soul Tasks of the Coming Age" in *Common Boundary* (November/December 1992): 42.

planet, emitting lethal concentrations of hydrogen sulfites. The vents arise through volcanic activity at the meeting place of the continental plates, known as the mid-ocean ridge, where the Earth's crust is formed. Here, in the lethal environment of the vents, scientists have discovered extraordinary sites of what some consider to be bio-genesis, the spontaneous emergence of new life. At a depth of 8,600 feet, where there is no light for photosynthesis, new species of subterranean flora and fauna spontaneously arise in prolific numbers and thrive in the toxic environment through the process of chemosynthesis. Vent organisms are unique to their geography and their habitat. They are found in no other location. Since vents were first discovered, over three hundred new species have been identified, and every expedition discovers more. Speculation as to how vent life arises ranges from ideas about dormant larva ignited by the superheated water that follows volcanic action, to interplanetary cross-fertilization from comets and meteors that have entered the Earth's orbit.[4]

Paradox Site Two: The Black Madonna

In approximately A.D. 797, St. Meinrad was born of royal parentage in Central Europe. In 822, he was ordained as a Benedictine priest, eventually becoming a hermit six years later. Ultimately, his hermitage was founded as the Einsiedeln Monastery, which now lies within the borders of Switzerland, and is dedicated to the Black Madonna, the Virgin Mary. A universal phenomenon, the Black Madonna still lies within the sphere of mystery. There are an estimated 400 shrines to the Black Virgin, yet she remains little known, a subterranean figure even within the mainstream Catholic cosmology in which she is firmly rooted. As will be more fully explained below, the Catholic Church has little explanation for her blackness, except to surmise that the figures have been long exposed to candle soot and therefore darkened. Seen from a psychological and historical perspective, however, the Black Virgin is an archetypal figure of pre-Christian origins and has always been black. She carries the dark pole of the feminine archetype. As such, the Black Madonna is the religious expression of one aspect of the Godhead, revealing its dark, unconscious, mysterious, and unpredictable side.

---

[4] All references to hydrothermal vents are taken from official transcripts: *Deep Sea, Deep Secrets, www.discovery.com*, September 1998.

St. Meinrad's initial approach into the realm of the Black Madonna began with his hermit's journey, delineating the religious expression of his desire for greater intimacy with the unconscious or the Unknown. To establish a hermit's refuge, St. Meinrad traveled deep into a dense and virgin forest: the dark and mysterious aspect of the unconscious, the Black Madonna in vegetative form. Soon after establishing his refuge, St. Meinrad was confronted by an overpowering multitude of spectral demons that arose from the forest. To these fearful figures, he surrendered completely, lying prostrate in prayer and terror on the ground. After a long time, an angel of deliverance appeared out of the east, and the demons were dispelled.[5] At the threshold of unpredictable and utter demonic destruction, a redemptive, fecund beginning presented itself. Through his prayerful surrender to the demons of the dark wood, St. Meinrad plumbed the darkest depths of the unconscious—existential terror and a sense of total abandonment—out of which new life, a new beginning, emerged. Here in the dark wood, the hermit built the first edifice of what has now become a foremost point of pilgrimage to the Black Madonna. Like Bonhoeffer, St. Meinrad survived the trauma of God's abandonment, in and with God.

Sites One and Two: Parallels

In both situations above, new life appears at the threshold of trauma and destruction: volcanic eruptions generate toxic vents where biogenesis occurs; and St. Meinrad's life-threatening confrontation with demons brings about a spiritual birth, an event of psycho-genesis. Hydrothermal vents present a biological correlate or analogue to the psychic reality represented by the Black Madonna. At vent sites, biogenesis occurs in total darkness at the ocean floor, and lethally toxic material is transformed into fuel through chemosynthesis. In the realm of the Black Madonna, we plumb the depths of our being where we confront and transform the toxic psychic substances of fear, betrayal, and profound uncertainty. As a result, we are presented with the opportunity for vital and creative growth.

Observation of toxic, hydrothermal deep-sea vents and recognition of the archetypal nature of the Black Madonna may offer us vital

---

5 Fred Gustafson, *The Black Madonna* (Boston: Sigo Press, 1990), pp. 2–3.

clues for undertaking the soul task that Sardello proposes. In these examples we find that life, or love, expressed at instinctual and spiritual levels, can thrive in spite of, and even more importantly, *because of*, what formerly we believed would bring about a total absence or annihilation of life.

In the ecosystem of hydrothermal vents, life thrives and flourishes through symbiotic relationships where chemosynthesis takes place. The tube worm, for example, takes in hydrogen sulfite (H_2S) and brings it down into a large sac filled with bacteria. The bacteria then process the H_2S and give the worm energy. The tube worm is able to detoxify a deadly substance by bringing it to its symbiont, the bacteria. A cooperative process breaks down and transforms a toxic substance into fuel for survival.

The Black Madonna has been compared to personages in other cultures and spiritual traditions, including Persephone of the Underworld, Kali, and Isis.[6] These are goddesses or deities whose rule lies within the dominion of surrender, death and rebirth. From the perspective of the ego, they are lethal forces. But without yielding to this composting and transcendent energy, no transformation is possible and therefore no renewal of life-force. As archetypal energies within the psyche, what these personages accomplish is the breaking down and transmutation of toxic substances, thereby fueling soul growth.

Psychically toxic substances, like the hydrogen sulfites that originate deep within the bowels of the earth through volcanic activity, are primitive and primal energies which erupt into consciousness—fear, pain, pride, rage, envy, our intolerance—which can be converted into fodder for spiritual regeneration. Primitive energies become transformed not by denying them, but by working them into new life through heightened consciousness; that is, by fully acknowledging them, as St. Meinrad acknowledged the spectral demons of the dark wood when surrendering himself in full prostration on the earth. Only when we are willing to fully and deeply acknowledge the presence of these dark forces can the angel—our redemption—come.

---

[6] Gustafson, *Black Madonna*, chapter 4.

Darkness and the Imago Dei

The Black Madonna is revered in many shrines and cathedrals of Western and Eastern Europe. She has existed there for centuries. It is only from the middle of this century that the Black Madonna has been present in the United States, the figures of which are descended from the Virgin at Einsiedeln in Switzerland.[7] The darkness of the Virgin is enigmatic. Different sites of the Black Madonna offer different stories for her blackness. The story within the tradition at Einseideln describes the original figure of the Madonna as needing restoration when long-standing candle soot had accumulated on the white skin of the Virgin. Gustafson, in *The Black Madonna*, includes a first-person account given in 1799 by Johann Adam Fuetscher, ornamental painter and restorer. Fuetscher states that the statue of the Madonna he received for restoration was blackened by intensive exposure to church candles, but that beneath the soot was white, flesh-colored skin. Cryptically, and without explanation, he notes that in his restoration, *he painted her black*, that is, as the statue had appeared when originally it came to him for restoration. He does not say why his restoration is to black rather than white, flesh-color. He goes on to say that over the black pigment he painted in eyes and some color for cheeks and lips, but that when the statue was viewed by church members they firmly requested that she be painted *completely* black, thus requiring Fuetscher to paint over the eyes and other areas on the face to which he had lent a rosy color.[8] Clearly, in her darkness, the Madonna gave something to her petitioners that she could give in no other form.

Marie-Louise von Franz offers another explanation for the Madonna's blackness, one that encompasses the archetypal and pre-Christian dimensions of this special figure. Von Franz explains that statues of the Black Madonna, including that of Einsiedeln, were always black, being original descendants of the Egyptian goddess Isis and her child Horus, who in the Late Roman Empire played an important role. Wherever the Roman Empire spread, the Isis cult rooted; and there you find statues of the Black Madonna. She goes on to say:

---

[7] For example, at Saint Meinrad Archabbey, St. Meinrad, Indiana. *www.saintmeinrad.edu/friends/history.html.*
[8] Gustafson, *Black Madonna*, pp. 41–42.

[W]hat is stressed about Mary is her spiritual aspect—the Immaculate Conception, the Assumption into heaven into the heavenly Thalamos or bridal chamber—but Isis had a much richer theme. Isis was represented as the highest divine spirituality, but she was also worshipped as the underworld goddess, ruler of the dead. . . . Isis was a black goddess . . . nocturnal, earthy. . . . She was a mother goddess who comprised, or contained in her image, the highest spirituality—she is the Mother of God, the new sun god Horus, and wife of the reborn Osiris—and also the darker chthonic aspects of the Great Mother. She unified them all. . . . The Virgin Mary inherited those traits, but in the official teaching she inherited only the sublime and spiritual, the attributes of purity and so on. The other aspects, of earth fertility and the dark side, were never officially recognized.[9]

Given the people's response to the restoration of the Black Madonna at Einsiedeln, it seems apparent that the official church image of the Virgin was incomplete. The people, then, provided necessary compensation for the Virgin's incomplete state in their request for a completely black-skinned Madonna and Child.

Whatever the explanation for the Black Madonna's presence, apparently it is the very blackness of the Virgin that gives special hope to those who come to her. She is able to encourage and sustain those who seek her certain solace precisely *because* of her darkness. Within the nature of her being, she holds the paradox: in and through darkness lies a fertile resurgence of life. No doubt, it was the reassurance of this experience that people fervently sought by having her returned to her blackened state.

The presence of the Black Madonna fulfills a collective need within the psyche. Her presence informs us that we can, and must, fully embrace the darkness of the unpredictable and unknown. While a thrashing torment may accompany the hopelessness and despair of a profound rupture in our connection to what we know, exactly at this juncture a penetrating vision of faith, and new life, comes into being.

---

[9] Marie-Louise von Franz, *The Cat: A Tale of Feminine Redemption* (Toronto: Inner City Books, 1999), p. 40.

The *Imago Dei*, the image we have of God, is not only what we, from our *egoic* stance, perceive as good. As Bonhoeffer and Sardello explain, we must open wide enough to believe in the goodness and love of God, even when we can perceive no good or loving God in which to believe. As the fecundating and dark side of the feminine Godhead, the image of the Black Virgin helps us to endure and survive this dilemma, born of piercing and deadly uncertainty.

As a counterpart in the natural world, bio-genesis at hydrothermal vents gives precedent to the psychically regenerative nature of the Black Madonna. It presents an apparently impossible yet living paradox: in the most lethal environment—in chemicals more toxic than deadly cyanide, under the crushing weight of water that measures five thousand pounds per square inch (enough to liquidate a tank), at the junction of near-freezing deep-sea waters and volcanic vent-waters reaching up to 750 degrees Fahrenheit, in pitch-black darkness where no photosynthesis is possible—plants, spaghetti worms, sea dandelions, orange sea stars, crustaceans and a litany of others spontaneously arise and thrive. Indeed, new life forms manifest and proliferate as abundantly as on any coral reef found in the ocean. On this point scientists agree: through vent life, a new vision of the world is brought to light. An event of this magnitude cannot be ignored or left fallow, neither in the outer world of nature nor, by analogy, in the inner world of the psyche.

Vent discoveries have prompted interdisciplinary scientific approaches that are mutually focused on the possibility of global detoxification and the discovery of new medical remedies. Greater understanding of the archetypal dimensions of the enigmatic Black Madonna may direct us to similar resolutions at the level of the psyche, both personally and collectively.

The New Vision: The Threshold of Psycho-Genesis

St. Meinrad's experience in the forest when confronted by spectral demons describes the daunting nature of an intrapsychic, depth-psychological journey often referred to as *The Dark Night of the Soul*, or *The Night Sea Journey*. In this inner journey, one plumbs the depths of a spiritual *nigredo*, mining a possibly more profound sense of faith. Comments made by marine biologists and other scientists about the experience of their adventures and discoveries in relation to hydrothermal vents are remarkably parallel to the nature of this journey into the deeper layers of the psyche. C. G. Jung's pioneering observations on the nature of the personal and collective unconscious aptly define these subterranean realms in psychological terms. One method by which he describes these realms is by comparing the maturation of the individual personality and the development of consciousness to alchemical processes found in ancient texts on alchemy. In the alchemical *opus*, the true beginning of the journey commences when the "matter" turns black. One alchemist writes, "When you see your matter going black [in the alchemical retort], rejoice: for that is the beginning of the work."[10] By comparison, Jung postulates that getting to a state of psychological wholeness means—at least for starters—confronting our own blackness: pride, greed, envy, fear, alienation. Without this first step, we cannot find true light, the inner gold.

In addition to facing a personal experience of darkness, one fundamental task in applying Jung's analytical psychology in our own lives is to open to the mysterious and often terrifying depths of the unknown, and through it to an experience of the *numinous,* to the touch of a transcendent force. Through the grace of the *numinous*, the transcendent enters our lives and brings us to a new level of consciousness. Only then do we find the inner gold of which the alchemists spoke, a condition of which is referred to here as psychogenesis. The journey through the unknown to wholeness is no ordinary journey. It requires unending courage and willingness to endure what often seems impossible to bear. An experience of the *numinous* arises not only from ecstatic-filled light, but just as often from the mournful darkness of isolation and despair.

The following comments that are made by vent explorers could also be made about the perils and ultimate riches of *The Night Sea Journey*, the psychological dimension of the alchemical *opus*:

> There's no template for this research. Most of the work here has to be newly engineered. . . .
> The abyss is no normal laboratory. . . .

---

[10] C. G. Jung, *Mysterium Coniunctionis, The Collected Works of C. G. Jung*, vol. 14, R. F. C. Hull, trans., Bollingen Series XX (Princeton: Princeton University Press, 1970), § 729, n. 182.

The trip to inner space [deep sea waters] in many ways is more treacherous than a trip to outer space. The pressures are enormous. . . .

Each trip [down to the ocean floor] is an opportunity to discover previously unknown life. It is a slow trip, but one brimming with excitement. . . .

You travel down . . . through the inky blackness of the deep sea and you get to the bottom and you see this growth of life. There's [sic] thriving communities. There's so much activity going on. It's like no place else in the universe.

Each and every dive we find something and discover something that we've never, ever seen before. . . .

One of the real challenges of working in the deep sea, and one of the reasons it's so exciting to us, is it probably represents the most extreme environment on the planet, particularly when we're dealing with hydrothermal vents.

Our appreciation for how little we know about life on Earth has really been manifest since the discovery of the vents. . . .

Within all creation myths of the world, the *Imago Dei* brings new life into existence. In considering our present "creation myth" of hydrothermal vents, the possibility of bio-genesis transpires even under the most lethal conditions. As vessels of the divine spark, it is also our nature to bring new life into existence through the development of the psyche into fuller and greater consciousness. This hard-won development necessarily includes an acceptance of death. Death itself brings us to a fuller experience of life, not from the standpoint of the ego, but from the standpoint of spiritual growth, where we surrender our smaller will to the mystery of the Unknown. A full acknowledgment of death prompts us to the procreative possibility of bringing new soul life, a deeper love, into the world. Those like Bonhoeffer who have experienced extreme trauma with a profound understanding of what they have endured, found their way to an unfathomable faith that grew from an incomprehensible abyss of demonic chaos and destruction. Their spiritual legacy is a beacon to the world, their innocent suffering a redemptive act for the collective. In our day-to-day lives we, too, are confronted with the challenge of redemption whenever we are

overcome with a personal experience of trauma, or a sense of alienation and despair. Bio-genesis in the toxic environment of hydrothermal vents reflects, in the natural world, the possibility of a
psycho-genesis generated by accepting, and transforming, toxic sites of
our personal experiences of darkness.

ॐ

After years of living a life of growing consciousness and simple spiritual devotion, one would think that the path of life becomes easier to
navigate, that an inner light will radiate at the flick of a switch. This is
not my experience. Nor, I am convinced, is it the experience for many
other people of similar circumstances. Only by grace have I been
spared the personal and direct experience of horrific traumas—natural
catastrophe, personal holocaust, and genocide. Yet, by the very fact
that I am alive and therefore not without wounding, I am vulnerable
to the periodic visitations of a quietly eruptive and deadly darkness, to
the terrifying chaos of complete uncertainty.

Experiences of despair and loss of connection—even after breakthrough, life-changing events, extensive analysis, and a profound sense
of communion with the forces of nature and spirit—have led me to
believe, and growingly accept that my own path leads me repeatedly
on pilgrimages to the inner shrine of darkness, not because I am
morally deficient, not because I am depressed, and not because there's
some form of enlightenment or personal maturation that I am just not
"getting." Rather, I am led to the shrine of darkness because, in spite
of a desire to consistently experience the peace and happiness of a certain spiritual liberation, the mournful face of God abides within me
and wants to be seen, and loved, through my eyes. At this shrine I have
learned to love when I experience nothing to love.

The Mournful Face of God

Sadness, I need
your black wing.
So much honey in the topaz
each ray smiling
in the wide fields
and all an abundant light about me,

all an electric whir in the high air.
And so give me your black wing,
sister sadness.

I need sometimes to have the sapphire
extinguished and to have
the angled mesh of the rain fall,
the weeping of the earth. . . . Now I am missing
the black light.
Give me your slow blood,
cold
rain,
spread over me your fearful wing!
Into my care
give back the key
of the closed door,
the ruined door.
For a moment, for
a short lifetime,
remove my light and leave me
to feel myself
abandoned, wretched,
trembling in the web
of twilight,
receiving into my being
the quivering
hands
of
the
rain.
            —PABLO NERUDA[11]

In the bittersweet of Neruda's poem, we are reminded of a primordial
longing for darker places, spaces where we can rightfully mourn, feel
our sadness, our grief and despair; a place where we can let ourselves
experience, without shame or guilt, the sense of abandonment and

─────────

11 Pablo Neruda, excerpt from "To Sadness/II" in *Fully Empowered*, Alastair Reid, trans. (New
York: Farrar, Straus and Giroux, 1967), p. 117. Used by kind permission.

wretchedness we encounter in the wake of our wounds, in the recognition of others' wounds, in receiving "the weeping of the earth." Neruda honors these places, acknowledging that this, too, is a necessary part of life. We are reminded that this mournful face of God, the shrine of darkness, is a holy place, a place that makes whole, and heals. True to the paradoxical nature of spiritual and conscious life, the wounds we bring to this shrine are both the suffering and the redemption. Through them, we are pierced and torn apart; but without them, we would not have the opportunity to forge a forgiving and compassionate response. We would not have the opportunity to make love conscious.

If we turn away from experiencing these darker places, seeking, as Neruda says, only the all "abundant light," "the electric whir in the high air," we risk denial of the vivifying dimensions of the underworld: surrender, vulnerability, death—the composting and transformative agents of regeneration and new life. If we turn away from these darker places, we risk great danger and damage. By turning away from experiencing our own sadness and darkness, we risk extensive projections that can lead, ultimately, to the persecution of individuals and groups left at the mercy of a striving, solar-polarized consciousness. We risk self-righteous scapegoating, sexism, racism, genocide, and other atrocities of marginalization, such as the tyranny of poverty and lack of education.

More often than not, those who frequent the shrine of darkness, making offerings to "sister sadness," carry or acknowledge something to which the collective remains blind, something that is trying to become conscious through pilgrimage to these darker realms. Those who frequent this shrine often carry the collective shadow. If they are fortunate, they realize that this is the case. They realize that their sadness, their profound grief, is not only personal, but collective as well. If they do not have this awareness, those who frequent this shrine may suffer the greater torments of being overshadowed by collective denial and feel that they, solely, are to blame.

In pilgrimage to the shrine of darkness, something is attempting to come into fuller consciousness. Through pilgrimage, the rites of mourning are asking to be lived; death is seeking to be fully embraced as part of life; the dark sister, the Dark Feminine, is asking to be honored. It is not the wholesale eradication of suffering that we must hero-

ically achieve, but the humble understanding that suffering is inseparable from life. The pilgrimage into the realm of the Dark Feminine is not without
sacrifice. As in any encounter with the unconscious, with the
Unknown, the ego suffers a blow. Because the descent is not without
cost, there is a desperate avoidance of these subterranean realms. We
delude ourselves into believing that by avoiding the encounter, we can
avoid existential chaos.

Existential Chaos

Perhaps one of our greatest misperceptions is that correctly following
the spiritual path, "getting it right," will put an end to suffering, to
existential chaos. The fantasy is that if we can only know the final and
definitive formula to ceasing eruptive visitations of suffering, we will
be able to reach the goal: We will have, *once and for all*, gained peace
and freedom, and never have to face suffering again. The mournful
face of God requires that we take another look at that fantasy.

In my previous discussion on psycho-genesis, I offered Robert
Sardello's description of the explosion of the atomic bomb and the
ensuing holocaust as a mythic event. From this perspective, what
arises is a global creation myth of vast and collective proportions,
which requires the human psyche to continually engage in the renun-
ciation of certainty and, therefore, in the continual encounter with
death, impermanence, and chaos. To re-create ourselves, physically
and psychically, we must pay homage to this reality. The depth
encounter with uncertainty must be accepted if we are to understand
this creation myth and its instructive potential. Uncertainty, chaos,
and impermanence cannot be denied; it is our perception of these phenomena that needs refocusing.

Ancient teachings have already revealed the truth of impermanence long before it was brought so undeniably and irrevocably into
collective consciousness through the atomic blast. Tibetan Buddhist
nun and teacher Pema Chödron offers insight into the experience of
uncertainty and impermanence, helping to realign our perception. She
says, "If we're willing to give up hope that insecurity and pain can be
exterminated, then we can have the courage to relax with the ground-
lessness of our situation." She continues by noting that turning "your
mind toward the dharma [spiritual teachings] does not bring security

or confirmation. Turning your mind toward the dharma does not bring any ground to stand on. In fact, when your mind turns toward the dharma, you fearlessly acknowledge impermanence and change and begin to get the knack of hopelessness. . . . Hopelessness means that we no longer have the spirit for holding our trip together. . . . We long to have some reliable, comfortable ground under our feet, but we've tried a thousand ways to hide and a thousand ways to tie up all the loose ends, and the ground just keeps moving under us."[12]

While Chödron is not suggesting that life is hopeless, she does offer that if we do not include chaos, death, and impermanence in our lives we will be denying the intrinsic nature of life itself. We will once again be rejecting what is referred to here as the mournful face of God, the Dark Feminine, and our suffering will not disappear but will only be compounded.

Chaos and the Dark Feminine

In *Addiction to Perfection*, Jungian analyst Marion Woodman refers to the Dark Feminine when she says, "what we now call the unconscious is in psychological reality a consciousness that has simply been underground for too long. In alchemy there is the concept of the *Deus Absconditus* (male), the hidden god in matter. But the unconscious also includes the *Dea Abscondita*, The Black Madonna. . . . "[13] She continues by describing how this dimension of the psyche reveals itself, how we are to recognize its very particular manifestation or expression.

> The return of God is one of the most ancient expectations of the human race. Every world religion has presented itself as preparing for his return. Every religion still awaits it. We already know God in his outward manifestation, by his laws, his commands, his works. That is the Logos, the masculine side of God. What we await in the Second Coming is what we lack: God's inner dynamic or process. This—*God in his cre-*

[12] Pema Chödron, *When Things Fall Apart: Heart Advice for Difficult Times* (Boston & London: Shambhala, 1997), pp. 38, 39.
[13] Marion Woodman, *Addiction to Perfection: The Still Unravished Bride* (Toronto: Inner City Books, 1982), p. 80.

ativeness rather than in his creation—is the essence of the feminine, traditionally enacted in the ancient Mysteries. The return is, therefore, the emergence of the feminine side of God, which has been gradually taking shape for centuries in what we call the unconscious.[14]

"Inner dynamic or process," "creativeness rather than creation"— these are essential conditions of the *Dea Abscondita,* and by their very nature demand interaction with the uncertain and impermanent, with flux and chaos. The Dark Feminine side of God does not act through the rule of law, nor through rigid control; rather, it acts through the quality of wisdom and the profound ability to engage the unpredictable and the unknown.

In October of 2000, Dr. Marvin Spiegelman presented a lecture at the C. G. Jung Institute in Zurich. He spoke of the Virgin Mary's various apparitions to children in France, Portugal, and Yugoslavia. Spiegelman points out that Mary's message to those to whom she appears has become increasingly insistent on our need to pray to her. He understands this as the urgent need to honor the feminine, not only within analytical psychology, but also in the world at large. Perhaps even more urgent now is to recognize the Dark Feminine, the Black Madonna or *Dea Abscondita,* whose intrinsically earthy nature has been left fallow and uncultivated for far too long.

Denial of Darkness: Experiences in the Psyche

When we do not consciously recognize the Dark Feminine, we place ourselves on dangerous ground. Denial of darker realms contributes to a profound betrayal of life, especially when the denial turns itself into projection—into one person, onto one people. Within the psyche of those betrayed, toxic projection can twist and drive, wrenching itself into despair, rage, and even terror. For those who have experienced betrayal at these levels, for those who have been overshadowed by the trauma of individual and collective denial, the betrayal can become a horrifying and bottomless abyss, an abyss that is experienced as the demonic and raging core of one's very own being. This experience can arise within those who

---

14 Woodman, *Addiction to Perfection*, p. 83. Italics mine.

have been radically marginalized and brutalized, forced to carry the projection of a malignant shadow that is not theirs, personally, to bear. This is experienced in the survivors of genocide, in sexual abuse, child abuse, sexism, racism, and maleficent oppression of all kinds that implant a life-threatening sense of shame, simply for being who one is . . . a woman, a defenseless child, of a different belief, or just different.

At extreme states, massive betrayal of innocence, against one person or against one people, can become massive trauma, turning the mournful face of God into a monstrous one. This is a monster which fiercely defends against further betrayal by destroying any threatening approach or experience, including that of being loved or feeling whole. The individual who has been so brutally betrayed cannot risk further violation. Even if the approach is genuinely loving and caring, that love is experienced as perilous and must be destroyed at all costs. It makes one far too vulnerable, and therefore at great risk of further betrayal. It is understood by those so violated, mostly unconsciously, that experiencing this level of vulnerability must be vehemently defended against, even at the cost of suicide or other forms of destruction aimed at self-dissolution. Those who have been traumatized at these levels are continuously retraumatized, through encounters with others, and by isolation from others. They live in a bleak and terrifying no-man's land.

A necessary response to this experience of trauma is the painstakingly slow dismantling of a self-protective impulse which has become aberrant, cruelly annihilating any approach of healing or love. With patience, and grace, the internal experience of love can be restored, at least well enough. Without it, the damage of betrayal can remain indefinitely, leaving the individual to relive again and again the terror of a raging disintegration.

It is not within the scope of this brief paper to enter deeply into the psycho-dynamics of trauma. There are others who have done this with exceptional skill. Among them are Jungian analyst, Donald Kalsched, who describes the phenomena in his opus, *The Inner World of Trauma: Archetypal Defenses of the Personal Spirit*. For the scope of this paper, it is sufficient to say that in working with trauma we are often working with the horror of marginalization imprisoned within both body and mind. We are working with the deadly denial of the Dark Feminine.

As individuals and as a collective, we are being traumatized by a world view that leaves no room for the mournful face of God. We are told by many indigenous cultures, including the Hopi of the American Southwest, that we must begin in great earnest to address and embrace what we are here referring to as the Dark Feminine. If we cannot, the world as we now know it will be lost to us. If we cannot mourn, if we cannot feel an authentic and profound sense of compassion and sorrow, for ourselves and for others, for all sentient beings including this planet, our losses will be even greater than they are now, spiritually, environmentally, psychically.

Pema Chödron writes about the nature of this particular spiritual path in the following passage from her book, *When Things Fall Apart: Heart Advice for Difficult Times*. In her particular terms, she clearly describes how the mournful face of God, the Dark Feminine, can bring us to the deepest experiences of an indestructible love, the very healing necessary for our traumatizing world view:

> In the process of discovering *bodhichitta* [an awakened heart], the journey goes down, not up. It's as if the mountain pointed toward the center of the earth instead of reaching into the sky. Instead of transcending the suffering of all creatures, we move toward the turbulence and doubt. We jump into it. We slide into it. We tiptoe into it. We move toward it however we can. We explore the reality and unpredictability of insecurity and pain, and we try not to push it away. If it takes years, if it takes lifetimes, we let it be as it is. At our own pace, without speed or aggression, we move down and down and down. With us move millions of others, our companions in awakening from fear. At the bottom we discover water, the healing water of bodhichitta. Right down there in the thick of things, we discover the love that will not die.[15]

Sightings and Celebrations of the Dark Feminine

In the first section of this inquiry, the phenomenon of deep-sea hydrothermal vents describes one site of the Dark Feminine. Through what other sites can we directly engage this dimension of the psyche?

---

[15] Chödron, *When Things Fall Apart*, pp. 91–92.

How do we "pray to her" as Spiegelman suggests we must? Where are the spaces and places we encounter uncertainty creatively, bringing depth and darkness to its rightful place of honor within the continuum of consciousness? Where can we find the inspiration that will allow us to enter the field of uncertainty and learn to move with it, rather than against it? And where do those marginalized find recognition and respect in the world? Here, I present a few examples—by no means exhaustive—that might help address these questions, and that acknowledge Her presence.

Day of Pardon 2000

In honor and celebration of the millennium, the Catholic Church issued a public apology for acts that encouraged and condoned centuries of cruel and abusive treatment against countless peoples. The apology asks forgiveness for deeds enacted that have violated the rights of those marginalized and made to unwillingly sacrifice their lives and their cultures by becoming scapegoats, carrying the shadow for the unrelenting collective. In referring here to this unprecedented apology, it is not to say that all is now well and redeemed. It is to say, however, that we are presented with a significant gesture suggesting serious reflection on the atrocities committed, atrocities that were once ordained and considered acceptable. This apology has the potential to prompt the creative chaos of an expanded vision, and to encourage the new growth in consciousness that arises as a result. Although the apology may not reach many ears initially, it is a prayer that, hopefully, may quietly and pervasively enter the listening heart in decades to come.

Below is an edited version of the prayer, asking God's forgiveness for sins committed throughout history by the "sons and daughters" of the Church. This was the central act of the Day of Pardon on March 12, 2000 and was an integral part of the Mass celebrated that day in St. Peter's Cathedral in Rome.[16]

---

[16] This excerpt is from a seven-part "Universal Prayer: Confession of Sins and Asking Forgiveness" posted at the Web site of The Holy See, *www.vatican.va/news_services/liturgy/documents/ns_lit_doc_20000312_prayer-day-pardon_en.html*. My thanks to Nick Cafarelli of the *Catholic Digest* for bringing this prayer to my attention.

IV. CONFESSION OF SINS
AGAINST THE PEOPLE OF ISRAEL

A representative of the Roman Curia:

Let us pray that, in recalling the sufferings
endured by the people of Israel throughout history,
Christians will acknowledge the sins
committed by not a few of their number
against the people of the Covenant and the blessings,
and in this way will purify their hearts. . . .

The Holy Father:

God of our fathers,
you chose Abraham and his descendants
to bring your Name to the Nations:
we are deeply saddened by the behaviour of those
who in the course of history
have caused these children of yours to suffer,
and asking your forgiveness we wish to commit ourselves
to genuine brotherhood
with the people of the Covenant.
We ask this through Christ our Lord. . . .

V. CONFESSION OF SINS COMMITTED IN ACTIONS
AGAINST LOVE, PEACE, THE RIGHTS OF PEOPLES,
AND RESPECT FOR CULTURES AND RELIGIONS

A representative of the Roman Curia:

Let us pray that contemplating Jesus,
our Lord and our Peace,
Christians will be able to repent of the words and attitudes
caused by pride, by hatred,
by the desire to dominate others,
by enmity towards members of other religions
and towards the weakest groups in society,
such as immigrants and itinerants. . . .

The Holy Father:

> *Lord of the world, Father of all,*
> *through your Son*
> *you asked us to love our enemies,*
> *to do good to those who hate us*
> *and to pray for those who persecute us.*
> *Yet Christians have often denied the Gospel;*
> *yielding to a mentality of power,*
> *they have violated the rights of ethnic groups and peoples,*
> *and shown contempt for their cultures and religious traditions:*
> *be patient and merciful towards us, and grant us your*
> *   forgiveness!*
> *We ask this through Christ our Lord. . . .*

VI. CONFESSION OF SINS AGAINST THE DIGNITY OF WOMEN AND THE UNITY OF THE HUMAN RACE

A Representative of the Roman Curia:

> *Let us pray for all those who have suffered offences*
> *against their human dignity and whose rights have been*
> *   trampled;*
> *let us pray for women, who are all too often humiliated and*
> *   emarginated,*
> *and let us acknowledge the forms of acquiescence in these sins*
> *of which Christians too have been guilty. . . .*

The Holy Father:

> *Lord God, our Father,*
> *you created the human being, man and woman,*
> *in your image and likeness*
> *and you willed the diversity of peoples*
> *within the unity of the human family.*
> *At times, however, the equality of your sons*
> *and daughters has not been acknowledged,*
> *and Christians have been guilty of attitudes*
> *of rejection and exclusion,*
> *consenting to acts of discrimination*

on the basis of racial and ethnic differences.
Forgive us and grant us the grace to heal the wounds
still present in your community on account of sin,
so that we will all feel ourselves to be your sons and daughters.
We ask this through Christ our Lord. . . .

Jesus of the People

In an another celebration of the millennium, the *National Catholic Reporter*, a Missouri-based weekly newspaper, launched a worldwide search for an image of the contemporary Jesus. It was to be a bold new image that best represented a new vision of Christ. The response to the search was global. There were 1,678 entries from 19 countries on 6 different continents. Judging the competition was Sister Wendy Beckett, a British Roman Catholic nun and world-renowned art critic. For first place, Sister Wendy chose *Jesus of the People*, a painting submitted by Janet McKenzie from the United States (see Plate 2).

The most obviously striking feature of the painting is that Christ is black: perhaps African, perhaps African American, perhaps Caribbean—it is left to the imagination of the viewer. Surrounding the central figure of Christ are cultural icons outside those we have traditionally come to associate with Jesus. On one side of Christ, McKenzie places the yin-yang symbol of the East; on the other, a sacred feather representing the indigenous peoples of the world. These elements arise from cultures and philosophies that have been severely marginalized in a world dominated by the prejudices of Western civilization. Bringing these elements together, including Christ's darkness of skin, reveals a vision that includes the neglected, rejected, and denied. McKenzie's image of Christ gives us the opportunity to acknowledge what has too long been crucified, made invisible.

The following comments are excerpts from a newspaper article about McKenzie and her painting, *Jesus of the People*. The article is quoted at length to illustrate the range of reactions in response to her image of Christ. You will note that while many welcome this image as long overdue, others do not.

Neither the fame nor the fury that has swallowed Janet McKenzie and her painting "Jesus of the People" since last December was the least bit expected. The fame has taken form in radio, television, and newspaper interviews, nationally and internationally. It has taken form in a deluge of letters and e-mails hailing her as prophetic, begging to buy the painting.... The fury has taken form in letters and accusations of blasphemy, political correctness, racism, paganism and ignorance. The framed Plexiglas that protects the painting's dark-skinned, slightly feminine face crowned by thorns is just one example of the fury.... [Plexiglas was installed as a precaution to the huge negative reaction.]

There isn't one single aspect of that painting that hasn't been ripped up, shredded, denied, misinterpreted, thrown back in my face; I've been told this is wrong on every level," says McKenzie....

[The] National Catholic Reporter has received, and continues to receive, thousands of letters and e-mails on the painting. Some readers said they saw the painting and cried at its beauty, and some priests wrote to say they had included the painting in their sermons....

Other readers said McKenzie's Jesus [was] ... "garbage," "utter stupidity," "an embarrassment" and demanded it be destroyed. More extreme reactions called the painting the Antichrist....

That her young, mixed-race nephew in Los Angeles would never have been able to see himself in the more traditional blond-hair [sic], blue-eyed Aryan representations of Jesus was part of the inspiration for "Jesus of the People," McKenzie says. The painting is intended to be all-inclusive.[17]

It is clear that a collective nerve had been struck. The image carries profound impact. People are compelled to respond. That the painting was actually selected as the winner is already telling. It was not overlooked, or overruled. It was found to be timely: a Jesus of the people, today's people. Like the Black Madonna of Einsiedeln, this image of Jesus is sorely needed in the collective.

---

[17] Mike Eckel, "Fury and Fame Swallow Janet McKenzie and Her Painting," in The Bennington Banner (South Burlington, VT: Associated Press, April 29, 2000). Used by permission.

The greatest synchronistic element within the painting (in relationship to this paper) is something the viewer can never know until
informed. Though not directly evident, it can indeed be sensed, as the
reference in the newspaper article suggests. The model for *Jesus of the
People* was not a man. The model was a woman, a black woman.
Here, symbolically and literally, Christ is not separate from the Dark
Feminine. They are inextricably one. The new Christ consciousness is
inseparable from the feminine side of God, and furthermore, from the
Dark Feminine side. To recall Woodman's words, "what we now call
the unconscious is in psychological reality a consciousness that has
simply been underground for too long." The return or the second coming is, therefore, "the emergence of the feminine side of God, which
has been gradually taking shape for centuries in what we call the
unconscious." With her extraordinary painting, *Jesus of the People*,
McKenzie reflects, visually, Woodman's far-reaching notions on the
Dark Feminine.

Butoh: Dance of Darkness

The word *Butoh* has been translated into *Dance of Darkness*. *Butoh* is
a Japanese dance form that emerged out of post-war Japan, which
includes the experience of nuclear holocaust. It was founded by
Tatsumi Hijikata, with the first performance given in 1959. Although
its roots can be found in the oldest Japanese folkloric traditions, *Butoh*
recognizes influences from post-war European movements, most pre-
dominantly, German Expressionism. Although one can make attempts
to describe *Butoh* according to these categories, conclusive classifica-
tion is not possible. Ultimately, the dance of *Butoh* arises outside con-
vention, outside form, outside any prescribed approach. It is, at its
most authentic, a protest against those very elements.

Butoh has been viewed by some as a search for a new identity, a
way of establishing meaning for a society that had directly and unmer-
cifully experienced a profound breach in their personal, cultural, and
existential reality. It is considered by its practitioners to be an exploration into the unconscious, into the realm of imagination and shadows. Movement in this art form does not typically focus on depiction,
nor is it choreographed in the usual way, that is, by shaping movement
from the conscious level. Movement intentionally begins and continues
from the inner recesses of the psyche. The focus is on tracking the

immediate metamorphosis of psyche through movement. The discipline in tracking the psyche in this way is then ritualized or formalized into performance.

In *Butoh*, the intention is to follow, through movement, an internal psychic image to the conclusion of becoming the consciousness of the image itself. You are no longer moving like a river, for example, you become, as closely as possible, the consciousness of river. This approach encourages an experience of the primal energies that animate and nourish the very core of our being. In this regard, it is an opportunity for an experience of the numinous that, as Jung says, "is the real therapy and inasmuch as you attain to the numinous experiences you are released from the curse of pathology. . . ."[18]

One well-known *Butoh* performer, Min Tanaka, traveled the entire length of Japan, dancing each day. His idea was to feel the difference in the ground at different places. He called the experiment *Hyperdance*. Of the experiment he says that he did not dance *in* the place, but that his dance *was* the place."[19] *Butoh* has been described by other practitioners as the dancer's attempt at capturing the subtleties of the soul through the body. Further, *Butoh* dancers do not feel that the soul is there for others to like it, to think it is beautiful or elegant; rather, the soul is there to express itself fully and authentically in whatever form it takes. The only requisite in *Butoh* is to stay committed to the arising expression of the soul, to not give up on oneself in the exploration. In *Butoh*, one pursues the images offered up in sensation, visualization, or dream and lets the images take root deeply in the body, becoming fertile treasures that sustain vitality and life. These images "dream the dreamer" until the dreamer awakes to them and receives their life-sustaining energy.

If we can consider *Butoh* to have arisen, at least in part, out of the mythic event of nuclear holocaust, if we can consider it an attempt, conscious or unconscious, to make meaning out of that mythic event, we might postulate that the discipline of *Butoh* can help restore psychic wholeness within the reality of that global myth. To be related to the mythological is to be in touch with the whole-making and order-

[18] C. G. Jung, *Letters*, Gerhard Adler, Aniela Jaffé, eds., R.F.C. Hull, trans. (Princeton: Princeton University Press, 1973), August 20, 1949.

[19] *http://www.artandculture.com/cgi-bin/WebObjects/ACLive.woa/wa/movement?id=891.*

ing principle of the psyche. Marie-Louise von Franz describes an occasion of this occurrence when speaking of Fijian Islanders:

> Whenever they are threatened by dissociation and panic and social disorder, they try to restore the creation and the whole cosmos by retelling the creation myth. They create again, as it were, the conscious order of things and then await the corresponding effect upon their souls, which would mean that they once again feel themselves to be in order.[20]

Butoh potentially gives us the rare opportunity to delve philosophically, somatically, and psychically into one of the most profound "creation" myths in the history of humankind, and to help restore meaning within the individual and collective psyche as a result.

For our spiritual evolution as a collective, and possibly for our very survival, there is a great need to develop a psychological technology, a "skillful means," that will more deeply connect us to the experience and understanding of the feminine, especially the Dark Feminine, which includes the body and its relationship to consciousness. *Butoh* bases its teachings firmly and squarely on the feminine in that it seeks and fosters "God's inner dynamic or process . . . God in his creativeness rather than in his creation . . . "[21] *Butoh*, therefore, has the potential to strengthen the awareness and integration of an aspect of the psyche that has been underground for far too long.

In Analytical Work, in the Analytical World: Personal Experiences

In my experiences as a Jungian analyst, there were many times when I intensely felt the presence of the Dark Feminine, and engaged in the very difficult lessons that may come when interacting with this archetypal energy. It is my hope that, in addition to the sightings of the Dark Feminine listed above, the ensuing story will help answer for you, the reader, as it did for me, some of the questions I pose at the beginning of this section: Where are the spaces and places we encounter uncertainty creatively, bringing depth and darkness to its rightful place of

---

20 Marie-Louise von Franz, *Creation Myths* (Boston & London: Shambhala, 1995), p. 23.
21 Woodman, *Addiction to Perfection*, p. 83.

honor within the continuum of consciousness? Where can we find the inspiration that will allow us to enter the field of uncertainty and learn to move with it, rather than against it?

Upon starting my training at the C. G. Jung Institute in Zurich, I had the following initial dream. I was 40 years old at the time:

> There is a group of people in a church-like building. On the altar of this sanctuary stands a short, dynamic man with whitish-gray hair (very much like my analyst), who is also myself. He is facing the group of people with his back to the altar, bending over, head toward his knees, with arms outstretched to the sides. He is uttering some kind of special incantation, a holy thing; but at the same time he is using obscenities—all in a rather humorous, yet still serious, vein. He is a solemn clown. At the recitation of his incantation, the Madonna with Child, elevated on the altar behind him, comes to life. Her white lace veil falls from her black and voluptuous body as she begins to step down. She is a strong Madonna, not a maiden. She is clearly an ancient and timeless fertility figure.

I finished my training at the Institute without having analyzed this dream. It was simply there as the guiding star, in all its magical splendor, left intact by the wisdom of my analyst, to unfold according to psyche's own sense of timing. As you will see in the story that follows, this dream unfolded precipitously a few years after my training when I recommenced my analytical practice in the United States.

After living, working, and training in Switzerland for 11 years, I decided to return to the U.S. I knew it would not be an easy re-entry, for several reasons, including the prospect of practicing in a country that was so very different from the mentality and culture in which I had been formally trained. In addition, I would be moving with minimal financial resources.

I was uncertain as to where I would return. For the first few weeks, I traveled along the West Coast, where I had roots since early childhood, to see what place felt right. One morning during my travels, I had a dream which determined my final direction:

> I am standing in front of a church. I am being told by a woman (a former analysand of great courage, endurance, and

integrity) that in order to enter the church, I will need the pair of red shoes that she is holding in her hands. I take the red shoes, open the church doors, and find a vast and infinite high-desert landscape stretched out before me. In the dream, I realize this landscape is Taos Valley. I awake.

As soon as I woke up, I realized that I had to go to Taos and investigate. I had lived in Santa Fe in the late 1970s and early 80s and was familiar with Taos. I had visited several times, but I had never lived there. The city of Santa Fe, with all its cosmopolitan sophistication, is a world apart from the town of Taos, which is well over a mountainous hour's drive north, and is quite isolated.

After two weeks of exploration in Taos I decided, with great trepidation, to follow what my unconscious seemed to be directing me toward: I moved to Taos, and started a practice. It was more challenging than I had ever anticipated.

Taos Valley stands at about 7,000 feet (over 2,000 meters), with mountains reaching to an altitude of over 13,000 feet (almost 4000 meters). The town of Taos has about 6,500 inhabitants, most of whom are Hispanic, some being direct descendents of the original Spanish Conquistadors who came in the middle of the 15th century. The second largest population group is represented by those who are referred to in New Mexico as Anglos ("white" folks), and the third largest population is American Indian, the Tiwa nation from Taos Pueblo. The approximate percentage breakdown is 45, 35, and 20 percent, respectively. Of the percentage of Anglos, there is a small number actively interested in Jungian psychology, and smaller still who are able to afford analysis. The Hispanic and Tiwa population have their own firmly-rooted spiritual traditions.

According to an issue of the Economic Newsletter for Taos County, "Average weekly earnings . . . in the Taos economy were almost a fourth less than for the entire state. Unemployment rates were triple the national figure. Major income supporting social welfare . . . declined. All in all, the boom characterizing the national economy in the past few years has bypassed Taos."

As you can imagine, the challenges of starting a practice in Taos from ground zero have been extreme. In spite of the mystique and mana of Taos, which Jung himself discovered (and contributed to) when he came to visit the Pueblo in the 1920s, the difficulties have been spiritually bone-breaking. I have worked in earnest to develop a radical sense of trust. In the process, I have experienced high and physically painful states of anxiety, my legs literally collapsing from under me. In the midst of this sense of urgency, however, I have also been acutely conscious of an invisible though vital awareness to sustain me.

I discovered this awareness, most particularly, in the parking lot of some rag-tag little store on a bitter-cold day in the middle of winter, wondering for the 10th consecutive month how I was going to buy the next bag of groceries (let alone pay the rent). I almost stopped short as I understood in the deepest strata of my being how a person could be driven to homicide (a great surprise, since suicide had always been the prior fantasy in times of chronic crisis). I realized how impotent one can feel in this persistently hopeless situation, and how any act, even an act of violence (which is statistically high in Taos County), can relieve this sense of utter powerlessness and desperation. I realized I was not separate from this . . . except for an invisible though vital awareness.

Upon reflection, I began to realize the nature of this awareness. It had arisen from seeds planted long ago, and was now bearing fruit. The awareness I refer to can best be described by saying that, at rock bottom, I realized there was within me the ability to love, even when I thought there was nothing to love. I realized within me the ability to contain absolute paradox, if only for brief moments at a time. As intermittent as it may be, it has been this awareness that has quietly and bravely accompanied my experiences of hopelessness, rage, and confusion, and that has kept me from utter despair.

In significant part, the awareness I speak of has arisen directly from the gut and soul of analytical psychology; that is, from the opportunity and privilege to search within myself with a ruthless honesty, guided by the wisdom and genuine respect of another person, an analyst who has come through the experience of the same intensively tempering journey. Along with pure grace, it has been the gut and soul of analytical psychology (as opposed to the endless academic and bureaucratic training requirements) that has provided the kind of moral strength needed to endure the rending forces of paradox, and to be sufficiently open to the creative chaos of a vital life. The experiences I have encountered in Taos have solidified my belief that a crucial factor in the development of the psyche is a continuous and visceral *experience* of what is required to mine one's essential creativity, and what it means to endure the painful dissonance of existential chaos. This visceral experience serves as the ground of being held within the Dark Feminine.

Conditions have improved for me in Taos, both personally and professionally. However, after surviving the infamous first years of initiation (people in Taos introduce themselves by the number of years they've lived here), I am uncertain I will remain. Being here, however, has provided opportunities to live the awareness I have gained beyond my wildest imagination. I have suffered, but in the process I have been driven to the core of what I personally understand analytical psychology and its practice to be. I have also been exposed to a profound experience of the Dark Feminine.

My initial dream upon starting analysis in Zurich was a shimmering and numinous mystery. Little did I realize that the Black Madonna in this early dream would come to life so vividly in Taos. Nine years later, the red shoes in my dream about Taos—shoes I associate with Dorothy's red shoes in the *Wizard of Oz* which she must don in order to return home—have brought me to a spiritual home, a place where I would, indeed, learn acutely and critically about the Black Madonna who had come to life at the beginning of my analytical journey. My initial dream has come full circle in Taos, and has shown me the terrible beauty of the Black Madonna, the *Dea Abscondita*.

ᛒ

And so give me your black wing
sister sadness,
I need sometimes to have the sapphire
extinguished and to have
the angled mesh of the rain fall,
the weeping of the earth . . .

The examples represented by the *The Day of Pardon, Jesus of the People, Butoh,* and my own personal story demonstrate different experiences that can help equalize an imbalance of power, both at the intra-psychic level where heroic, solar consciousness can dominate, and at inter-psychic levels in our relations with others where the willingness

to experience vulnerability can generate trust and, ultimately, true intimacy and healing. If the essence of these experiences and others like
them were more widely admitted into the realm of consciousness, it
might be easier for those who frequent the shrine of darkness to find
the inherent redemptive power that lies there. They would be able to
recognize that it is not necessarily a personal deficiency that drives
them to the shrine, but a natural need to recognize the *Dea
Abscondita,* The Mournful Face of God. It is only when the Dark
Feminine is not recognized that She is tormented, through us. When
denied, She disappears from our conscious life only to become an
unconscious, unquenchable and destructive drive to disavow all suffering, at all costs, to no avail.

> *And so give me your black wing*
> *sister sadness,*
> *I need sometimes to have the sapphire*
> *extinguished and to have*
> *the angled mesh of the rain fall,*
> *the weeping of the earth . . .*

On the Black Madonna

An interview with Andrew Harvey

Andrew Harvey is a poet, novelist, mystical scholar, seeker, and teacher. He is the author of more than 30 books, including the critically-acclaimed *The Direct Path* (Bantam, Doubleday, Dell, 2000), *Son of Man: The Mystical Path to Christ* (J. P. Tarcher, 1998), and *Journey to Ladakh* (Houghton Mifflin, 1984). He is co-editor, with Patrick Gaffney, of Sogyal Rinpoche's best-selling *The Tibetan Book of Living and Dying*. Born in South India, he studied at Oxford University and became the youngest Fellow ever elected to the prestigious All Soul's College. He has devoted the past 25 years of his life to studying the world's various mystical traditions, while living in London, Paris, New York, and San Francisco, and teaching at Oxford, Cornell, and the California Institute of Integral Studies.

This interview took place between Andrew Harvey and Fred Gustafson on January 24, 2001. Following the terrorist attack on the World Trade Center on September 11, 2001, they reconvened to reflect on the bearing that the Dark Feminine has upon that terrible event.

Fred: Andrew, when you hear "Black Madonna" or "dark virgin," what thoughts, feelings, dreams, and personal experiences come to you?

Andrew: The Black Madonna is a very important part of my inmost life and has been now for almost 10 years. I first met her in a book by Anne Baring titled *The Myth of the Goddess*. I realized when I read Anne's book that what was coming together in this symbol were the two sides of my own quest for the divine feminine. I was then a devotee of an Indian woman, Mother Meera, whom I believed, at that time, to be the divine mother. I was also very moved by the whole vision of Mary that was being opened up to me by the Christian mystics such as Louis Grignion de Montfort. However, I had not found the inner connection between an Eastern understanding of the divine mother as the force of destruction as well as creation and the Western vision of her as this transcendent force that unifies and unites all things.

When I met the dark Black Madonna in a book, I suddenly realized that was the force that I had been looking for to bring together my Eastern passions and my Western inheritance. Although this realization was quite profound, it remained on a mental level, until I actually left my guru under very painful circumstances. Briefly, Mother Meera told me on December 27, 1993 to get rid of my lover, Eryk (who is now my husband), get married to a woman, and write a book about how I was transformed into a heterosexual. At that moment, I realized that 15 years of passionate devotion to Meera had been lunacy. This sent my whole life into a whirlwind of suffering. During the weeks that followed as I was battling with myself and with my past and with the craziness of this extraordinary situation, I made a pilgrimage to Chartres where I worshiped for the first time with the fullness of my being the Black Madonna in the "Virgin of the Pillar." I came to begin to understand very deep things about Her because I had come to the moment when Her agony, power, and extreme vibrant, violent purity of compassion could be revealed to me.

That day I realized that I had been projecting onto Meera my soul's secret passion to come into direct connection with the Black Madonna beyond name and form. In meeting the Black Madonna in my state of misery and psychological and spiritual torment, I was being opened to Her presence in the cosmos and in present history. On that day, I think what I understood most of all was that the Black Madonna is the force of divine destruction and creation, the non-dual Mother whose absolute ferocious power is manifesting the entire cosmos. I also understood that what was astounding about this particular symbol was that in Her burnt blackness, it was quite clear that the Black Madonna was sharing the pain of the whole creation; in fact, She was suffering and sobbing and howling and screaming and dying in and with all of her creations so that there was an extreme sense not only of Her transcendent power but also of Her absolute and final, immanent compassion. I realized that the only force that could see me through the tremendous crisis that Eryk and I were in would be the Black Madonna.

The whole of the rest of the crisis that Eryk and I were to live through was lived through very consciously on my part in the atmosphere of the Black Madonna. What I came to realize was that She was helping me birth my inner non-dual Christ consciousness, which is only possible in and under Her because only She can take the adept into the depths of a non-dual identification both with the transcendent and with the suffering of the immanent. Only She has the symbolic and actual power to birth the realization that can only be born through an experience of the dark night of the soul, the total shattering of all the agendas, concepts, visions and spiritual understandings that have accompanied the adept up to then. So, to me, the Black Madonna was the force of the divine Mother that I met at the very moment when I needed to plunge into unfathomable pain and suffering in order to dissolve the old structures of myself. It was only Her force that could sustain and see me through that suffering and, through divine grace, birth the new being that that suffering was preparing. So I saw Her as the womb, if you like, in which the crucifixion of the false self takes place. It is Her power that both enforces the death and engenders and protects the new life of the Christ-Self that is born from the death.

At the end of a particular set of devastating experiences in which I had to face the betrayals of my old friends as well as my own complicity in those betrayals because I had been deliberately blind to what they had been doing for years, I decided that the only way to survive such knowledge would be to "die" in life. So I lay down on the ground and found myself sinking through layer after layer of divine knowledge and awareness until finally I reached an unfathomable darkness, which was calm and broad as the universe and wide as infinity and ultimately peaceful. At that moment, I understood beyond knowledge that I was the child of the Black Madonna. I had been birthed into a dimension of transcendent and immanent divine identity.

When I surfaced from this experience, the whole of the room around me (I was actually in the bath), the bath, the taps, the walls, all were brilliant with divine light. I understood that the unraveling of my own agendas, programs, and visions of myself had taken me to a point of total surrender where She could reveal the dark divinity at the core of myself. This experience led to many other unfoldings that I also recognized to be Her gift. I had first of all projected onto a guru my own self secret need to meet the Black Madonna. Then, through the shattering of that illusion of the guru, I actually came in increasing intensity to meet the Black Madonna and, in increasing intensity, to be stripped, seared, and burned by Her in Her crucible of the dark night of the soul. It was also here, however, that I was reborn by her. I feel I have been graced the initiation of the Black Madonna, and that this is a very crucial initiation for our planet at this moment.

While I was living through the initiation, I remembered that I had already been informed of its deepest secrets by somebody that I had met only a year before, Father Bede Griffiths. I was invited by an Australian film director to go to south India to the ashram where Father Griffiths lived to be involved in the making of a film about him. He was 86 at the time. When we met, we fell spiritually in love, and he opened the treasure chest of his emotional and mystical journey to me. The account of what he said in the tapes we made is published in a book titled *The Human Search*,[1] which has a marvelous description of his meeting with the Black Madonna. What happened to Bede was that in his 80s, he had a series of strokes that he interpreted as the dark mother coming to shatter his patriarchal addiction to the left-brain understanding that he had adhered to all his life. Through Her shattering of this, he had come into a deeper and much broader, wider, wilder vision of the cosmos, of his own relationship with it and into a far deeper understanding of what the sacred marriage between body and spirit really is. So as I was going through my own initiation I was being fed, if you like, the wisdom of what Bede himself had told me. Now I was living it for myself in the terms of my own temperament and the terms of my own dark night.

Fred: And what did you actually discover as you lived this initiation?

Andrew: What I discovered was two things, which many people discover when they come into the crucible of the Black Madonna. The first thing is, of course, that all your plans, agendas, projects, and visions are systematically and with a terrifying precision unraveled by Her. They are annihilated because they belong to a world of division and separation. They belong to the pride of the false self and to a way of acting that has to become immeasurably deepened by radiant awareness. The second thing that you discover is that She is not only transcendent, She is also the most passionately profound natural process and that the birth into Her and through Her is very much a physical birth. This is what Bede, in his 80s, discovered. He discovered

---

[1] John Swindells ed., *A Human Search: Bede Griffiths Reflects on His Life* (Liguori, MO: Triumph Books, 1997).

that being annihilated by Her actually birthed him into the dimension of the body for the first time and into the dimension of a consecrated and sublime sexuality and into the marriage of the body and spirit at a level and intensity that he never before imagined.

What happened during the annihilation process that I went through with the Black Madonna is that just as my external life and concepts were being destroyed, so in my love for Eryk and in our lovemaking, in our deepest and most passionate meeting, She revealed to me some of the most transfiguring truths of the Tantra. The birth in Her was simultaneously the destruction of all fantasies and an initiation into the divinity of the body, and the divine secrets that consecrated, Tantric love reveals about the body and physical life when transfigured by spiritual passion. So it was clear to me and became clearer still that this birth into the Black Madonna is a birth simultaneously into this "dark transcendent," the source and womb and spring of all manifestation, and a birth into the splendor of Tantric fullness and the glory of Tantric being. The two *together,* as they deepen, create what only can be described as the resurrection consciousness, the consciousness of divine humanity. Though this process is very far from complete, I have experienced how She is the birthing force of authentic divine humanity. What She does to birth it is to destroy all of the fantasies that block the transcendent as well as destroy all of the fears, loathing, self-hatreds, and all of the terrors of the body that block the glory of the flaming out of the body's own most sacred truth. This is essential information for all seekers at this moment because, unless we come to this birth of divine humanity here on the earth with fully consecrated sacred powers and sacred creativity of every kind, we are simply not going to be able to survive.

Fred: How would you describe what the Black Madonna is now doing on a world-scale? With the whole planet?

Andrew: First of all, I believe She is allowing the crucifixion of the planet by our arrogance, pride, greed, and horrible lust of power to take place, because it is the only way in which we will now, at this late moment, wake up to the terror and horror of our pride, greed, and arrogance and lust for destruction.

Secondly, and as part of this, She is shattering all human agendas. All of our fantasies about ourselves are being exposed horribly by this crucifixion that is clearly the result of our own madness. Every single belief that humanity ever had about itself, about its worth, its holiness, its sweetness, its reason, its technological power, its divine truth—all of them are being rubbled by this destruction which is increasingly revealing to anybody with half a mind and half a heart that everything that we have ever known, or believed about ourselves, is illusion. This is a terrible process and involves not only a crucifixion of nature but also a crucifixion of our inmost spirit and agendas as well as everything we believed in that is now an outmoded version of our own nature. The Black Madonna is doing this because it is only through this that we will become abandoned and surrendered and humbled enough to Her to call upon Her to take us through the dark birthing process of the "annihilation adventure" into the new consciousness that She alone can bring us. Everything in human history now depends on whether or not this fierce and frightening knowledge with its glorious conclusions and possibilities can be revealed to human beings clearly and accurately enough so that as many people as possible can give themselves over to the birthing powers of the Black Madonna, and go through whatever is necessary to birth the divine human creatively.

Fred: I can't help but see a parallel between your personal journey—specifically, your being with Mother Meera with the pain that brought, and how you dealt with that—and what is happening on the planet and the planet's need, the peoples of the Earth's need, to withdraw their projection and to take a look with how they are living on the Earth and crucifying it. It seems to me the Black Madonna was behind the events around Mother Meera for you.

Andrew: Three weeks before I broke with Mother Meera, I received a postcard from a friend's exhibition in Zurich. It was of Kali. The week before that I had a dream that I now realize was my first experience of the chthonic power of the Black Madonna. I had just finished writing *The Way of Passion*[2] about Rumi. I had a dream in which I went to a window, opened it, and saw this great, blue wave, which reared like a vast cobra and turned black. From the center of this swarming, boiling darkness flashed out a lightning flash that actually caused me to faint

---

[2] Andrew Harvey, *The Way of Passion: A Celebration of Rumi* (Berkeley: Frog, Ltd., 1994).

away. After that, the Kali picture came and then the dark night I have described started to unfold.

It became very clear to me that the entire process was ruled by the Black Madonna. The crucifixion initiation I underwent burned me free from my own projections of my own divinity onto someone else and forced me to take back those projections, and to honor them, and to consecrate my whole life to honoring them not only in myself but also in other people, without illusion. It compelled me to stop being a secret junkie of transcendence and realize my own body, sexuality, love, and desire were all potentially, wholly, and completely sacred.

Also, because I suffered in my inmost core the horror of the abuse of power, it made me a permanent mystical revolutionary. If you suffer the abuse of power in one area, it initiates you into all the nuances of abusive power in all the different institutions of the world. One of the major gifts of the Black Madonna to anybody who worships Her is that She wakes them up starkly to all the games of manipulation that mask abuse and to the presence of the corruption of power in every institution, media, and way of being and doing that is not directly illumined by democratic egalitarian compassion. This is a terrifying initiation because, once you see, or begin to see, with Her eyes, what you see is a world gone mad, a world in which the essential truths of divine humanity are rubbled, betrayed, and degraded on every side, not merely by the materialists or by those who deny God, but with horrible ingenuity by those who claim to represent God both in the established religions and in the guru systems—all of which are addicted to power and not to the true transmission of sacred empowerment.

Fred: I do not see the Black Madonna in any way being benign. But I do see Her being patient except when we ignore what She represents. Then She becomes like Kali. Then She will tear you apart, lovingly.

Andrew: Yes, She will tear you apart within yourself to rebirth you in your true, divine self. I have found that the most important way of seeing the Black Madonna is actually to bring together three seemingly contradictory aspects. It is my experience that you experience them all together like music. The first aspect is that She is the Transcendent Queen of Darkness—the "dazzling darkness" of Dionysius Areopagite. This is the darkness beyond name and form. It is the darkness of the Tao. It is the transcendence from which even the light, even the godhead is born. The phrase of Ruysbroeck that Bede used when he was talking of her is very moving. He says, "She is the darkness in which lovers lose themselves." The Dark One is the Queen of final Mystery, the One who through all transformations is leading us on, ever onward, while "hiding" in a kind of cloud of darkness forever distant from any formulation or concept we may have of Her.

In the second aspect, the Black Madonna is the Queen of Nature, the Queen of Tantra, and the Queen of all the dark, rich, gorgeous, fertile processes of nature and of Tantra. The sum of these processes is often destructive because for the true divine nature to emerge and for true Tantra to be born, all kinds of fears and self-presentations have to be rubbled. That can be searingly painful but the purpose of the pain is to open you up to the gorgeous textures of Her transformations. That is what streams through the destruction: one of Her hands is tearing you apart while the other is pouring into the torn-apart self the perfumes and unguents and revelations of a new kind of being. This is important to remember. The more you experience the holiness and the exquisite and acute precision of her destruction, the more you will be helped by her to understand why She is stripping you, because almost immediately afterwards into the dark empty hole that She has dug in your psyche, She will pour a wholly new vision and new awareness.

The third aspect is also revelatory. I think that one of the reasons why the Black Madonna haunts us all so much is that She very clearly represents the cost, the price, the anguish, and the sacred agony of the Divine Feminine in each of us. She is that part of us that is burnt, wounded, seared, and broken by the world, by what we suffer in the world. There She is, standing in front of us as the Queen of the great and final mystery, and as Queen of Nature and Tantra, but also as what Jacopone da Todi[3] calls Mary in one of his great poems to the Virgin, "La Donna Brucciata," the burnt woman, the woman who has been burnt by love, burnt by the price of love, by the constant, unavoidable opening of the heart to the misery of life, and to the injustice of human beings, and to the cruelty of the false self. I think what she is doing in standing in front of us in Her burnt, black dignity is giving us a way of enduring without closing down, of standing in the fire and being burnt and charred by the fire without ever turning away

---

[3] Jacopone da Todi was a Franciscan poet who was born in the first half of the 13th century.

from the necessity of loving in a complete and total way and of giving everything.

There is a great Sufi text of the ninth century which I think goes right to the heart of this third aspect of the Black Madonna. It says, "Those who are taken into union are drawn near. And those who are drawn near never fall asleep, and the sublime rays of heartbreak engulf them." When you connect with Her in the third aspect of *La Donna Brucciata*, what you connect with in the depths of yourself are those "rays of sublime heartbreak." What She gives to you is the ability to participate in Her own life of final fiery compassion beyond hope, beyond agenda, beyond all plans, beyond any kind of transcendental justification. This aspect of the Black Madonna is an initiation into the burning furnace of charity, that is, the broken and burnt heart of the Mother. You are taken into the depths of the mystery of the Mother because the Mother is not simply the great, dark cloud of final mystery that is uplifting everything from revelation to revelation. She is not simply the Queen of Nature and the Queen of Tantra, the Queen of all the fertile processes that transform life itself into a mirror of the divine. She is also Herself living as every dying animal, as every dying plant, as every raped child, as every broken-hearted gay man and woman, as every abused person, as every killer, as every being of every kind on the planet suffering all the different forms of torment, ignorance, and grief.

Knowing Her in these three aspects together is a mind-, heart- and soul-shattering experience because, if you only know Her in the transcendent aspect, then you can leave this world and reality behind. However, your realization is going to be incomplete. And, if you only know her as the Queen of Nature and Tantra, you have no knowledge of Her as the transcendent Mystery or as absolute and final compassion. Again, your realization will be incomplete. However, if you only know Her as final suffering and final compassion, you will not be able to bear such knowledge because you will not know Her also as the Queen of the Processes and as the Queen of the Mysteries. You really have to come to a knowledge of Her in all three aspects and link them all in the inmost part of yourself beyond thought and paradox so that you can come into her true dimension. When you do this, what you find happening within yourself is that you start to birth a being and a way of being and doing which reflects all of the three aspects, together, of Her great identity. It is only through facing, inviting, and saturating your whole practice with all of those three aspects that you can do that. You have, in fact, to "invite in" consciously the whole glory of the sacred feminine, since in the Black Madonna you have the whole radical glory of the Sacred Feminine in one symbol.

The universe and all mystical traditions tell us about a sacred marriage between Matter and Spirit, the "Feminine" and the "Masculine." For millennia, the bride in the marriage, the Black Madonna, has been kept in a dark, filthy, stinking cellar with her hands tied behind her back and her feet tied to a chair with black tape over her mouth. No sacred marriage has been able to take place within human beings, no marriage of spirit and matter, of transcendence and immanence, body and soul. Releasing the bride from the cellar, taking the black tape from over her mouth so she can speak her own sacred wisdom in us is the present task before all of us. If she does not turn up at our inner wedding in her full splendor, there will be no sacred marriage. The only way in which the world can be saved is through a personal initiation into that sacred marriage by millions of people and a flooding of all the world's arenas and institutions with the powers awakened by that sacred marriage. These powers are celebratory, earth-rooted, earth-grounded, justice-making, and create in the name of love and justice a new world of equality for all beings. That is the future if there is a future. So bringing the Black Madonna back is not a luxury for a few intellectuals or a private passion of a few mystics.

Fred: Yes, and isn't honesty the chief thing that the Black Madonna asks of us?

Andrew: In my experience, she demands something even more frightening than honesty. She demands the most extreme abandon because She demands the most total acceptance of the terms on which She manifests the whole universe. And those terms are extremely shocking not only to the rational mind but also to the religious mind. Remember how Ramakrishna describes the Mother. He had a dream about Her. He dreamed he saw this beautiful pregnant woman arising out of the waves of the Ganges looking glorious. Pregnant, she goes to the shore, births her child, and with a smile of ecstasy on her face, tears her child limb from limb, eats the child with the blood running down the sides of her mouth and, still ecstatic, goes back into the Ganges and drowns.

Then, the whole process begins again. What Ramakrishna is trying to make us aware of is the shocking, terrifying coexistence of crucifixion and resurrection at every single level of the universe.

This simultaneously creative/destructive force is something our rational minds have been constructed to try and block us from. Our religious minds also have been "constructed" to try and save us from the full shock of recognition of Her real nature. The deep reason for the addiction to transcendence in all the patriarchal mystical systems is that they simply cannot face the extremity of what She is up to. They choose to devalue the creation, life, relationships, the body, and the earth because they cannot embrace the cost of crucifixion and resurrection that the immanent aspects of the Mother demand and exact. In refusing to embrace the immanent aspects of the Mother, what they have done is effectively to castrate themselves. They have made themselves impotent. If you are addicted to transcendence, you may have a certain kind of realization of divine Being, but you can never have the realization of divine becoming that belongs to the Mother and is the Mother's supreme gift. In choosing to privilege the realization of divine Being exclusively, what you ensure is that those realizations never flood Becoming, never transfigure or transform it, never form a radical, revolutionary core of insight and transfiguring wisdom that can actually turn the institutional axis of the world around.

It is only by facing what Ramakrishna faced in the story and plunging beyond the mind and the frightened heart, beyond the lust for transcendence into the full, outrageous, gorgeous lunacy of Her non-dual bliss that you can ever be taken into the divine truth of your own divine humanity and initiated into the creative powers that come from an acceptance of the terms in which this whole experience happens.

So, it is not just honesty the Black Madonna requires. She requires the most searing imaginable abandon and the most extreme imaginable plunging into the total embrace of Her conditions. When that is mature in you, in the depths of yourself, you become a part of the Cosmic Resurrected Christ simultaneously awake to your divinity and also initiated into your total connection in suffering with every being everywhere. Think of those vivid Mexican representations of the Cosmic Christ. You are at once divine and yet carrying the stigmata whether outwardly or inwardly. Marrying Transcendent Identity with a broken and crucified immanent identity, you finally become useful. On the one hand, there is a transcendent being or light body that you feel at one with and part of; that light body, and held up and nourished by it, is the crucified Christ. The Black Madonna ensouls and sustains both as necessary for her initiation. It is not just honesty She wants. She wants, in the end, your commitment to be crucified so as to be resurrected.

Fred: When you lived in India and prior to Mother Meera, did you have any personal or spiritual connection with Kali or Amba?

Andrew: India is itself a living Kali because India is the total coincidence of opposites.

As a child, I experienced with the child's vulnerability, nakedness, and sacred imagination the coincidence of opposites that is India. On the one hand, there are the glorious tombs and the Taj Mahal, jasmine in the air, the aromas, Maharanis wrapped in silk that looks like spun moonlight. On the other hand, mad people masturbating in the street, crazy yogis eating shit, rabid dogs howling in the night, and the poor starving and dying under crumbling bridges.

Fred: That is the full spectrum of life right there.

Andrew: The genius of India is to expose you to both the glory and horror of life at the same time. So I feel it is not that I just experienced the Black Madonna in some meeting with Kali or Amba. By being born in India, I was born into Her directly.

Fred: And through your crisis with Mother Meera, you completed, in a certain way, a process that had begun at birth.

Andrew: Yes, when I look back, it makes sense that I would try and project onto an Indian woman what I experienced of India as a child. I came to understand the difficulties and horror of my own imperial inheritance. As a child, I woke up to the fact that I belonged to a culture that had used, exploited, and betrayed India in all kinds of ways. The equivalence as an American would be waking up to the fact you were the son or daughter of a Southern plantation family and had the blood of black Americans on your hands.

Fred: Yes, or red Americans.

Andrew: Yes, or red Americans. Basically what I did in retrospect was to project the choice to love Meera because what I wanted to do was to honor the Black Madonna as India. Meera was a wonderfully convenient way of psychologically killing my own mother and of revenging myself psychologically on my "imperial" family. Nothing you could imagine would make them crazier and angrier than their distinguished, intellectual son choosing to worship an illiterate Indian woman with a mustache and call her the divine Mother on Earth! Looking back at it, I realize psychologically I needed to project India onto Meera and to try and destroy my own mother by projecting true motherhood onto someone else. I needed to have this bizarre revenge on my own imperial past. Thank God I unmasked these games and was able to take back these projections and heal my relationship with my mother—my real mother—by finding the real Black Madonna. I also was able to heal my relationship with my family and my past. I came to understand all this in a much subtler way. As a young person, however, I could not see any other way out of my own psyche except by doing what I did.

What I see now is that I was born to the Black Madonna. I could not face that early on because I did not know enough about Her. I probably, psychologically, was too fragile and complicated to face Her full on so She gave me a false master and mother on which I could project Her. Out of Her even more paradoxical mercy, She shattered that projection in a terrible way. She also gave me as a companion to that shattering, my husband, who has been an amazing warrior for Her and in Her. She birthed me into a wholly new awareness that I pray and hope is now helping a lot of people.

Fred: That is an excellent analysis of your story. I think, in America, it is similar for our own imperial past in terms of the need to reconnect with our own indigenous roots. This has a direct connection with the Black Madonna that is our own Earth, here in America.

Andrew: It is the only way because, on the one hand, what She will do is to make you face the full horror of it and, on the other hand, Her compassion will give you the strength to go through it. Her strength will hold you up as you are crucified. That is what America has to go through both in its relationship with black people and Native Americans. She is the only force that can bring about the debt of recognition, the debt to sorrow, and the debt of crucifixion.

Fred: I am now reading *The Woman with the Alabaster Jar* by Margaret Starbird.[4] She relies heavily on the work in *Holy Blood, Holy Grail*.[5] What do you think of that? That is a movement that suggests Jesus was married, has a bloodline, in southern France . . .

Andrew: Well, I think the bloodline stuff cannot be proved or disproved. However, the understanding that Jesus may have been married to Mary Magdalene is what I think would be crucial. It is entirely possible and opens up what I have been talking about. It opens up the real truth of the resurrection: namely, that resurrection is about the transfiguration of the body. One of Jesus' tremendous powers as well as the Mother's is Tantric. I believe actually that Jesus was bisexual and that he had a sacred relationship with John as well as with Mary Magdalene. There is a heterosexual and homosexual Tantra which comes out of the Black Madonna, and Jesus realized them both. One of the tremendous benefits of opening up to the Christ as the Cosmic Androgyne would be the healing of all human sexual shame and all human sexual division and the initiation of the human race into the great secret of the Tantra that springs directly from the force of the Cosmic Christ and is birthed by the force of the Black Madonna. Awakening to this Tantric force might give us as a race the power and sacred energy to change all things in Her and for Her before it's too late.

In every arena of life, there is a massive shift to be made, and very fast. Only the Black Madonna, I feel, can give us the passion, vision, strength, and complete realization necessary to make this shift in time. These days there is a prayer I keep saying in Her honor, a prayer I first prayed in Chartres to the Black "Virgin of the Pillar":

> O Black Madonna, my Dark Mother, who births all those who love and surrender enough into Divine Humanity, keep me close to your wild and burning heart, and grace me the courage to go through all I need to become your instrument.

---

[4] Margaret Starbird, *The Woman with the Alabaster Jar* (Rochester, VT: Bear & Company, 1993).
[5] Michael Baigent, Richard Leigh, and Henry Lincoln, *Holy Blood, Holy Grail* (New York: Dell, 1983).

I have found that if you pray this prayer sincerely or "danger-ously" enough, it will be answered.

After September 11, 2001

This interview addresses the attack on the World Trade Towers, September 11, 2001, in New York City. It is meant as an addendum to the previous interview with Andrew Harvey and describes, through this specific, historical event, the relevance of the eruption of the Dark Feminine archetype. The interview was held on November 18, 2001.

Fred: The tragic event of September 11 changed not only the American psyche but also the world psyche.

Andrew: Yes, for me it seems like the eruption of the Black Madonna into the center of life. Fundamentally, I think of the planes going to the towers in two ways: the first image that comes to me is that of the spear opening the heart of Christ on the cross. It is the spear that lances the boil of a very long coma of denial. The other way in which I think of those planes going into the side of the towers is like the breaking of the waters. When the towers dissolved, it seemed as if the waters of a vast, pregnant woman had broken. A birth was going to take place. For me, both ways of looking at this disaster are as a huge immersion in the acid of the shadow. I see the crisis as a vast shattering-open of all the fantasies so as to confront the world with the seriousness, grav-ity, and horror of real evil, and people on all sides with the necessity for a real transformation of the heart and mind, if we are going to sur-vive. This event has brought together in a death or birth dance the two different sides of the world: Jihad and McWorld. Jihad is the fanatical extremist wing of Islam, and McWorld,[6] the fundamentalism of the dollar, of the corporate mind, of the oil multimillionaire, and the world of the domination over nature by economic greed. Both sides are fun-damentalists disconnected from the feminine, mass-murders, in fact, of the feminine in women, in relationships, in nature. They are being brought together now to fight each other to the death so that the dark in both will be destroyed.

---

6 See Benjamin Barber, *Jihad Versus McWorld: How Globalism and Tribalism Are Reshaping Our World* (New York: Ballantine, 1996).

This is terrifying. Both sides are not only responsible already for enormous suffering but also have to face enormous suffering. Both sides will have to claim the truth of their shadows if they are going to change and be creative, if there is going to be a birth of a new humanity and not a death.

I believe strongly this tremendous clash has come for a prophetic purpose. It comes at the very time in which all the terms for a great birth of a divine humanity are ready, despite everything, and waiting to be implemented. All the technological and philosophical possibilities and skills are there. All of the mystical systems have flooded the world with the treasures of their knowledge and the treasure of their sacred technology.

The birth can only take place in democracy. In the Western world, there is a growing awareness of the body as sacred, of the value of freedom, of recognizing the power and potency of the Sacred Feminine, and seeing the blessing in human variety and diversity. There is also here tremendous scientific, biological, ecological, and economic knowledge that, if it were dedicated to divine love and to the re-creation of the world in and under God, could help a massive transformation take place really quite fast. That is really why this crisis is manifesting at this moment—to bring the West to a knowledge of its fundamental role in bringing about this potentially all-transforming birth. We really do have to dedicate ourselves to this birth seriously, with all our powers, if it is going to take place.

This is very much the time in which human history is going to be decided. It is going to take a real turning in the psyche toward the dark side of the feminine, toward the side that reveals the horror of what we have done, the cruelty the shadow inflicts, and the depths of the vastness of the major problems that threaten humanity. These are not simply terrorism but are environmental, psychological, spiritual, and political.

Only the Dark Feminine can open us up to the vastness of the suffering we all need to go through to become responsible for what the human shadow has inflicted both on the life of humanity and on the life of nature. We are going to have to open up to the necessity of suffering as part of the great, sacred, dark heart of the Dark Feminine, the dark heart that bleeds and suffers with all living things. We are going to have to be taught by the Dark Feminine how to go through what is about to occur, which is really the crucifixion of all of our illusions, fantasies, and beliefs in humanity as separate from God. We are going to have to turn to the Dark Feminine in order to be able to endure the various stages of deceit, disintegration, and disillusion that are about to be unfolded in meticulous and ruthless geometrical stages. We are going to have to turn to the positive Dark Feminine, the glowing Guadalupe aspect of the Dark Feminine, because only that will reconnect us to the sacredness of embodiment. She will give us the blood knowledge, the green-heart knowledge, the connection to the living streams of life that we must recapture very fast if we are going to have a chance of birthing ourselves in all dimensions as a renovated divine humanity. We are going to have to turn to the transcendent aspect of the Dark Feminine, the one who goes beyond all dogma or religion, the absolute eternal marriage of all opposites, the final mystery of paradoxical grace that will be the only source of guidance and of stamina to take us through the process of annihilation into resurrection, the only one who could feed us the mystical awareness that we will need.

The clearer the individual sees the overall global reach of what is happening, the clearer the archetypal patterns will be understood. The more that people see, the greater the chance they will be able to turn to the Black Madonna and ask directly for help and start opening up in the ways She demands.

The Black Madonna is a very demanding archetype. She demands radical honesty about one's own motive. She demands total connectedness to the living glory of the world. She demands total submission to the mysteries of Her paradoxical dance. She demands total, passionate commitment to giving your life to serve justice and transfiguration in the real world. She really is asking humanity to kick away not only the material toys but also all of the religious divisions that have kept humanity from the heart of God and from each other's hearts. We need to kick away the dogmas and the crazy fundamentalist systems whether they are Islamic, Hindu, or Christian and to place ourselves in contact with her naked heart that transforms everything. That will take a massive breakdown on all levels. She is preparing us for that. I think we are going to be put through this because we have been given absolutely every chance to change for the last 150 years. We have been given extraordinary messages of warning and potential hope by the divine Mother Herself as Mary at Fatima and elsewhere. We have been given extraordinary evidence of our destructiveness revealed in, for example, two world wars, the creation of atomic bombs, the devastating information about the environment and worldwide diseases and the extent of poverty that threatens the world at the moment. We have paid no attention. Now what has happened is the Divine Dark One has organized a crisis perfectly horrible in all of its aspects, perfectly tuned to drive us from every single illusion that we have held dear, every single dogma that we have clung to into the arms of Her own Kali knowledge and transcendent awareness. We can either go into those arms and become free, become one with Her heart and start giving everything to turn this lunacy around before it destroys the planet, or we can simply pretend it is not going on and retreat into denial and join the destructive forces and hasten the end of everything. Now, more than ever, the choice is ours. What I am certain of is this: the Black Madonna will give us all the strength and passion we need if only we can find the courage to surrender to Her.

These days I find myself praying continuously a prayer that came to me on September 12:

O glorious Dark One,
do what is necessary
to wake us up,
and give us
the strength and sacred passion
to bear our illumination.

Transformation through Integration of the Dark Feminine

Carol B. Donnelly

Carol B. Donnelly, L.C.S.W., is a diplomate Jungian analyst, trained at the C. G. Jung Institute of Chicago. She has lectured and presented courses on fairytales and dreams and has a particular interest in the dark side of the feminine archetype. She lives and practices in Three Rivers, Michigan.

INTEGRATION

What is brewed
in the cave
is cupped
and drunk to the dregs.

I am not the same.
Yet, Self-same I remain.

In Darkness I rise up
to greet the Light.

I am blinded;
She is terrified.
The dance begins, the pounding drums
cadence in the night.
We step together, Darkness and the Light,
becoming one, wholeness and delight.[1]

I am in Switzerland, attending the winter seminar at the C. G. Jung Institute in Kusnacht. Afternoons are free; groups of us wander around the country via its fine railway system to enjoy the beauty of the country. This day we disembark at Einsiedeln in the midst of a blustery snowfall. We walk through the charming, narrow streets to the massive Benedictine monastery that houses the shrine of the Black Madonna. Struggling with the huge, heavy doors in the cold wind, we enter another world. Moving first to the front of the church, I observe the structure as a whole and absorb its ancient sense of sacredness. Then, as I am about to move back to the shrine, a group of monks in black robes appear in the sanctuary and proceed toward the gated shrine. I follow, standing as close as space allows. The monks begin to sing a pleading hymn in the ageless Latin language that is so familiar to me: "Salve Regina, Hail Holy Queen, Mother of mercy, our life, our sweetness, our hope. . . ." Magnificently gilded and attired in rich colors, this Virgin to whom they sing is black. The Child in Her arms is black. Standing on Her pedestal, She is surrounded by a backdrop of clouds, streams of energy emanating from Her.

I stand riveted, unable or unwilling to move away from this powerful image that is enlarging my heart beyond measure. Suddenly, I feel redeemed. The purity of the voices that sing that beautiful prayer seems to intermingle with the dark, earthy, feminine energy emanating from that Black Madonna. I experience a sense of my own darkness, this time with peaceful acceptance, untinged with heavy guilt and remorse. In this moment, I am consciously aware of the split within my psyche, of the fierce conflict between the internalized, virginal values that I embraced from my religious childhood and the earthy, passionate, sensual nature that had been imprisoned in the unconscious for so long. In my body, I feel a pair of invisible nurturing hands gather up the "Good" and the "Bad" and meld them together into a lovable and acceptable wholeness. Long after the monks retire to the sanctuary, and several minutes after my traveling companions begin their exit from this shrine, I reluctantly follow, not quite grounded until the cold snowy air slaps me in the face as the heavy door is pushed open.

This mystical meeting with the Black Madonna at Einsiedeln initiated my personal search for the Dark Feminine, which has extended over a period of years and continues as an ongoing process. A previously unexplored dimension of my femininity has unfolded, providing me substance, richness, and depth as woman. It is my firm belief that a woman cannot attain wholeness without recognizing and confronting this powerful, and often dormant, aspect of her psyche.

The dark can be defined by the light. I was raised in an era when culture and religion urged a young woman to model her behavior on the Blessed Virgin Mary, the carrier of disembodied virtue and devotional purity. Even the birth of Her Son was virginal. I was taught that Original Sin tarnished this perfection in ordinary men and women, and we must make every effort to resist the temptations of the body in order to elevate the spirit. My encounter with the Black Madonna provided a jolt of recognition and a joyous acceptance of the dark side of my being. The ensuing process of paying homage to this neglected side of myself became a long and terrible ordeal before I was able to embrace the creative power and instinctual beauty of that guilt-laden "Dark Feminine." I have since found that the challenge to awaken this sleeping giant belongs to many women today. It becomes a primary task in the analytical container as a woman moves on to the discovery of the fullness of her feminine self. Her own inner authority then becomes her primary guide to wholeness.

Defining the term "Dark Feminine" is difficult. If I think of words as containers for inner speech, it helps me comprehend its meaning. Although I can look for archetypal explanations in the mythological figures of Kali, Demeter, Innana, and other goddess figures, I am still left to analyze what all that means in my own psyche and to the women with whom I work. One of the etiological sources of the word "dark" comes from the Old English term *deorc*, which means to hide, to render obscure. "Feminine" has part of its root in "fecund," to render fruitful. If I put together these loose analogies, my inner language can translate "Dark Feminine" to be that place within psyche that is deeply hidden and obscure, but is the source of the fruitful renderings of the creative soul. It is the secret dwelling place of the potential to unite as fully as possible with the Divine.

Plumbed to the depths and without boundaries, the Dark Feminine has the power of death, but it can just as well send a woman to the heights of life. A woman engaged with her Dark Feminine is capable of exploring life and the world with a "no-holds-barred" attitude, with nothing that says, "No, don't." In the process, she may cause agony for herself and those close to her because she must be

willing to go into wild terrain, unknown territory. Leaving the comfort of well-established attitudes and opinions to encounter her dark
nature means confrontation and analysis of guilt that clings with
static persistence to the synthetic aspects of her psyche. The Dark
Feminine, positive and negative, rises out of the fierce landscape of a
woman's soul. She must journey inward in order to identify and own
all parts of herself.

Often, as a woman engages in this mythic struggle, she faces periods of confusion, doubt, and depression. But the gradual journey into
wholeness also enables her to experience freedom and welcome release
from the burden of "Bad." It opens that place within her psyche where
she is able to allow, and trust, depth of spirit in all of her encounters
with emotional experience. Now the repressed energy becomes available as a source of muse-like inspiration to live, create, and relate from
a much broader, deeper perspective.

One of the primary areas of being cut-off from the Dark Feminine
for me was disembodiment. My religious background had informed
me that the body was a mere holding-place for the soul, a Temple of
the Holy Spirit, to be cared for but not indulged. The split between
body and soul had to be healed. Six years of body work, in conjunc-
tion with analysis and meditation, helped to repair the damage. I found
Marion Woodman's observation to be very accurate:

> Body work must be approached with the same respect and
> attentiveness that one gives to dreams. The body has a wis-
> dom of its own. However slowly and circuitously that wis-
> dom manifests, once it is experienced it is a foundation, a
> basis of knowing that gives confidence and total support to
> the ego. To reach its wisdom requires absolute concentra-
> tion; dropping the mind into the body, breathing into what-
> ever is ready to be released, and allowing the expression
> until the negative, dammed energy is out, making room for
> the positive.[2]

The negative, dammed energy that Woodman refers to results when
one undergoes forced separation from the natural, dark forces in the

---

[2] Marion Woodman, *The Pregnant Virgin: A Process of Psychological Transformation* (Toronto: Inner City Books, 1988), p. 60.

feminine. It is the fear that is engendered in the body from years of denial and repression of the sensual, seductive, mysterious realm of the Dark Feminine. Confrontation with this fear as it exits the body through the mechanics of body therapy is the necessary access to genuine Light. Instead of confessing, in guilt, her knowledge and pleasure in that part of herself, a woman must learn to rejoice in her darkness and to own responsibility for living out creative energies in pursuit of her wholeness.

Wholeness requires an integration of darkness and light. I knew that part of the integration process of dark and light feminine, for me, would be to bring together the images I held of the Madonna. There was the Virgin on Her pedestal in the Church where I had knelt with great devotion throughout my childhood. The elaborate rituals surrounding devotion to Mary were rich and imaginative, and the virtues She represented catered to my need to be reflected as good and pure. Now, in my later adult life, I had encountered the Black Madonna with life-changing results. I discovered that Black Madonnas received homage in several parts of the world. Most recently, while traveling in Costa Rica, I visited the Shrine of *La Negrita*, the "Dark Lady," as She is affectionately called by the Costa Ricans, who have adopted Her as the Patroness of Costa Rica. I watched as people knelt before Her shrine in rapt devotion in the grand cathedral of Nuestra Senora de Los Angeles in Cartaga. Why, I ask, is there such devotion to the Dark Madonna in so many countries, but little recognition of Her darkness in America? Perhaps some of the explanation lies in cultural reasons, where the people have merely projected the dark-skinned quality of their own ethnicity. That does not explain the avid devotion to Black Madonnas in European countries such as Switzerland, Poland, and France. Does She, in Her Blackness, speak to that archetypal darkness that lies so deeply hidden in the psyche? There are probably more scholarly explanations for the European devotion. But as I gaze at the collection of Madonna images and statues that I have accumulated during the course of my search, I know that She has identified for me "dark" as defined by light and "light" made more brilliant by definition of the dark. Finally, the dance has begun, bringing the two together.

Recently, I came across Jim Brandenburg's book of extraordinarily profound nature photography, *Chased by the Light*. These were not "calendar" scenes. The photographs were one artist's endeavor to purify his work, which he felt had become overladen with technique and overproduction. So he limited himself to just one shot a day over a period of time between the autumn equinox and winter solstice as he wandered about his land near the Boundary Waters in Minnesota. I was drawn into each picture as one is drawn into a profound bit of poetry, until I became unaware of time and place. With great reluctance I finally had to close the book and return to the so-called "real" world. Brandenburg provided a comment about one of the sites he chose to photograph. It was a spruce forest, not so overtly beautiful, he said. It did not contain the usual subjects of popular photography. For that reason it had remained untrampled. "And perhaps that is why I have always felt that something spiritual lived there, something dark and old. . . ."[3] And perhaps that is, for me, the realm of the Dark Feminine—a spiritual place, dark and old, untrampled, and not so overtly beautiful that it dazzles, but quietly existing in its own underworld terrain at the center of the psyche.

---

[3] Jim Brandenburg, *Chased by the Light* (Chanhassen, MN: NorthWord Press, 1998), p. 10.

Lodestone

Meinrad Craighead

Meinrad Craighead is an artist and writer. Born in the United States, she lived much of her early adult life in Europe, principally in Italy and Spain, and later in England, where she spent 14 years in a Benedictine monastery. Her paintings are in public and private collections in North America and Europe. Her highly-acclaimed book, *The Mother's Songs*, published in 1986, brought to a wider public the unique and deeply personal imagery in mythological language, the union of spirit, woman, and nature. In 1991 her book *The Litany of the Great River* was published. Her life and art have been discussed in many books and featured in film documentaries in England and through the Public Broadcast System in the United States. She makes her home in New Mexico. "Lodestone" will also appear in *Meinrad Craighead: Crow Mother and the Dog God: A Retrospective*, forthcoming from Pomengranate in October, 2003.

I have become a painter, but as a youngster in the 1940s my first love was for charcoal. My father gave me a narrow gray box of six charcoal sticks. Knotty, crooked, still coated with the metallic sheen from the fire, messy. Black. My young soul had found the way to mark a surface significantly and see itself reflected. I had crossed a threshold and, from time to time, in the eternal round of my fifty some years of creative work, I return to that naked place of the purity of black on white.

In the 1960s, a Fulbright in hand to study medieval Catalan art, I set out on a pilgrimage to the many-breasted mountain of Montserrat in Catalonia, Spain. There I would live and pray to the Black Madonna for nearly a year. This solitary, sculpted mountain rises from the surrounding plain just as, in the beginning, it rose from the sea. Remote and forested, the many caves are a natural home for anyone seeking solitude, and a thousand years ago, hermits had already seeded the site where the legend of this Black Madonna would grow. I sought the mountain because I, too, sought solitude, sought the metaphorical darkness of the same caves and forests, sought her.

Down the mountain, several kilometers below the Benedictine basilica and pilgrimage center, I rented a room in a small monastery of Benedictine nuns. Near their chapel was a free-standing bell tower. My little room was in the tower, beneath the bells which tolled throughout the day, summoning the nuns to prayer. Alone, yet with them, I, too, worked at my prayer.

I had brought large sheets of white Fabriano paper with me from Florence, where I had lived for some years, and now, hidden in the mountain, I entered the chaos and wilderness of solitary creative work. Twenty-eight years old, I would move deeply into my life pilgrimage of search, prostration, and worship through image making. Large charcoal drawings were the vehicle and manifestation of this search. Her dark face, which I beheld each morning up in the basilica, was my focus and became the receptacle for intuitions that became clear during and because of this chosen solitude. The charcoal imagery that emerged from isolation and concentration announced themes still evident in my work. Leaning over the heavy paper, rubbing and smearing the charcoal, I felt like her, a black transformer, eating the seeds, growing the images, harvesting the food, my hands and arms black with the powdery mess of burnt earth.

I worked standing at a table before the room's single long window, the charcoal drawing flat before me. My eyes shifted continually from the unfolding charcoal imagery to the imagery beyond the window, where boulders crouched and, rounded like beasts asleep, walked up the mountainside, and rain ran down small gullies and steep ravines to the Leobregat River below. Hawks, crows, ravens, and magpies hunted the mountain by day, and owls by night, as I slept in my narrow monastic cot.

Before dawn each morning, before the daily flow of pilgrims began arriving in busloads, I walked the several kilometers up the mountain and heard Mass in the crypt of the basilica. Afterward, going still higher, I climbed the many steps up to her shrine, set high behind the main altar. There in the semidarkness, I stood alone before La Morenita, the Little Black Virgin of Montserrat. This daily rhythm—walking up the mountain, walking down to my bell tower—shaped the solitude of those ten months, as if I were inhaling the silence and exhaling her potent darkness into the charcoal drawings. The double spiral of beginning-midpoint-ending imprinted each day as the phases of the moon imprinted the nights.

If the forest is a metaphor for the unknown, a drawing is the stroke-by-stroke journey through the unknown: a laying this in, a wiping that out, all the time watching for the image to take shape and lead you into its very specific story. The image begins to give itself to you; you follow it, you serve it. Hence the kinship of making and prayer manifests, with each evoking and shaping the other, creating images that walk right out of the emptiness which has contained them.

෴

It was at Montserrat that I first understood Crow Mother's fierce presence moving within a Black Madonna. Although I had been in Italy for some years, away from the land of New Mexico, I was never not there, for the spirits of that land clung to me in dreams, in memories, and in the animals sacred to the spirituality of its native peoples.

More recently I have felt Crow Mother in other shrines, especially at Rocamadour in southeastern France, where the silhouette of the Black Madonna is raw and strangely birdlike. In these intuitions Crow Mother unfolds her vast wings and slowly enfolds the Black Madonna.

Crow Mother, as a kachina, visits the Hopi people twice each February. She embodies two traditional images: she holds out a shallow basket of corn, and she carries a whip of barbed yucca leaves. What do these images mean? In the first, as one of the Mothers of the Kachinas, she is Crow, black as the night sky and the richest soil, dark as the miracle of deeply watered earth in the arid Southwest. She is the mother who fertilizes all life and feeds us the sacred cornmeal.

The other image of Crow Mother is startlingly different. She comes to the villages for the second time in February to initiate young boys and girls in the predawn winter darkness of the kivas. She purifies them with her yucca whip, strapping the calves of their legs. This severe, ritual cleansing prepares them to receive the sacred knowledge of their people. During the boys' maturation they submit to Crow Mother's whip several more times, but the girls have only the one experience. Each girl, in her own time, is initiated into her own blood mysteries and becomes a container for the mother wisdom of her people.

New Mexico is a land of harsh sun and black shadows. Before and after midday, everything beneath the sun throws a black shape on the earth in some direction. I move tied to earth. I walk in the empty semi-arid land and see everything bound to its black projection. For many years I lived in England. There were many aspects of the landscape I found wanting, but the hardest to bear was the absence of shadows. Everything was missing half of itself.

Wind moves white clouds below a hard sun. They will blackly overshadow acres and acres anywhere in this vast landscape. From a height, and at some distance, I often watch these dark patterns racing over the land and understand her sweeping presence, the overshadowing embrace of Crow Mother, holy mother of this high desert and my Rio Grande valley.

&

In New Mexico, where I now live, images of Our Lady of Guadalupe are ubiquitous, as is to be expected, since using the image may now also be read as a Hispanic political and cultural statement of pride. Seen less often, but also revered, are images of Our Lady of Sorrows and Our Lady of Solitude, *Dolorosa* and *Soledad*. Although they can be found in museums as treasured *bultos* and *santos* from the 1700s and 1800s, they are also widely available in shops and open markets, their images carved and painted by contemporary New Mexican folk artists who carry on the ancient tradition of the *santeros*. People want these dark mothers in their homes: severe Black Soledad, her hands knotted in grief; Black Dolorosa, her heart riven by the sword of her seven sorrows.

Various reproductions of these two images of her are placed on altars throughout my home and studio. More often than not her eyes are closed, her gaze utterly inward, her mouth slightly open, keening. I hear in these pictures the muted cry voiced in the liturgy of Good Friday and I remember those verses from the Lamentations of Jeremiah: "She weepest sore in the night and her tears are on her cheeks . . . All you who pass by, behold and see if there be any sorrow like unto my sorrow."

We hear the sound of her sorrowful dirge, we behold the face twisted in grief, the universal face of Mother grieving for Child—or Child grieving for Mother. Like most of us, I have indelible memories of the faces of my own mother's grief—or what I was allowed to see of it—those grimaces of loss or pain or fear that, once seen, can never be effaced from memory. But the sorrow is radiant, like light shining in the darkness of a black stone lying over the heart.

In ancient Egypt, during the binding of a corpse, a scarab amulet was laid over the heart and bound to the body. I often see these large, stone amulets in museum collections, the surface of each inscribed with this prayer to the Great Mother: "O heart of my mother, do not outweigh me before the Keeper of the Balance." The prayer recalls a time in the early 1950s when I went to church with my mother each Tuesday evening for the devotions to Our Lady of Perpetual Help. I don't remember those prayers. I do remember kneeling next to my mother and feeling the intensity with which she laid down her own heart to the Keeper of the Balance.

When I was about eight years old my family moved from Arkansas to Chicago, but my mother sent me back to North Little Rock each summer, to stay with my grandmother. It is my mother, then, who imprinted the poetry of pilgrimage in my soul. Summer after summer she sent me back home to her mother. In Memphis I changed to a Rock Island train running to Little Rock, driven by my grandfather. Then, in his blue Pontiac, we drove up Main Street. Memaw sat on the front porch watching for us. Still at some distance I saw her see me. And, sweetly, the finding of each other was reenacted on those summer nights, hiding and seeking and finding. After supper, as soon as it was dark enough, we children gathered to play the day's final game. Sometimes it was Memaw who looked for me and found me and then lifted me in her arms and put me to bed.

When Memaw died, my family and I arrived from Chicago to attend her funeral. The little white clapboard house on Main Street was filled with grieving adults. They gathered in my mother and she disappeared into her family. I had never seen so many people in the living room, and now they were embracing each other and bending over Memaw's casket. While the adults comforted each other, many bewildered children, strangely forgotten, wandered around seeking a container for their own loss. We were of no use to each other. I fled to the backyard, to the dogs, but soon came in, cold. It was mid-December.

In a bedroom I found my father's sister, the only relative of his who had come to the wake. A stranger to most of my mother's family, she sat alone in a dark bedroom. I paused in the doorway. "Come here, baby," she called, and I ran into her wide open thighs, her embrace, into cloth and comfort, into the dark enclosure of her enormous body where I could lay down my grief.

Through a lifetime of pilgrimages to many Black Madonnas, this memory of Aunt Louise has passed through each of them. Even anticipating each sweet discovery, I still approach these dark altars grieving, and I find there the deepest place to lay that grief down.

For over forty years I have prayed before the Black Madonna. Throughout Europe, images of her are enshrined in countless pilgrimage churches, in remote monasteries, in tiny chapels and vast cathedrals, down in dark crypts and up on high altars. Enclosed in these many homes, she has been visited by millions of pilgrims for hundreds of years. She is the Lodestone, always pulling us into her mystery.

Each Black Madonna is unique. Each one's story is a composite of legends, differing from place to place. But most evolve from a common, mythic tale. Set around the time of the turning of the first millennium, it is the story of a shepherd or a child or children, who, perhaps searching for a stray animal, enter a forest and find a statue of a black Mary in a cave or in a tree, often guarded by animals.

The movement toward pilgrimage begins as a hunch, perhaps a vague curiosity. We cannot anticipate these whispers, but we do hear them, and the numen aroused has teeth in it. Thus a quest is initiated, and we are compelled or shoved into places of possible epiphanies.

At the shrines, the anticipation of approaching her weaves a connective tissue between pilgrims. We all gaze in the same direction. We are immersed in a collective search, yet we remain deeply solitary. On pilgrimage, there is an abiding contradiction inside each visitation: I seek her, yet, when I kneel before her, it is I who am found. Shoulder to shoulder with countless other pilgrims, I have come to recognize this common response. There is a surprising transparency, a sweetness, and courtesy between us strangers. We have all left home to find home. We have all been found and we recognize each other. We have all come home to her and we experience a profound communality of spontaneous ingathering. For me, this paradigm of searching and finding defines the experience of coming before the Black Madonnas. Many of her shrines have the comfortable feeling of casual chaos. They smell sweetly of banks of candles, incense, and lamps, but they stink of smoke and the close press of crowds pushing along toward her. In the smaller, deeply shadowed shrines, the milling churn of pilgrims, the heat, and the lack of air carry the distinct weight and shape of a hot cave matrix. I have been in some shrines as small as dark bedrooms. These you enter alone, as if to speak intimately to an elderly relative. But at other shrines I feel no invitation to approach her. I just stand before a statue. I kneel, light candles, pray, search the image— perhaps marvel at the superb carving. But I am not invited to cross the threshold into her mystery.

Returning from pilgrimages to Black Madonnas, women (Catholics, Protestants, or women of no professed religion) will often say to me, "I don't know what possessed me to go to them, but now I can't imagine not having gone." Many stories are carried back from each shrine, and those of us who have traveled her pilgrimage routes in the European countries find that we need to tell these stories to each other. We need to talk about her. Along these routes, each Black Madonna has a local history, a roster of legends specific to the particular place. She *belongs* to the people of those places, like the matriarch honored at family gatherings. Several years ago I experienced this most poignantly in Orcival, a village in the mountainous region of the French Auvergne. Its stunningly beautiful Romanesque pilgrimage church is in a deep valley wrapped closely in low, grassy hills. It was mid-May, green, and throngs of people were there, celebrating the feast of the Ascension. A sea of pilgrims and parishioners flowed in and out of the church, and in the interior hundreds of people, shoulder to shoulder, sang and celebrated the High Mass. The local bishop and many priests presided. At the center of the ritual, enthroned on a column beside the altar, was the Black Madonna of Orcival. As is often the case, she is not "black" but shades of rich brown, a wooden statue covered with copper and silver plate, aged to a dark patina.

After Mass ended, a procession formed, and she was carried from the raised sanctuary down several steps to ground level and placed on a simple wooden table covered with a linen cloth. When the bishop came down and stood next to her, the roar of organ and hymns ceased.

He raised his arms, gestured to Our Lady, and then gestured to us, saying, "Now come forward and kiss her." The people formed a procession and moved forward to venerate her. The devotions of the people would go on into the night. A friend and I stayed in the church for some hours. I inched my way forward in the procession to touch the statue and then went to the back of the massive volcanic stone church, joined the procession again and walked up the aisle to kiss her a second time. I have always envied the serious women of Greece who flagrantly bend to kiss their saints and stroke their saviors. I often feel the desire to do this before certain Black Virgins but, unlike the statue of her in Orcival, they are usually inaccessible.

Some years prior to that blessed day in Orcival I spoke and showed slides of my paintings at an international conference of Methodist clergywomen. After the presentation I was approached by a Methodist bishop who embraced me and asked, "Do you understand how blessed you are to have prayed to her from childhood?"

When I am asked about my name, I tell the old story of Saint Meinrad and his ravens. In the early ninth century, when Saint Meinrad was about thirty years old, he left his monastery, the celebrated Carolingian Abbey of Reichenau on Lake Constance in Switzerland, seeking a deeper solitude. But, even in forested wilderness, people tracked their way to this legendary wise man (his name means "great counselor"), and so he withdrew again, moving further into the forests, seeking the solitude he craved. Meandering in this search for just the right place to be, Meinrad found two raven nestlings at the base of a fir and rescued them from two harassing hawks. Accepting this as a sign, he decided on this site for his second hermitage. It was the ravens, then, who chose the place. In the far future, the Benedictine Abbey of Einsiedeln, near Zurich, would be built here. When Saint Meinrad walked away from a communal monastic life, legend says that he carried with him into the forest a statue of Our Lady. Only she and the ravens were to live with him in eremitical solitude.

In the winter of 861, two men came to his hermitage. Although he knew them to be thieves, he invited them in and treated them generously, but they clubbed him to death, thinking to find something of value hidden in the hermitage. Finding nothing, they fled. But the ravens followed them and screamed the story of the slaying of their friend to villagers, who set out after the thieves and caught them.

Playing with Saint Meinrad's dates, I see that he was then about sixty-four years old and the ravens about twenty-five years old when they witnessed and then broadcast the murder of their solitary companion. When I was sixty-four, my dogs, at thirteen, were half the age of Meinrad's ravens. Time and again, through the days and months and years in my place near the Rio Grande, I watch my own crows and ravens, speculating on their ages. Through fifteen winters I have fed and watched these birds, my own black guardians who continue to feed and watch me.

One morning when I was working on this essay, a raven fell to the ground several yards from the studio. It had dropped from a height; the great beak was driven into the earth, but it bore no wound. The raven was huge, dead weight. As I handled the bird, I was startled by the synchronicity of this visitation just as I was meditating on the nearly one-thousand-year-old tale of Saint Meinrad and his ravens. These are tame words, vitiated and weightless compared to the raven's astonishing presence. The heft and roll of its shining black bulk in my hands and the fierce thrust of this striking dark encounter were so compelling that I was loath to bury the magnificent creature.

ॐ

Artists live a spirituality of epiphanies. We are called to see and be seen, and the veil between the two is often thin. Living at the line between the visible and the invisible, we make our images of the Divine (however we define this) and have ever done so.

Repeatedly I know the times (the life times) when I go to ground. Let me alone, I say. I need to rot and rise up and say, "Look, I have fashioned something which has never existed before." In a sustained, rhythmic, creative life, the essential urge for solitude and the fall into our *prima materia* is utterly trustworthy, despite the fear of failure, of chaos. Artists thrive in the deepest layer of mulch; we seed those pockets where the search has reached deepest, places where the hunt consumes the very ground that hosts it. We sit down deeply into the compost from which all imagery rises. We sit down into that darkness, that somber place, uncertain whether any image will rise from those containers in our soul that never dry out, where deep memories spill forth even denser memories until we marvel at the wellspring and do obeisance to the source, Her dark matrix.

In museums, in those houses of the muses, I often want to kiss paintings and run my hands over sculpture. In Rome I once found smooth marble hounds at the feet of divine Artemis. They still break my heart, as does Bacon's dog at the Tate and Matisse's *Dance*, as do the hands of Piero's *Madonna della Misericordia* and Dosso Dossi's butterflies—an endless litany. Everywhere there are sacred images to approach, each a sacramental sign, a source of grace. As I might enter a church, I enter a museum to pray to beauty. I listen to what André Malraux called "the voices of silence." Silent images stand time still. They are now and always present, ever playing round the edge of memory. Recently I was bedridden for a while. In the liminal zone between waking and sleeping, and often drugged, I drifted to many altars to pray. A lifetime of memories pulled me back into galleries and museums to specific paintings, and, as if in a dreamtime, the pictures overlaid each other intimately with eidetic vividness. In bed, inside their pulse, their presence, I knelt to serve my soul at these altars, and in that threshold place, I healed.

$$\text{\emph{so}}$$

The umbilical connection I feel for Saint Meinrad's story began many years ago. In 1956 I lived in Vienna and attended drawing classes at the Akademie. It was winter; the afternoons grew darker and colder, the walk around the Ringstrasse, longer. Passing Karlskirche on my way to the Strassenbahn, I often stopped in to pray there. One evening, a spindly table had been placed in the empty vestibule, centered under a naked, dim bulb, the only light in the dark vastness of the basilica.

Over the years I have mused on the clarity with which I noticed some pamphlets on this table, despite the dimness of the light. They offered the face of an elderly monk, smiling sweetly up at me, whose resemblance to my maternal grandfather, John, was startling. I struggled to translate the German text and gradually realized that the story of an ancestor of mine was being given to me. I was looking at the face of my grandfather's uncle, Brüder Meinrad Eügster. Born Joseph Gebhard Eügster in Altstätten in the Swiss Rhine valley, he was the youngest of a large family. The eldest son, Johann, and his wife emigrated to the United States where my grandfather was born in the

1880s. As I stood reading the account of Brüder Meinrad's life, I knew I had to visit the monastery of Einsiedeln, where he had lived for fifty years and where he was buried. I was also curious about the Black Madonna associated with this monastery. In Vienna, I sometimes saw images of "the Black Madonna of Einsiedeln" here and there, in churches and bookstores, not infrequently on large public posters announcing group pilgrimages to her shrine. I had never seen an image of Our Lady with a black face before.

But ten years passed before I finally went to Einsiedeln, in 1966. I planned to enter a Benedictine monastery and I wanted to go to my uncle Meinrad's grave to ask a blessing on the contemplative life I had chosen to enter. I also wanted to see this Black Virgin. I clearly remember that first visit to Our Lady of Einsiedeln. I recall her presence as a deep, transparent stillness and sweetness, and I remember her enigmatic eyes, which opened and closed as candlelight passed across her dark face. Just as Saint Meinrad carried a statue of Our Lady into his wilderness, so did I now carry this experience of her into my own journey into the unknown. Some months later I arrived at my monastery. In the course of my reception, the Abbess, knowing my family story of Brüder Meinrad, said, "I would like to call you Sister Meinrad."

ᢟ

In 1998, my sister Carole and I stayed in Einsiedeln for some days. It was her first visit. One morning we took the long pathway from Einsiedeln up to Etzel, to the shrine of Saint Meinrad's first hermitage. This path moves across sweeping meadows, past small, scattered homesteads, up to forested elevations. Portions of the pathway are signed "Jakobsweg" (Saint James's Way). So, that September morning, we walked a bit of one of the ancient ways to Santiago de Compostela, part of the complex network of routes that for hundreds of years has funneled pilgrims through Europe southward, across the Pyrenees, and to the great pilgrimage center in Spain.

After praying at Saint Meinrad's shrine, we hoped that the black dog who met us when we arrived at Etzel might walk back down with us. He did not. We soon passed some unseen line that marked one of his boundaries. He stopped at this invisible threshold, peed, and turned back uphill. When we first saw the dog, he had stepped forward sharply, inquisitively, as befitted his role of guardian of the shrine.

By afternoon, a mist had settled over Einsiedeln. Despite the driz-zle we took another path that sloped away from the monastery, up into thick woods. I had brought gifts from New Mexico with the intention of leaving them here: a raven's skull, a hank of my braided hair, and chunks of turquoise, tokens for my mother's family. We were alone in the woods. The foggy mist cloaked sounds from the village below. For a time we followed the meandering trail steeply uphill and then stepped off into the tangle of thick vegetation on either side of the path. How sweet was that sudden aura of mystery as we left the path-way and wandered into the woods, deeper into the darkening after-noon, holding hands! At a likely spot, silently agreed upon, we squatted opposite each other and scooped aside the loose rot and soft rubble. The ripe and rank odors of life and death rose, and small crea-tures ran away. I dug to shoulder depth and never felt firm earth. We mixed the gifts down into the crumble and chew of the mouth we had opened to receive them.

⁊⁊

The Black Virgin of Einsiedeln is deeply enshrined in black marble, an architectural cave shining with banks of candles. The shrine stands alone, near the two church entrances, providing easy access to the con-stant stream of pilgrims. Our uncle Meinrad's tomb is near the Black Madonna, beneath a rectangular slab set into the floor tiles at the entrance to a side chapel. It is unusual for a grave to be placed here. In 1941, sixteen years after his death, his body was brought here from the monastic crypt. Healings, increasingly attributed to Brother Meinrad, have attracted growing numbers of pilgrims who come to pray to him. They leave him votive candles, food offerings, and fresh flowers.

Throughout the day the bells of the monastery toll in the village and echo far out over the hills into the evening, marking the liturgical hours of communal monastic prayer. Carole and I happily fell into this rhythm and came to the Abbey church regularly to pray at the Black Virgin's altar and visit our uncle's tomb. We attended daily Mass and then, later in the day, Vespers, and finally stood with the monks who sing the *Salve Regina* before her each evening.

In the church we watched people come to her. Many local people became familiar to us, as they passed through the church in easy pedes-trian rhythms. She stood at the center of their lives. They moved with a sense of belonging, graciously but privately. This was their home; she was their treasure. I feared transgressing unspoken codes and customs. I envied them their sure position in her family. They entered the church in a circular movement, coming before her shrine, then walking over to Brother Meinrad's gravesite, lingering at each place and then leaving the church by the opposite door. All through these days, Carole and I watched this continual procession of people circling through their devotions to Our Lady and to our uncle. Praying inside this processional circle, I felt the thrum of the old story into which I am woven by blood and soil and soul. Herein lie the layers of sounds and silences of innumerable monastic lives and deaths and legends, of needy pilgrims seeking solace, nine centuries measured in chant and burning candle wax, moons, mulch, and many ravens.

On the eve of our departure from Einsiedeln, after the monks had sung the *Salve Regina*, we settled into a final visit with her. *O clemens, O pia, O dulcis Virgo Maria*. The music still vibrated in the silence. "O clement, O loving, O sweet Virgin Mary." We lingered in her gaze, the melody of her stillness, the sweetness of her ancient and mythic youth.

Eventually the elderly sacristan appeared, turning out lights and rattling keys, nodding invitations to the small group of us to leave. The church dimmed; now only candlelight shone inside her chapel, a rich image of golden, moving light shadowing and suffusing her and shimmering down the long, black marble pillars. We left the silent church and entered silent night. A thick, rainy mist overlaid Einsiedeln. Below us, the Platz and the streets were empty, and we paused in the silence. After a while Carole said, "I don't want to leave here."

&.

There is a grave aura about many of the Black Virgins, an expression of utter solitude so intense that the child on her knees or in the embrace of her left arm seems strangely appended. She sits, solitary, weighted, at the crossing-over place, the place where we fall, face down, and do obeisance. Rooted in her own aboriginal darkness, her eyes are opaque, blank, veiled in the deepest interiority. She sits deeply, a curtained container, a tabernacle, the eternally bloody cave of birth, disintegration, and rebirth. *Sedes sapientiae*. Seat of Wisdom.

Her *gravitas* defuses the Christian story. The older mystery of the ancient Black Mother God seeps and spills out of the Catholic container. We hear her oldest names chanted in our ancestral dreams and subliminal memories: Black Stone, Black Ishtar, Black Isis, Black Cybele, Black Artemis, Black Mary, Hail, full of grace, favor, mercy, blessing! Hail, Gate, Garden, Morning Star, Evening Star! Permit me again and again to enter your prayer, your place of dismemberment and remembering. Despite the Fathers, it is you whom we still worship. You, Black God Mother.

%

A PRAYER

Lodestone, you have sucked my prayer to yourself from my beginning. I have questions for you.

You are privy to every plea the human heart has ever shaped; is this the weight you carry, as any mother accumulates the weight of each tear and every touch?

Is this the weight of our grief's journey, groping its good way home to you?

Is this the weight, your waiting for us, which we lift like a treasure and bear away to give ballast to our lives?

All of us pilgrims, we seers and seekers, are drawn down into your measuring place, the shrine we have been moving toward, where we feel the magnetic pull of your gravitas.

This is the deepest place; here you mine our naked rawness.

Is this what we hear at your dark shrines, your invitation to work our rawness?

Is it here that you weigh our hearts against the weight of your own?

Is this the exact place where we find the treasure and fill up and spill over and call out

"I never want to leave here"?

The Return of the Black Madonna: A Sign of Our Times or How the Black Madonna Is Shaking Us Up for the 21st Century

Matthew Fox

Matthew Fox is a postmodern theologian and an ordained priest since 1967. He holds master's degrees in philosophy and theology from Aquinas Institute and a doctorate in spirituality from the Institut Catholique de Paris. He is president of the University of Creation Spirituality and codirector of the Naropa Oakland MLA program in Oakland California. He is the author of 24 books including *Original Blessing, A Spirituality Named Compassion, Passion for Creation: The Earth-Honoring Spirituality of Meister Eckhart, The Reinvention of Work, Sins of the Spirit, Blessings of the Flesh, Natural Grace* (with Rupert Sheldrake), and *Confessions: The Making of a Post-Denominational Priest.*

E very archetype has its seasons. They come and go according to the deepest, often unconscious, needs of the psyche, both personal and collective. Today the Black Madonna is returning.[1] She is coming, not going, and She is calling us to something new (and very ancient, as well). The last time the Black Madonna played a major role in Western culture and psyche was the 12th-century renaissance, a renaissance that the great historian M. D. Chenu said was the "only renaissance that worked in the West."[2] It worked because it was grassroots. And from this renaissance was birthed the university, the cathedral, the city itself. She brought with Her a re-sacralization of culture and a vision that awakened the young. In short, it was the last time the

---

[1] See, for example, China Galland, *Longing for Darkness: Tara and the Black Madonna* (New York: Viking, 1990).

[2] See M. D. Chenu, *Nature, Man and Society in the Twelfth Century* (Chicago: University of Chicago Press, 1957), chapter one.

goddess entered Western culture in a major way. But now we need to re-acknowledge what the Black Madonna archetype awakens in us and why She is so important for the 21st century.

My first encounter with the Black Madonna occurred in the spring of 1968 when I was a student in Paris and took a brief trip—my first—to Chartres Cathedral, located about 35 miles from Paris. While all of Chartres was an amazing eye-opener for me—its sense of cosmology, humor, human dignity, and inclusion of all of life—I stood before the statue of the Black Madonna and was quite mesmerized. "What is this? Who is this?" I asked myself. A French woman came by and I quizzed her about it. The answer was as follows. "Oh, this is a statue that turned black over the years because of the number of candles burning around it," she declared. I didn't believe her. It made no sense. I looked carefully and saw no excessive candle power around the statue.

The story is an old one, one of ignorance and of racism. Even the French, at their most central holy spot, have lost the meaning and the story of the Black Madonna. And racism has contributed to this neglect.

The Black Madonna is found all over Europe, in Sicily, Spain, Switzerland, France, Poland, Czechoslovakia, as well as in Turkey and Africa, and in Asia as Tara in China and as Kali in India. She is also named by Our Lady of Guadalupe in Mexico. (Sometimes called the "brown Madonna.") What is she about and why is interest in her returning today?

An archetype by definition is not about just one thing. No metaphor, no symbol, is a literal mathematical formula. The Black Madonna meant different things in different historical periods and different cultural settings. Why is she re-emerging in our time and what powers does she bring with her? Why do we need the Black Madonna today? I detect 12 gifts that the Black Madonna archetype brings to our time. They are more than gifts; they are challenges. She comes to shake us up which, as we shall see, is an ancient work of Isis, the Black Madonna.

1. The Black Madonna Is Dark and Calls Us to the Darkness

Darkness is something we need to get used to again—the "Enlightenment" has deceived us into being afraid of the dark and dis-tant from it. Light switches are illusory. They feed the notion that we can "master nature" (Descartes' false promise) and overcome all darkness with a flick of our finger.

Meister Eckhart observes that "the ground of the soul is dark."[3] Thus, to avoid the darkness is to live superficially, cut off from one's ground, one's depth. The Black Madonna invites us into the dark and therefore into our depths. This is what the mystics call the "inside" of things, the essence of things. This is where Divinity lies. It is where the true self lies. It is where illusions are broken apart and the truth lies. Andrew Harvey puts it this way: "The Black Madonna is the transcendent Kali-Mother, the black womb of light out of which all of the worlds are always arising and into which they fall, the presence behind all things, the darkness of love and the loving unknowing into which the child of the Mother goes when his or her illumination is perfect."[4] She calls us to that darkness which is mystery itself. She encourages us to be at home there, in the presence of deep, black, unsolvable mystery. She is, in Harvey's words, "the blackness of divine mystery, that mystery celebrated by the great Aphophatic mystics, such as Dionysus Areopagite, who see the divine as forever unknowable, mysterious, beyond all our concepts, hidden from all our senses in a light so dazzling it registers on them as darkness."[5] Eckhart calls God's darkness a "superessential darkness, a mystery behind mystery, a mystery within mystery that no light has penetrated."[6]

To honor darkness is to honor the experience of people of color.[7] Its opposite is racism. The Black Madonna invites us to get over racial stereotypes and racial fears and projections and to go for the dark.

2. The Black Madonna Calls Us to Cosmology, to a Sense of the Whole of Space and Time

Because she is dark and leads us into the dark, the Black Madonna is also cosmic. She is the great cosmic Mother on whose lap all creation exists. The universe itself is embraced and mothered by her. She yanks us out of our *anthropocentrism* and back into a state of honoring *all our*

---

[3] Matthew Fox, *Meditations with Meister Eckhart* (Santa Fe: Bear & Co., 1982), p. 42.
[4] Andrew Harvey, *The Return of the Mother* (Berkeley, CA: Frog, Ltd. 1995), p. 371.
[5] Harvey, *Return of the Mother*, p. 371.
[6] Fox, *Meditations with Meister Eckhart*, p. 43.
[7] See Eulalio R. Baltazar, *The Dark Center: A Process Theology of Blackness* (New York: Paulist, 1973).

relations. She ushers in an era of cosmology, of our relationship to the whole (in Greek, *kosmos* means "whole") instead of just parts, be they nation parts, ethnic parts, religious parts, or private parts. She pulls us out of the Newtonian parts-based relation to self and the world—out of our tribalism—into a relationship to the whole again. Since we are indeed inheriting a new cosmology in our time, a new "Universe Story," the timing of the Black Madonna's return could not be more fortuituous. She brings a blessing of the new cosmology, a sense of the sacred, to the task of educating our species in a new universe story.[8]

3. The Black Madonna Calls Us Down to Honor our Lower Chakras

One of the most dangerous aspects of Western culture is its constant flight upward, its race to the upper chakras. A chakra represents our physical and spiritual energy centers and the upper chakras denote intellect and rationality. Western culture flees from the lower chakras of groundedness and the source of our common, human experience. A classic example of this is our popular investment in the Cartesian belief that "truth is clear and distinct ideas." The Black Madonna takes us down, down to the first chakras, including our relationship to the whole (the first chakra, where we pick up the vibrations of sounds from the whole cosmos), our sexuality (second chakra), and our anger and moral outrage (third chakra). European culture, especially in the modern era, has tried to flee from all these elements both in religion and in education. The Black Madonna will not tolerate such flights from the earth, flights from the depths.[9]

4. The Madonna Honors the Earth and Represents Ecology and Environmental Concerns

This is a natural expression of the Black Madonna's honor for the direction of down and the lower charkas that take us there. Mother Earth is named so by her very presence. Mother Earth is dark and

---

[8] See Brian Swimme and Thomas Berry, *The Universe Story* (San Francisco: HarperSanFrancisco, 1992) and Brian Swimme, *The Hidden Heart of the Cosmos* (Maryknoll, NY: Orbis Books, 1996).
[9] For a fuller development of the chakras, see Matthew Fox, *Sins of the Spirit, Blessings of the Flesh* (New York: Harmony, 1999), pp. 94–116 and pp. 167–327.

fecund and busy birthing. So is the Black Madonna. Andrew Harvey says: "The Black Madonna is also the Queen of Nature, the blesser and agent of all rich fertile transformations in external and inner nature, in the outside world and in the psyche."[10] Mother Earth nurtures Her children and feeds the world and the Black Madonna welcomes them home when they die. She recycles all things. The Black Madonna calls us to the environmental revolution, to seeing the world in terms of our interconnectedness with all things and not our standing off to master or rule over nature (as if we could, even if we tried). She is an affront to the capitalist exploitation of the Earth's resources, including the exploitation of the indigenous peoples who have been longest on the Earth interacting with Her in the most subtle ways. The Black Madonna sees things in terms of the whole and therefore does not countenance the abuse, oppression, or exploitation of the many for the sake of financial aggrandizement of the few. She has always stood for justice for the oppressed and lower classes (as distinct from the lawyer classes). She urges us to stand up to those powers that, if they had their way, would exploit her beauty for short-term gain at the expense of the experience of beauty of which future generations will be deprived. She is a conservationist, one who conserves beauty, health, and diversity.

Furthermore, if Thomas Berry is correct that "ecology is functional cosmology," then to be called to cosmology *is* to be called to its local expression of ecology.[11] One cannot love the universe and not love the Earth. And, vice versa, one cannot love the Earth and ignore its temporal and spatial matrix, the universe.

5. The Black Madonna Calls Us to Our Depths

She calls us to live spiritually and radically on this planet—not superficially, unthinkingly, and oblivious to the grace that has begotten us in so many ways. The depths to which we are called include the depths of awe, wonder, and delight—joy itself is a depth experience we need to re-entertain in the name of the Black Madonna. She calls us to enter

---

[10] Harvey, *Return of the Mother*, p. 371.
[11] Thomas Berry is the founder of the History of Religions program at Fordham University and the Riverdale Center of Religious Research. Among his several books are *Dream of the Earth* (Sierra Club Nature and Natural Philosophy Library, 1990) and *The Great Work* (New York: Bell Tower, 1999).

into the depths of our pain, suffering, and shared grief—not to run from it or cover it up with myriad addictions ranging from shopping to drugs and alcohol and sport and superficial religion. She calls us to the depths of our creativity and to entertain the images that are born in and through us. And she calls us to the depths of transformation, of social, economic, gender, racial, and eco-justice and the struggle that must be maintained to carry on solidarity with the oppressed of any kind.

She calls us to the depths of our psyche which, as Meister Eckhart says, are "dark," and to the depths of the Earth, which are surely dark, and to the depths of the sky that have also been rediscovered for all their darkness. Black holes abound in space as well as in the mysterious breadth of our souls. We need to explore them. They, too, are fecund. They have much to teach us.

6. The Black Madonna Calls Us to Our Divinity, Our Creativity

Because She is a goddess, the Black Madonna resides in all beings. Birnbaum makes the point that since humanity and all human culture emerged from Africa, it is logical to surmise that everyone's genetic "'beautiful mother' is African and dark, and that she is the oldest divinity we know. . . . Everyone has an African black mother."[12] She is the divine presence inside of creation. She calls us inside, into the "kingdom/queendom of God" where we can co-create with divinity and feel the rush of divinity's holy breath or spirit. But to call us to divinity is to call us to our responsibility to give birth.

If Carl Jung is correct when he says that creativity comes "from the realm of the mothers"[13] then the Black Madonna, who is surely a realm of the mothers, calls us to creativity. She expects nothing less from us than creativity. Hers is a call to create, a call to ignite the imagination. What, but our collective imaginations, can succeed in moving us beyond our energy dependence on fossil fuels to an era of self-sustaining energy based on solar and renewable, clean fuels? What, but an education in creativity, can reinvent learning so that the joy, wonder, and

---

12 Lucia Chiavola Birnbaum, *Dark Mother: African Origins and Godmothers* (New York: Authors Choice Books, 2001), pp. xxv, 11.
13 C. G. Jung, "Psychology and Literature," in Brewster Ghiselin, ed., *The Creative Process* (New York: Mentor, 1952), p. 222.

enticement of learning displaces our failing and boring educational systems? What, but moral imagination, can move us beyond the growing
divide between materially impoverished nations and materially sated
but spiritually impoverished nations?

The Black Madonna would usher in an era where more and more
artists will get good work and thrive on good work and reawaken the
human soul by way of moral and political imagination.[14]

7. The Black Madonna Calls Us to Diversity

There is no imagination without diversity—imagination is about inviting disparate elements into soul and culture so that new combinations
can make love together and new beings can be birthed. Because the
Black Madonna is *black*, she addresses the fundamental phobia
around race and differences of color and culture that come with race
and ethnic diversity. Meister Eckhart says: "All the names we give to
God come from an understanding of ourselves."[15] To give God the
name "Black Madonna" is to honor blackness and all people of color
and to get over an excessive whiteness of soul and culture; it is also to
honor the feminine. Divinity is diverse—in color, in traditions, and
gender; God as Mother, not just Father; God as Birther, not just
Begetter. Gender diversity is honored by the Black Madonna and so,
too, is gender preference. The Black Madonna, the Great Mother, is
not homophobic. She welcomes the diversity of sexual preferences that
are also part of creation, human and more than human. (We have now
counted fifty-four species of birds and mammals that have significant
homosexual populations. The medieval notion that homosexuality is
"against nature" has been disproved: A homosexual minority is very
much part of nature.)[16]

John Boswell, in his groundbreaking scholarly work titled
Christianity, Social Tolerance and Homosexuality has demonstrated
that the 12th century, which birthed the great Renaissance and the
Black Madonna in France, rejected homophobia. For a period of 125
years—years that were the most creative years in Western civiliza-

---

[14] See Suzi Gablik, *The Reenchantment of Art* (New York: Thames and Hudson, 1991).

[15] Fox, *Meditations with Meister Eckhart*, p. 42.

[16] See Christian de la Huerta, *Coming Out Spirituality: The Next Step* (New York: Jeremy
Tarcher, 1999).

8 8   THE MOONLIT PATH

tion—diversity was welcomed at all levels of society.[17] Creativity thrives on diversity.

8. The Black Madonna Calls Us to Grieve

The Black Madonna is the sorrowful mother, the mother who weeps tears for the suffering in the universe, the suffering in the world, the brokenness of our very vulnerable hearts. In the Christian tradition, She holds the dying Christ in Her lap but this Christ represents all beings—it is the cosmic Christ and not just the historical Jesus that she is embracing, for all beings suffer and the Black Madonna, the Great Mother, knows this and empathizes with us in our pain. She embraces as a tender mother would, for compassion is Her special gift to the world. She invites us to enter into our grief and name it and be there to learn what suffering has to teach us. Creativity cannot happen, birthing cannot happen, unless the grieving heart is paid attention to. Only by passing through grief can creativity burst forth anew.

Grieving is an emptying, it is making the womb open again for new birth to happen. A culture that would substitute addictions for grieving is a culture that has lost its soul and its womb. It will birth nothing but more pain and abuse and misuse of resources. It will be a place where waste reigns and where Divinity itself wastes away, unused in the hearts and imaginations of the people. Andrew Harvey writes of how the Black Madonna provides "an immense force of protection, an immense alchemical power of transformation through both grief and joy, and an immense inspiration to compassionate service and action in the world." She is also "queen of hell," or "queen of the underworld . . . that force of pure suffering mystical love that annihilates evil at its root and engenders the Christ-child in the ground of the soul even as the world burns."[18] She holds both creative and destructive aspects within her.

To grieve is to enter what John of the Cross in the 16th century called the "dark night of the soul." He instructed us not to run from this dark night but to stay there to learn what darkness has to teach us. The Dark Madonna does not run from the darkness of spirit and

---

[17] John Boswell, *Christianity, Tolerance and Homosexuality* (Chicago: University of Chicago Press, 1980).
[18] Harvey, *The Return of the Mother*, p. 372 f.

soul that sometimes encompasses us. She invites us not to flee from pain and suffering. Mechtild of Magdeburg in the 13th century wrote of this darkness in the following manner: "There comes a time when both body and soul enter into such a vast darkness that one loses light and consciousness and knows nothing more of God's intimacy. At such a time when the light in the lantern burns out the beauty of the lantern can no longer be seen. With longing and distress we are reminded of our nothingness. . . . I am hunted, captured, bound, wounded so terribly that I can never be healed. God has wounded me close unto death."[19] Mechtild does not run from the darkness but stays and learns. "God replied: 'I wish always to be your physician, bringing healing anointment for all your wounds. If it is I who allow you to be wounded so badly, do you not believe that I will heal you most lovingly in the very same hour?"[20] What is it we learn in this darkness of soul and spirit? "From suffering I have learned this: That whoever is sore wounded by love will never be made whole unless She embrace the very same love which wounded Her."[21]

9. The Black Madonna Calls Us to Celebrate and Dance

The Black Madonna, while She weeps tears for the world, as the sorrowful mother, does not wallow in Her grief, does not stay there forever. Rather, She is a joyful mother, a mother happy to have being and to have shared it with so many other creatures. She expects joy in return. Celebration of life and its pleasures lie at the core of Her reason for being. She expects us to take joy in Her many pleasures, joy in Her fruits. Sophia, or Wisdom, in the Scriptures sings to this element of pleasure and eros, deep and passionate love of life and all its gifts:

> *I have exhaled a perfume like cinnamon and acacia,*
> *I have breathed out a scent like choice myrrh. . . .*
> *Approach me, you who desire me,*
> *And take your fill of my fruits,*
> *For memories of me are sweeter than honey,*

[19] Sue Woodruff, *Meditations with Mechtild of Magdeburg* (Sante Fe: Bear & Co., 1982), pp. 60*f*., 64*f*.
[20] Woodruff, *Meditations with Mechtild of Magdeburg*, p. 68.
[21] Woodruff, *Meditations with Mechtild of Magdeburg*, p. 69.

Inheriting me is sweeter than the honeycomb.
They who eat me will hunger for more,
They who drink me will thirst for more.
Whoever listens to me will never have to blush. . . .
(Ecclesiasticus 24.15, 19-22)

Celebration is part of compassion. As Meister Eckhart puts it: "What happens to another be it a joy or a sorrow happens to me." Celebration is the exercise of our common joy. Praise is the noise that joy makes. Joy, praise, and celebration are intrinsic to community and to the presence of the Black Madonna. She did not birth Her Divine Child by whatever name in vain. She opts in favor of children, in favor of life, in favor of eros and in favor of biophilia. She is a lover of life par excellence. She expects us, Her children, to be the same.

10. The Black Madonna Calls Us to Our Divinity, which Is Compassion

Compassion is the best of which our species is capable. It is also the secret name for Divinity. There is no spiritual tradition East or West, North or South, that does not exist to instruct its people in how to be compassionate. "Maat" is the name for justice, harmony, balance and compassion among the African peoples. The Black Madonna calls us to Maat. Grieving and celebrating and acting justly are all parts of compassion. In both Arabic and Hebrew, the word for compassion comes from the word for "womb." A patriarchy does not teach compassion, for it ignores the womb-like energies of our world and our species. If it mentions compassion at all, it trivializes it and renders it impotent. (For example, Webster's dictionary declares "obsolete" the idea that compassion is about a relationship among equals.) Patriarchy neglects what Meister Eckhart knew and taught: "Compassion means justice."[22] Compassion has a hard side; it is not about sentiment but about relationships of justice and interdependence.

Because the Black Madonna is the goddess that dwells deeply and darkly within all beings, ourselves included, She brings with Her our

---

[22] Fox, *Meditations with Meister Eckhart*, p. 103.

capacity for compassion. We are not whole—we are not ourselves—until we partake in the carrying on of compassion. Meister Eckhart taught that the name of the human soul properly is "Compassion" and that until we are engaged in compassion we do not yet have soul.[23]

Compassion knows when enough is enough; compassion does not overindulge; compassion does not hoard and does not run its life on addictions of insecurity and pyramid-building to overcome these addictions. Compassion trusts life and the universe ultimately to provide what is necessary for our being. But compassion works hard as a co-creator with the universe to see that a balance and basic fairness is achieved among beings. Compassion is present in the Black Madonna in Her very essence for "the first outburst of everything God (and Goddess) does is compassion."[24] To return to compassion *is* to return to the Goddess.

Cultural historian and feminist Henry Adams writes about the role of Mary in the 12th century at Chartres Cathedral. "The convulsive hold which Mary to this day maintains over human imagination—as you can see at Lourdes—was due much less to Her power of saving soul or body than to Her sympathy with people who suffered under law—justly or unjustly, by accident or design, by decree of God or by guile of Devil."[25] Adams understood Mary as the Buddhist element in Christianity for with Her as with Buddha, compassion is the first of all the virtues. "To Kwannon the Compassionate One and to Mary the Mother of God, compassion included the idea of sorrowful contemplation."[26] Only the Great Mother could provide the compassion needed by the sorrowful human condition.

> The Mother alone was human, imperfect, and could love; She alone was Favour, Duality, Diversity. Under any conceivable form of religion, this duality must find embodiment somewhere, and the Middle Ages logically insisted that, as it could not be in the Trinity, either separately or together, it must be in the Mother. If the Trinity was in its essence Unity, the

---

23 Matthew Fox, *Passion for Creation: The Earth-Honoring Spirituality of Meister Eckhart* (Rochester, VT: Inner Traditions, 2000), p. 442.

24 Fox, *Passion for Creation*, p. 441.

25 R. P. Blackmur, *Henry Adams* (New York: Harcourt Brace Jovanovich, 1980), p. 203.

26 Blackmur, *Henry Adams*, p. 203. Kwannon is the Buddhist goddess of mercy.

Mother alone could represent whatever was not Unity; whatever was irregular, exceptional, outlawed; and this was the whole human race.[27]

She was beyond the law, a friend of the outlaws who appealed to the masses who "longed for a power above law—or above the contorted mass of ignorance and absurdity bearing the name of law."[28] This power had to be more than human. It required the Goddess.

The Black Madonna, the Goddess, provides the womb of the universe as the cosmic lap where all creatures gather. An ancient hymn dedicated to Isis underscores her cosmic role as sovereign over all of nature and queen of all the gods and goddesses.

I am Nature, the universal Mother, mistress of all the elements, primordial child of time, sovereign of all things spiritual, queen of the dead, queen also of the immortals, the single manifestation of all gods and goddesses that are. My nod governs the shining heights of Heaven, the wholesome sea-breezes, the lamentable silences of the world below.[29]

This ancient hymn to Isis is remarkably similar to a 12th-century poem to the Christian goddess Mary as embodied in Nature, written by Alan of Lille:

O child of God and Mother of things,
Bond of the world, its firm-tied knot,
Jewel set among things of earth, and mirror to all that passes
    away
Morning star of our sphere;
Peace, love, power, regimen and strength,
Order, law, end, pathway, captain and source,
Life, light, glory, beauty and shape,
O Rule of our world![30]

Interestingly, Alan of Lille speaks of the "Mother of things" as a "firm-tied knot" and the Thet, which is an important symbol of Isis, is also

[27] Blackmur, Henry Adams, p. 204.
[28] Blackmur, Henry Adams, p. 203.
[29] Eloise McKinney-Johnson, "Egypt's Isis: The Original Black Madonna," Journal of African Civilizations, April, 1984, p. 66.
[30] Chenu, Nature, Man and Society in the Twelfth Century, p. 19.

understood to be a knot.[31] We play in Her cosmic lap, we bump up against one another there, and we work for balance, Maat, and justice there.

The Black Madonna is the Throne of Compassion, the divine lap. That is the meaning of the name "Isis" and Isis is the African goddess who gave us the Black Madonna both in Ephesus, Turkey, and through Spain and Sicily directly into Western Europe. From 1,000 B.C.E. to A.D. 500 "the major divinity of the Mediterranean world appears to have been Isis of Africa, dark mother of many names."[32]

Indeed, certain passages of the Christian Gospels such as the birth narratives, which are clearly not historical but are stories of the Cosmic Christ, are passages taken from stories about Isis and her son, Horus. Sir Ernest A. Wallis Budge, the late keeper of the Egyptian and Assyrian antiquities at the British Museum, writes:

> The pictures and sculptures wherein she is represented in the act of suckling Horus formed the foundation for the Christian paintings of the Madonna and Child.
>
> Several of the incidents of the wanderings of the Virgin with the Child in Egypt as recorded in the Apochryphal Gospels reflect scenes in the life of Isis. . . . and many of the attributes of Isis, the God-mother, the mother of Horus . . . are identical with those of Mary the Mother of Christ.[33]

11. The Black Madonna Calls Us to a Renaissance of Culture, Religion and the City

Isis often wears a regal headdress that symbolizes Her name as meaning "throne" or "queen." Erich Neumann has written about Isis as "Throne":

> As mother and earth woman, the Great Mother is the "throne" pure and simple, and, characteristically, the woman's motherliness resides not only in the womb but also in the seated woman's broad expanse of thigh, her lap on

---

31 See McKinney-Johnson, "Egypt's Isis," p. 71.
32 Birnbaum, *Dark Mother*, p. 13.
33 McKinney-Johnson, "Egypt's Isis," p. 67.

which the newborn child sits enthroned. To be taken on the lap is, like being taken to the breast, a symbolic expression for adoption of the child, and also for the man, by the Feminine. It is no accident that the greatest Mother Goddess of the early cults was named Isis, the "seat," "the throne," the symbol of which she bears on her head; and the king who "takes possession" of the earth, the Mother Goddess, does so by sitting on her in the literal sense of the word.[34]

The 12th-century Renaissance was especially conscious of the role of "throne" and the goddess. In Latin, the word for "throne" is *cathedra*. The medieval church gave birth to cathedrals—over 125 were built the size of Chartres—and every single one was dedicated to Mary with such titles as Notre Dame de Chartres, Notre Dame de Lyons, Notre Dame de Paris, etc. Over 375 other churches equal in size to these cathedrals were also built and dedicated to Mary. In many of these cathedrals a statue to the Black Madonna can be found even to this day. A cathedral by definition meant the *throne where the goddess sits ruling the universe with compassion and justice for the poor.* Anthropocentrism, clericalism, and sexism have co-opted the invention of cathedral to mean the place where the bishop has his (usually) throne. This is false. The cathedral is designed to be the center of the city, bringing the goddess to the center of the city to enliven it with goddess energies and values. Cities were birthed in the 12th century with the breakup of the land-based economy and religious and political system of the feudal era. The youth fled to the cities where religion reinvented itself apart from the monastic establishment that ruled for eight centuries and where education invented itself apart from the rural monastic educational system in the form of universities. Worship reinvented itself in the city cathedral, apart from the monastic liturgical practice in the countryside.

Today, for the first time in history, more than 50 percent of the world's human population is living in cities; By 2015, over two-thirds of humans—a great proportion of them young people—will be living in cities. The Black Madonna and the "throne as goddess" motif contribute to the resurrection of our cities. They give us a center, a cos-

[34] Erich Neumann, *The Great Mother: An Analysis of the Archetype*, Ralph Manheim, trans. (Princeton: Princeton University Press, 1974) pp. 98-99.

mic center, a synthesis and unity, and a life energy by which we can redeem our cities and take them back from lifelessness and *thanatos*. Artists gather in a city. Celebration and ritual happen in a city. Nature and human nature congregate in a city. No wonder Meister Eckhart and other medieval mystics celebrated the human soul as city and the city as soul. It is the task of a renaissance to bring soul back to city. We might even define renaissance as a rebirth of *cities* based on a spiritual initiative.

12. The Black Madonna Calls Us to Reinvent Education and Art

The goddess also ruled at the university—She was "Queen of the sciences" and "mistress of all the arts and sciences" who was "afraid of none of them, and did nothing, ever, to stunt any of them."[35] All learning was to culminate in Her. She was about wisdom, not just knowledge. The renaissance that the Madonna represented was both religious and educational.

Isis's headdress often depicts the full moon between curved horns and has the shape of the sistrum, a musical instrument that the Egyptians played in her honor. Plutarch stated that the purpose of the sistrum, which is a kind of rattle, was that "all things in existence need to be shaken, or rattled about. . . .to be agitated when they grow drowsy and torpid."[36] The Black Madonna *shakes things up.*

Is this not an archetype for our times? Is She not a forebear of a renaissance, one who comes to give new birth to a civilization, a birth based on a new sense of spirituality, cosmology, and learning—a learning that reawakens us to our place in the universe? How will work in the world become wise as opposed to exploitive without wisdom? How will the human soul move from knowledge to wisdom without the kind of effort the Goddess can bring—without a balance of male/female, heart/head, body/spirit truly happening at all levels of education from childhood to professional degrees? How will a renaissance happen if education is left behind? What role will art play when the artist, too, lets go of the internalized oppression of the modern era

---

35 Blackmur, *Henry Adams*, p. 206.
36 McKinney-Johnson, "Egypt's Isis," p. 71.

and recommits to serving his or her community and to serving the larger community of ecological sustainability?[37]

These are some of the questions raised by the return of the Black Madonna in our time. They beg for response. They beg for listening ears and attentive institutions. They beg for self-criticism of nation-states, governments, corporations, academia, religion, law, professions of all kinds that are called to something new (and very ancient): a new relationship between Earth and humans; one of mutuality, not mastery; one of joy and wonder, not boredom; one that honors all our relations. For this to come about some rattling of our modern cages and mindsets is in order. The Black Madonna provides such a shake-up. Still. After all these centuries.

[37] See Gablik, *The Reenchantment of Art.*

Lilith

Jane Kamerling

Jane Kamerling, L.C.S.W., is a diplomate Jungian analyst and member of the Chicago Society of Jungian Analysts. She is a senior training analyst with the C. G. Jung Institute of Chicago and has lectured both nationally and internationally on the relationship of Jungian psychology to mythology and religion. She has made significant contributions to our present-day understanding of the Jewish mystical tradition of Kabbalah and has been a feature presenter on Balinese mythology in Bali. She has a full-time analytical practice in the Chicago area.

He is alone tonight. Tired from a full day's work, he lies awake, wanting to fall asleep as quickly as possible, the night to be over, to be safe. The children were put to bed hours ago. His wife is needed to assist in childbirth. He knows he is vulnerable, unprotected, and available for exploitation. He is anxious. He intently reviews the passage in the Zohar, written by Moses de Leon in the 13th century and considered the *magnum opus* of Kabbalah, imagining himself victimized by the She-Demon, Lilith! "She roams at night, and goes all about the worlds and makes sport with men and causes them to emit seed. In every place where a man sleeps alone in a house, she visits him and grabs him and attaches herself to him and has her desire from him, and bears from him. And she also afflicts him with sickness, and he knows it not, and all this takes place when the moon is on the wane."[1] With a fearful heart, he says to himself, *She fornicates men who sleep alone.* He repeats it over and over, trying to create a consciousness, which he hopes will dispel her magic. He feels himself sinking into the comfortable bedding. He loses control of his thoughts. It's dark and quiet in his room.

---

[1] Zohar, vol. 1, 19b. Translated by Harry Sperling and Maurice Simon (London: The Soncino Press, 1984).

She enters ever so quietly. She moves like she is sliding across the room, so slender, voluptuous, and beautiful. He sees her face in the faint light of the moon. She smiles, her hair is long and wild and red as a rose. Her face is a fragile white, with red cheeks and gold earrings, all accentuating her long neck and luscious lips. Her scent inspires his desire for her; he begins to long to touch her. She moves closer, seducing him with every step. He's on fire. She lifts her scarlet dress and exposes her nakedness with wild animation. She opens herself for him to touch and taste and smell. She's orgasmic, instinctual, hungry, and natural. His whole body has awakened, loudly pulsating, throbbing. He feels primitive, virile, and strong. They collide with one another in fury and animalistic lust. He expands beyond himself and explodes within her. He has been one with the goddess. She moves away and takes off her adornments. She has the feet of an owl and no hands. He wonders how she created the illusion of hands and feet. She has wings and her garments quickly turn to fire. The She-Demon emerges. He is terrified and desperately begins reciting incantations, but to no avail; she now has his seed to procreate demonic offspring. He recoils, feeling humiliation and defilement. She further ignites his terror as she murders his sleeping children and finally kills him.

Lilith is to be reckoned with. She is a multifaceted entity, who entices and terrorizes. Like a diamond, each facet leading to the next, she reflects the past, summoning the future; sparkling, splitting, deepening, endlessly transforming. In her duality she is desired and dangerous. Lilith is organic, of the earth, pure sexuality, and power. She is a seductress and murderous, raging, infant killer. Is she a goddess or demon? Is she the perfect fantasy or a witch, a vampire, a creature who can transform herself into animals and fire?

Lilith energy dates back to 3000 B.C.E., appearing in the Sumerian culture as the storm or wind spirit, Lil. She developed into a she-demon between A.D. 2 and 5, the Talmudic period, and emerges in the Middle Ages, the Kabbalistic era, as a consort at the side of God.[2]

The legend is born from what appears as an inconsistency in Genesis, whereby Adam and Eve are initially understood to be created simultaneously, "Male and Female He created them" (Gen. 1:27), and then later introduced as a sequential creation. God creates

---

[2] Raphael Patai, *The Hebrew Goddess* (Detroit: Wayne State University Press, 1967), p. 221.

Eve from the rib of a sleeping Adam, "This at last is bone from my bones, and flesh from my flesh! This is to be called woman, for this was taken from man." (Gen. 2:18-24). Talmudic *midrash* tells of the primordial Lilith, the first wife of Adam, resolving the conflicting creation myths of man and woman. Adam wanted to dominate the relationship between Lilith and himself, but, Lilith wanted equality.

As a result of this irreconcilable difference, Lilith spoke the name of God in anger and flew from the Garden of Eden to the Red Sea. She lived in a cave and was promiscuous with demons living there, creating an army of her own demons. Adam complained to God about his situation and God responded by sending three angels, Senoy, Sansenoy, and Semangeloff to command Lilith to return to Adam. The angels followed God's instructions, but Lilith did not move in her refusal to return to Adam. The angels threatened Lilith with the death of 100 of her demon offspring. Lilith, unwilling to reconsider, vowed to snatch the souls of human infants. She conceded to spare those infants who are protected by amulets bearing the names of the three angels; Senoy, Sansenoy, and Semangeloff.

Lilith seeks her revenge by visiting men at night, especially those who sleep alone, tempting and seducing them into emitting their seed into her womb, creating more demons. Most horrific, she strangles human infants in pursuit of their souls. Infant boys are most vulnerable the first eight days after birth, prior to circumcision, and girls the first 20 days of life, unless protected by the amulets bearing the names of the angels, and the words "Out Lilith," which dispels her power so she disappears. Lilith is also responsible for infertility, miscarriages, and difficult, even tragic, births. She is especially fierce during times of transition such as marriages, bar mitzvahs, births, times of stress, holidays, and the Sabbath.

As Lilith is building her mythology, Adam has eaten of the Tree of Knowledge and he and his second wife Eve are expelled from the Garden of Eden. Adam, feeling overwhelming guilt, prostrates himself before God and performs penance of fasting and celibacy for 130 years. Adam becomes vulnerable to Lilith, sleeping alone, and Lilith takes this opportunity, seducing him, and because of his inability to control his sexual desires, she copulates with him creating the demons known as the "plagues of mankind."[3]

---

[3] Patai, *The Hebrew Goddess*, p. 232.

In addition to Lilith being Adam's wife, she mythologically evolves as the consort to God himself. She is the Dark Feminine side of God who takes the place of the *Shekhinnah*, the Light Feminine aspect of God, while the Shekhinnah is exiled from God along with the Israelites, after the fall.[4] The Kabbalah of the Middle Ages pairs Lilith with Samael, the Devil, as well as naming her Queen to Osmodeus, King of the demons.[5]

Lilith comes from the other side, *Sitra Ochra*. She begins as the dark side of humankind, rises to the status of She-Demon, to Queen of Demons, to the supernal status of the dark side of God, the Dark Goddess. Amulets and incantations are created to obliterate her power, but the suppression of Lilith brings on more devastation since Lilith cannot be banished. Instead, she must be brought into consciousness and integrated into the collective psyche, since she is a projection of our most basic fears and desires. She is a counterpart to the obedient Eve, who is passive, faithful, and supportive. Lilith is determined to seek revenge through her assertive seductiveness and her destructive beauty. She is created as a result of the diminishment of the moon, which reflects the light of the sun, rather than shining light of her own.[6]

The 20th century emerges from a superstitious past into a time of enlightenment, rationality, and scientific explanation. Lilith follows eastern European Jews as they emigrate to America and the Western world. Amulets are still being used and ribbons are tied around the cribs of newborn infants to keep a consciousness of Lilith's presence. During times of transition, distractions are incorporated into ritual to keep Lilith at a safe distance. An example is the shattering of the glass at the end of a wedding ceremony, a symbol that is no longer understood for its initial intention of creating a noise to scare off Lilith, the She-Demon. As new generations assimilate and the old world dies out, Lilith goes underground.

What happens to the Dark Feminine when there is no longer a conscious awareness, mindfulness of Her; when there is no vigilance due to the rationalization and intellectualization that there is nothing to fear? C. G. Jung speaks to these phenomena in his statement:

---

[4] Filomena Maria Pereira, *Lilith: The Edge of Forever* (Irving, TX: Ide House, 1998), pp. x–xi.
[5] Patai, *The Hebrew Goddess*, p. 246.
[6] Barbara Black Koltov, *The Book of Lilith* (Berwick, ME: Nicolas-Hays, 1986), p. 10.

The demonism of nature, which man had apparently tri-
umphed over, he has unwittingly swallowed into himself and
so become the devil's marionette. This could happen only
because he believed he had abolished the demons by declaring
them to be superstition. He overlooked the fact that they
were, at bottom, the products of certain factors in the human
psyche. When these products were dubbed unreal and illusory, their sources were in no way blocked up or rendered
inoperative. On the contrary, after it became impossible for
the demons to inhabit the rocks, woods, mountains, and
rivers, they used human beings as much more dangerous
dwelling places.[7]

Jung suggests that the demons become relegated to the dwelling places
of the unconscious. There they reside and build energy in the form of
our personal and collective shadow. Jung defines the concept of
shadow as the "negative side of the personality, the sum of all those
unpleasant qualities we like to hide."[8] A woman, manifesting unconscious Lilith energy (*Lilith* means "belonging to the night"), is identified with her shadow. She represses her shadow and identifies with the
initial presentation, the image, the persona, and the illusion of Lilith.
This woman may see herself as strong, determined, seductive, earthy,
etc.; the outer, ego-satisfying aspects of the Lilith personality. The
energy from the neglected shadow, however, breaks through and overwhelms the ego, creating devastation and havoc to her psyche. A man
who falls slave to Lilith's seduction is projecting his anima, in this case
dark anima, and his hidden feminine personality, onto the She-
Demon. Recall the image I described of the husband who becomes
vulnerable when he sleeps alone. This metaphor describes the man
who represses his anima, who sleeps alone; he has no access to his
feminine side. His ego, therefore, becomes vulnerable to the destruction of an angry anima. Both the shadow and anima are parts of ourselves that we are reluctant to acknowledge, but may become known

---

[7] C. G. Jung, *The Symbolic Life, Collected Works of C. G. Jung*, vol. 18, William McGuire,
ed., R. F. C. Hull, trans., Bollingen Series XX (Princeton: Princeton University Press,), § 1365,
p. 594. Further references to this work will be cited as CW 18.

[8] C. G. Jung, *Two Essays in Analytical Psychology, Collected Works of C. G. Jung*, vol. 7,
R. F. C. Hull, trans., Bollingen Series XX (Princeton: Princeton University Press,), § 103n.
Further references to this work will be cited as CW 7.

through our dreams or when they take " possession of our ego-consciousness."[9]

These archetypal patterns are both personal—in that we profoundly feel their effects—as well as impersonal, or collective. Lilith represents these dual psychological formulations in her status as a personal She-Demon as well as a universal Goddess.

> Cultural symbols are those that have expressed "eternal truths" or are still in use in many religions. They have gone through many transformations and even a process of more or less conscious elaboration, and in this way have become the *representations collectives* of civilized societies. Nevertheless, they have retained much of their original numinosity, and they function as positive or negative "prejudices" with which the psychologist has to reckon very seriously. . . . Nobody can dismiss these numinous factors on merely rational grounds. They are important constituents of our mental make-up and vital forces in the building up of human society, and they cannot be eradicated without serious loss. When they are repressed or neglected, their specific energy disappears into the unconscious with unpredictable consequences. The energy that appears to have been lost revives and intensifies whatever is uppermost in the unconscious—tendencies, perhaps, that have hitherto had no chance to express themselves, or have not been allowed an uninhibited existence in our consciousness. They form the ever-present destructive "shadow." Even tendencies that might be able to exert a beneficial influence turn into veritable demons when they are repressed.[10]

The cultural symbols and archetypal characteristics carried in the legends of Lilith unfold in the tale of the Queen of Sheba, a story from the oral tradition in 16th-century Germany. There was a poor innkeeper who was competing with a more successful inn within the same town. He was about to give up, feeling hopeless and helpless

---

[9] C. G. Jung, *The Archetypes and the Collective Unconscious, Collected Works of C. G. Jung*, vol. 9i, Michael Fordham, ed., R. F. C. Hull, trans., Bollingen Series XX (Princeton: Princeton University Press,), § 222. Further references to this work will be cited as CW 9i.
[10] Jung, CW 18, § 579-580.

when the most beautiful woman appeared before him in his storeroom, promising fulfillment and good fortune. He became overwhelmed with passion and lust and gave himself freely to her without considering where she came from or why she was there. After their encounter, she handed the innkeeper a bag filled with silver coins. The following day the man returned to the storeroom at the same time of day to again find this most beautiful woman taking a bath. Again, her beauty seduced him, and again they made love and he received another bag of silver coins. The innkeeper continued to return every morning and he became a rich man with a new and beautiful inn filled with travelers and a wife dressed in beautiful new clothes.

The innkeeper became obsessed by this woman known as the Queen of Sheba, and desired her even in the hours when they were apart. He thought of her every waking moment and dreamed of her all night. She promised him all that he could ever want but warned him never to tell the secret of their meetings or he would surely die.

All went well as the innkeeper became a slave to her temptations and his unquenchable desires, except the man's wife started to ask questions, curious about the sudden turn of fortune. He was successful in keeping her off track until one day she followed him to the storeroom and began to notice a pattern in his daily visits to the same place for the same time period. She copied his storeroom key and again followed him at the allotted time. Once the door closed and the man and the Queen of Sheba were in the intensity of their lovemaking, she opened the door, was shocked, and quickly closed it again. The Queen of Sheba noticed the intrusion and accused the innkeeper of telling their secret and breaking his promise. He protested, pleading for his life, blaming the event on his curious wife. Lilith, revealing her true demon identity, spared his life and declared that she would strangle the children she bore of his seed. In addition, all his wealth would disappear and he would return to being a poor innkeeper. Then, as quickly as she had originally appeared, she vanished. He realized, still feeling his terror, that he had been in the possession of a demoness, Lilith herself, which was again confirmed when he went to find his bags of silver and found them as empty as his wife's closets.

Lilith takes her revenge on those who ask no questions in the service of keeping Lilith unconscious. The personal and collective experience of the innkeeper is the feeling of being possessed by the obsessive and compulsive need to be in the numinous, bigger-than-life expression of the archetype. What would have happened had the innkeeper asked the questions, thereby confronting himself?

This confrontation is the first test of courage on the inner way, a test sufficient to frighten off most people, for the meeting of ourselves belongs to the more unpleasant things that can be avoided so long as we can project everything negative into the environment. But if we are able to see our own shadow and can bear knowing it, then a small part of the problem has already been solved: we have at least brought up the personal unconscious. The shadow is a living part of the personality and therefore wants to live with it in some form. It cannot be argued out of existence or rationalized into harmlessness. This problem is exceedingly difficult, because it not only challenges the whole man, but reminds him at the same time of his helplessness and ineffectuality. Strong natures—or should one rather call them weak?—do not like to be reminded of this, but prefer to think of themselves as heroes who are beyond good and evil, and to cut the Gordian knot instead of untying it. Nevertheless, the account has to be settled sooner or later. In the end one has to admit that there are problems which one simply cannot solve on one's own resources. Such an admission has the advantage of being honest, truthful, and in accord with reality, and this prepares the ground for a compensatory reaction from the collective unconscious: you are now more inclined to give heed to a helpful idea or intuition, or notice thoughts which were not allowed to voice themselves before. Perhaps you will pay attention to the dreams that visit you at such moments, or will reflect on certain inner and outer occurrences that take place just at this time. If you have an attitude of this kind, then the helpful powers slumbering in the deep strata of man's nature can come awake and intervene, for helplessness and weakness are the eternal experience of mankind.[11]

---

[11] Jung, CW 9i, § 44, pp. 20–21.

Had the innkeeper confronted his anima projection, he would have immediately realized that this beautiful figure was an illusion, but his personality is too outer-directed. In accordance with Jung's suggestion above, he prefers to think of himself as beyond good and evil, as a hero with a strong nature. Consequently, he is weak and vulnerable because of this attitude. The innkeeper has not integrated his anima, cannot face this dark side of his psyche, so instead he grasps for the bags of silver (symbolic of the feminine), compensating for the inadequate feelings that he has pushed deep inside himself. There is not enough silver or fame to balance for the neglected richness within. This dynamic is symbolized again in the abundance of clothes the innkeeper's wife is given to appease his anima figure; again outer-directed. Eventually, his wife expresses his anima's will by exposing the plot, revealing the dark anima. In so doing, the wife breaks the illusion, bringing the innkeeper to his knees (relativizing the ego), revealing the inner impoverishment of the anima imaged in the empty closets.

Had the innkeeper reflected on his obsessive, compulsive behavior, explored his secretiveness, or examined his dreams, he would have understood this innermost being offering him the opportunity for an expanded sense of self. The innkeeper would have experienced more fully the totality of his personality, which includes his feelings of helplessness and weakness. He would no longer be the inflated hero innkeeper. In discovering and acknowledging his vulnerability he would not as likely have been possessed and ultimately ruined. A man engages his anima by giving equal attention to his feminine side. He must alter his condescending attitude toward the feminine both externally as well as internally.

What about Lilith, herself? As told in legend, Lilith was unwilling to submit to the authority of her husband, Adam. The demand was humiliating and diminishing. Lilith responded with rage. Instead of obeying Adam, she chose flight and desolation. She threatened revenge and destruction. As the patriarchy strengthened, Eve became the prototype of the submissive female, and Lilith energy was repressed into the unconscious. Unacknowledged humiliation and diminishment strengthened the Lilith archetype, manifesting her throughout history. She carried the revenge of our grandmother's unexplored rage in the tales and rituals that expressed her power. Today she is divulging her wrath psychologically and somatically in women worldwide. By the end of the 19th, beginning of the 20th century, Freud began treating women suffering with conversion symptoms of hysteria, such as physical paralysis without physical cause. His seduction theory (1896) postulates an earlier sexual molestation or incest, usually perpetrated by the father, which the woman repressed, thereby becoming subject to hysterical symptoms later in life. Unlike Lilith's ability to flee or express her emotions, these women became trapped as a consequence of a woman's psychological and social experience of the day. Freud's patients symbolically were enacting through their symptoms entrapment and passivity. It is interesting to note that Freud abandoned this theory (1897) due to pressure from the patriarchy.[12] He modified his position claiming that the sexual abuse was the fantasy of the victim's infantile desires, effectively releasing the father of culpability, and shifting the hysteria causes from external to internal, thereby rejecting or diminishing the patient's victimization.[13]

A woman's inability to express her power continues to bring shame, humiliation, and diminishment. This in turn elicits rage! The split-off aspect flees into the wilderness (the unconscious), as does Lilith, and creates havoc. She becomes an outcast, neglected and rejected, unclean and unchaste. She is solitary and destroys everything in her path. Revenge is her goal and she detaches from her body to be sexually cold and in control. Women have used sexual politics for generations to attain power and influence. As she withholds or seduces, she becomes unrelated to her body, using it as a tool.

Women are the mainstay of the psychiatric and psychotherapy practices today. They outnumber men two to one with the diagnosis of major depressive disorder[14] and three to one with dysthymic disorder,[15] a milder form of depression. The feelings of isolation, rejection, neglect, marginalization, hopelessness, and self-criticism are all descriptive symptoms of depression. Rage is turned inward, causing a severe reduction of energy in one's life. Sexual desire is withdrawn, her

---

[12] Sigmund Freud, "The Aetiology of Hysteria," *Standard Edition of the Complete Psychology of Sigmund Freud* (London: Hogarth Press, 1953–1974), pp. 186–221.

[13] J. Masson, *The Assault on Truth: Freud's Suppression of the Seduction Theory* (New York: Farrar, Straus & Giroux, 1984), p. 264.

[14] *Diagnostic and Statistical Manual of Mental Disorders*, 4th Edition (Washington, DC: American Psychiatric Association, 1994), p. 341. Further references to this volume will be cited as *DSM-IV*.

[15] *DSM-IV*, p. 347.

Lilith fire is out, she's cold, and she feels physically disconnected, dead. Lilith energy is needed to assert and express her rage to become conscious and vital again.

Eating disorders have replaced hysteria as the woman's pathology of the day. There are women who do not eat at all, *anorexia nervosa* (90 percent female),[16] and are usually profiled as the high-achieving cooperative female whose only internal control is over her not eating.[17] Other women who binge and purge, *bulimia nervosa* (90 percent female),[18] are trying to keep their weight down to achieve a Barbie-doll figure. Then there are the overeaters who stuff their feelings with food, using it to sooth, sedate, or repress negative feelings. Weight is on the minds of most modern women, trying to imagine themselves the small figures that men fantasize about. This image, "small figures," represents visually how women collude in diminishing the feminine into "less," to accommodate the patriarchal diminishment of the feminine. Women use food to either proclaim their power or give it away. Using food as the symbol, many women are expressing the need to claim their authority.

Borderline personality disorders are more aggressive in today's array of pathological scenarios and about 75 percent diagnosed are female.[19] Women diagnosed with this disorder are characterized as unstable, and have difficulty with relationships because of either idealizing or devaluing others as well as themselves. They have exaggerated emotional responses, and intense rage.[20] One is reminded of Lilith's murderous rage and disconnection. Lilith becomes mad as a screeching owl, seeking revenge with her paranoid thoughts, insisting everyone is responsible, somehow, for her oppression, humiliation, and diminishment. Her psychic dismemberment causes somatic symptoms and complaints, unleashing more rage and fury.

The most severe psychiatric diagnosis is psychosis. In the Greek tragedy *Medea*, Euripides (431 B.C.) depicts a woman so outraged at her husband that in revenge she kills their sons. "He shall never see alive again the sons he had from me. . . . Let no one think of me as

---

[16] *DSM-IV*, p. 543.
[17] *DSM-IV*, p. 540.
[18] *DSM-IV*, p. 548.
[19] *DSM-IV*, p. 652.
[20] *DSM-IV*, p. 654.

humble or weak or passive; let them understand I am of a different kind: dangerous to my enemies, loyal to my friends. To such a life glory belongs."[21] There have been an increasing number of incidents reported recently of mothers murdering their children. Lilith appears draped in fire, determined to destroy. She is psychotic, powerful, and murderous. Women visited by Lilith to enact these unimaginable deeds often have histories of major depressive episodes, which episodically erupt from deep within the unconscious, making the patient totally out of control and vulnerable to her will.

Lilith resides in the consultation hour in her positive and negative aspects. She informs the analyst regarding conscious and unconscious material between analyst and analysand. A male patient projects Lilith onto all women. A sixty-something man, who is committed to religious life, has been terrorized most of his life. A female is a powerful defilement that tempts his sexual desires into, what he perceives, an eternity of burning in hell. He obsessively recounts the terror of being a meek child frightened to look at a woman's breasts, certain he would die on the spot. He fears his body and its sexual expressions, only to be a slave to compulsive masturbation. Religious life fosters his fear of eternal damnation and reinforces the repression of Lilith, the dark anima, so he is relegated to a life of continual masturbation, and feelings of guilt and shame. Lilith has sucked the vitality and fire for life out of this patient, leaving him depressed and with an obsessive/compulsive disorder.

A beautiful, talented woman in her mid-thirties struggles with depression. She has been respected both as a singer and musician. She abandons both means of self-expression for 10 years. As her story unfolds in treatment, she reclaims her talents. She becomes angry as she remembers her talent as belonging to both her father and herself. She recalls several rapes that occurred during adolescence, adding to her feelings of powerlessness and victimization that drive her underground. She notices that she is very flirtatious and fears the consequences of those actions, although they feel powerful. She complains that she is out of touch with her body and her sexuality. She observes her rage as she claims Lilith's energy, and the depression begins to lift. Lilith consciousness, in the form of bringing her talent out into the world, is helping her regain her sense of self.

---

[21] Euripides, *Medea and Other Plays* (London: Penguin Books, 1963), p. 42.

Exploring counter-transference assists the therapist in discovering Lilith's presence in the consulting room. Wanting to connect the Lilith energy with a patient in order to assert herself informs the therapist of the deep feelings of humiliation and diminishment suffered by the patient. Holding the image of Lilith's fire offers insight into the overwhelming rage, which has yet to be explored. Lilith becomes embedded in my psychology when a male patient is showing off his intellectual muscle, assuming that "weak" feminine can't compete. The therapist may want to impulsively react, targeting all his/her weapons at him across the room, retreating only when he/she becomes conscious that the Lilith in the room belongs to us both. She is the fire and the rage against diminishment. She is the fear of being devoured by the therapeutic relationship; in the transferential experience he believes he will be obliterated. Lilith needs to become conscious in the work for both so that we both grow from the interaction with her.

Lilith consciousness transforms the demon into a goddess. Lilith energy needs expression to redeem the Shekinnah by restoring balance to the universe. The feminine principle has suffered humiliation, diminishment, flight, and desolation. As a consequence, rage, revenge, and isolation manifest. When these primary and secondary emotions are rejected, sent into the wilderness, split off from consciousness into the shadows of the unconscious, one's personality becomes demonic, disconnected from the cycles of life and death, unrelated to instinct and sexuality, and detached from self and others. Claimed, Lilith offers an opportunity for an expanded sense of self. Lilith provides the transformative energy from demon of the night to goddess of wisdom. Her archetypal spirituality reincorporates body and sexuality, freedom and healthy narcissism, restoring psyche to wholeness. All the neglected parts, the outcast aspects of the psyche are integrated into a creative, resourceful personality. It is not surprising that Lilith has become a symbol of the feminist movement, including a magazine titled *Lilith*, expressing her power and energy. When conscious, she represents wisdom of the night, depicted in her owl feet. Her hair, her crowning glory, is red, free, and wild, symbolizing her freedom to selfhood, versus her sisters who, historically and in some parts of the world presently, cover, cut, and bind their hair, representing submission and obedience. She is once again connected to her body and reclaims her sexuality for herself. Her transformative energy is creative and brings enlightenment. Her inner self is free as she becomes conscious of the rejected and neglected side of herself. It is only in the wilderness, where the instinctual, dark aspects of Lilith reside, that a women must journey in order to individuate, to come out of exile, manifest the Self and feel whole. A woman today, conscious of her dark Lilith, is beautiful, sensual, powerful, and orgasmic. She is in the world mothering her children, loving her partner, and forging a career without dependency or submission.

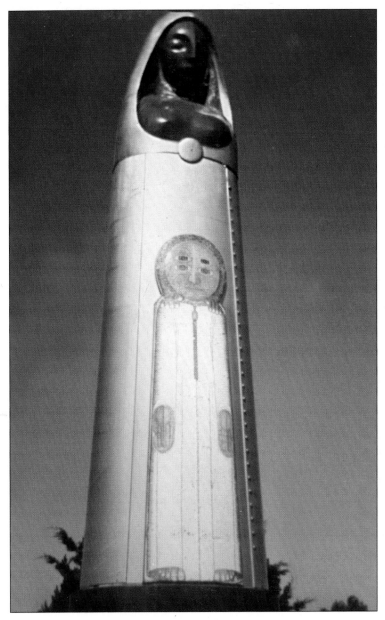

PLATE 1. *Peace* by Beniamino (Benny) Bufano, at San Francisco Airport. The Dark Mother holds St. Francis. Photograph courtesy of Fred Gustafson.

P LATE 2. *Jesus of the People*, copyright © 1999 Janet McKenzie. Used
by kind permission of Janet McKenzie.

PLATE 3. The Black Madonna of Einsiedeln, Switzerland.

PLATE 4. In this painting, *Crow Mother, Her Eyes, Her Eggs* (copyright © 1999 Meinrad Craighead), the artist depicts her as the Black Madonna of the Southwest. Deeply enthroned, nesting, she lays the eggs of potential in our lives. Her eyes are her wings. The rug at her feet represents the Rio Grande.

PLATE 5. Our Lady of Czestochowa appears in this modern rendition by Laura DuBois, announcing a celebration of the Black Madonna organized by Matthew Fox, Michelle Jordan, D. J. Yehudit and friends in Oakland, California.

PLATE 6. Goddess Kali. Photograph courtesy of Ashok Bedi.

PLATE 7. Our Lady of Guadalupe.

PLATE 8. Our Lady of Montserrat in Spain. Photograph courtesy of Fred Gustafson.

The Dark Irish Goddess Morrigan

Sylvia Brinton Perera

Sylvia Brinton Perera is a Jungian psychoanalyst who lives, practices, teaches, and writes in New York, Connecticut, and Vermont. Originally trained as an art historian and museum curator, she turned to psychology after working with disadvantaged children during the 1960s. After receiving her M.A. in psychology, she trained at the C. G. Jung Institute in New York. Her publications include *Descent to the Goddess: An Initiation for Women* (Inner City Books, 1989); *The Scapegoat Complex: Towards a Mythology of Shadow and Guilt* (Inner City Books, 1986); *Dreams: a Portal to the Source* (with E. Christopher Whitmont, published by Routledge, 1992); *Celtic Queen Maeve and Addiction: An Archetypal Perspective* (Nicolas-Hays, 2001); and *Mythic Rites in Modern Therapy*. This paper first appeared as "War, Madness, and the Morrigan, a Celtic Goddess of Life and Death" in *Mad Parts of Sane People in Analysis*, edited by Murray Stein and Nathan Schwartz-Salant (Wilmette, IL: Chiron Publications, 1993), pp. 155–193.

> *A political situation is the manifestation of a parallel psychological problem in millions of individuals. This problem is largely unconscious (which makes it a particularly dangerous one).*
>
> —C. G. JUNG[1]

When I was struggling to understand the reactions aroused in my clients, my friends, and myself during the war in the Persian Gulf, I found myself drawn to and supported by images of the Morrigan, goddess of life, death, war, fate, and transformation. Her mythologem helped me to fathom the social and personal chaos that enveloped many Americans even though most of us did not live in close geographic proximity to the palpable atrocities of that war. We were not under bombardment, nor did we have to flee our homes and endure thirst, starvation, and exposure. We did not have to don

---

[1] C. G. Jung to Dorothy Thompson, 1949, in *Letters I: 1906-1950*, Gerhard Adler, ed. (Princeton: Princeton University Press, 1973), p. 535.

gas masks while living under the threat of chemical attack. We were fortunate. Nonetheless, even though it was publicly denied, many of us felt the collective tensions of the war's buildup after Iraq invaded Kuwait in August, 1990.[2] In January and February, 1991, we participated on a more personal level through our concerned connection to individuals living or serving in the Middle East, our fear of terrorism, and the incessant television images of the war itself.

The Gulf War brought vast human destruction and environmental pollution. Its video coverage precipitated increased consciousness of both regional and global issues. In the following decade, although overt hostilities were limited to attacks in the no-fly zone, many of us have remained particularly sensitized to the up-heaving horrors of the war's aftermath and the devastation wrought by numerous other regional conflicts that have erupted around the world.[3] For some of us, the images of Gulf War also facilitated the uncovering of psychotic pockets in ourselves as functioning adults, permitting old wounds to open, and, in some cases healing, transformative personal initiations to begin.

In 1991 several psychoanalysts in New York told me they had never had to contain and metabolize so much primal emotion in analysands at once, never saw so many urban and suburban middle-class clients catapulted at one time into fear, despair, and emotional chaos. Those of us concerned with global and personal ecology know these emotions are relatively common in an age of catastrophic upheavals and in the process of deep analytic work. What marked this period as different in our practices was the acute nature of the effects of what the military called a "desert storm" on both neurotic analysands and on those functioning at more infantile or borderline levels. Its effects were similar to those of a sudden natural disaster or family death, because the war opened the psyche to anguish, fear of annihilation, impotence, rage, chaotic fragmentation, and loss of meaning. It gave many otherwise insulated people

---

[2] In some sensitive individuals the clinical symptoms of profound anxiety about the oncoming war cannot necessarily be attributed to paranoia and pessimism. It may be that certain individuals were intuiting this truth in spite of overt denials.

[3] Since the end of the cold war, regional violence has "killed at least 5 million people and created tens of millions of refugees and orphans" (Bruce Bower, "Inside Violent Worlds: Political Conflict and Terror Look Different Up Close and Local," *Science News* 158, no 6. [August 5, 2000]: 89).

a taste of what many third world and ghetto populations live with on a daily basis. The psychotherapeutic literature was full of articles about the war's impact on daily life. "A constant barrage of television, newspaper, and magazine coverage has brought the Persian Gulf War into almost every American's living room. . . . The electronic media is covering new ground with regard to the vividness and immediacy of war images, and no viewer is able to remain remote—cognitively or affectively—from these stimuli."[4] "Counselors in all sorts of settings report that their clients are having anxiety attacks, increased anger reactions, reduced frustration tolerance and other similar symptoms that can be traced directly or indirectly to Desert Storm."[5] "Post traumatic stress reactions may now surface . . . [among] returning military personnel, but in other clients as well. . . . Adults and children in the general population may need counseling, especially those who have gone through trauma or crisis, as they see pictures of the war and its victims."[6]

Part of the initial potency of the war in our psyches was due to the continuous television barrage of immediate war pictures, what was commonly referred to in New York as "CNN fever." As Jungians, we know that images can compel consciousness and libido. Our psyches are always using and reacting to images of outer phenomena. Everything from day residues to large, collective events and natural catastrophes may interface with our inner processes. The Gulf War provided a prime manifestation of the vital and perhaps ultimately world-saving fact that we live in a new age, one in which telecommunications enable us to experience far events as near, hidden events as exposed, and events we would like to deny as real. We are challenged to become conscious.[7] The shadow side of this awareness is a capacity in television viewers to become both excessively preoccupied with repetitions of scenes that arouse anxiety and defended against their fear

4 Rojean Wagner, "The Effects of War," *The Psychiatric Times* 8, no. 3 (March, 1991).
5 Carol Hacker, "AMHCA Responds to the Traumas of Desert Storm," *The Advocate* 14, no. 6 (February, 1991).
6 Carol Hacker, "AMHCA Helps the Healing of Desert Storm," *The Advocate* 14, no. 7 (March, 1991).
7 Part of such consciousness requires that we learn to differentiate what we are shown, for we are also forced to experience fraudulent or distorted scenes as if they were exciting and probable realities. Such propaganda now serves business interests as well as political agendas.

by denying or trivializing what they see. In our attacks of CNN fever, we were gripped by video images. Our empathy and horror were deeply stirred. As the war progressed, the news became more carefully guarded. Even as we rationally understood the military necessity for censorship, we hungered more anxiously for accurate information. Frustrated, we focused on the television source as if it were a seductive, persecutory, and withholding mother. Eager to take in whatever we saw, we were then forced to swallow the same exciting and disturbing images over and over again, because nothing fresh was forthcoming fast enough.

Bombarded by media coverage and empathically joined to family members and neighbors stationed across the globe, we were ineluctably drawn to share imaginally and emotionally in distant events and to recognize our interconnectedness with those in a remote and yet utterly immediate and palpable world. Most of us were privileged and blessed to be only participant observers of catastrophe. Our survival was not dependent upon taking such necessary actions as seeking refuge in bomb shelters or sealing off rooms against the threat of chemical attack. Actions of all kinds—those required for safety and survival and those we chose to do thousands of miles away from the war theater—helped to mute raw emotional responses. One friend in Haifa told me she felt her terror focused on her children under bombardment in Tel Aviv, because she was not near them and felt helpless to protect them. Nonetheless, necessary acts such as securing tape around the openings of the community's bomb shelter distracted and calmed her. Simple routines like the nightly ritual of gathering what would be needed when the air-raid warnings sounded functioned as guardians and made sleep possible. A Muslim friend in New York began to organize relief work. Her action, too, was an outlet for unbearable emotion and helped her to feel more closely connected to those who were endangered. In the United States many people roused themselves to act and counsel families with spouses or parents in the Gulf, march in demonstrations, write letters to service people, and even display yellow ribbons. Such actions help to channel and mitigate whole-body responses.[8] Other actions—such as attending prayer vigils

---

[8] These extroverted and active levels are reflected in the Celtic mythology of war goddesses, who fought with swords and shields, trained heroes in feats of skill, and challenged them as lovers and adversaries to prove their strength.

or participating in discussion groups—met needs for containment and community. Such transmutation of anxiety into assertive action and dependent bonding has been found to be characteristic of neurotics under threat of war.[9] Far from actual disaster, many of us nevertheless felt the potency of multiple, repeated, and intense images of war. They broke through the electronic buffer zone we like to think television offers. Many of us sat at home feeling ourselves assaulted by media images, which fell like bombs into our psyches, gashing open deeply buried emotions. Because the immediacy of the television images hit us vividly and repeatedly with a power that destroyed normal boundaries between outer and inner, collective and personal, present and past, we were often forced into depths where our own oldest wounds are scarred over. This may have been particularly true of those engaged in deep analytic work either as analysands or analysts. One analysand who viewed the early scenes of war said: "I am compelled—that's the word—to watch the news. Some awful truth out there has stretched open a tunnel to anarchy that I already know and don't want to know—an inside battlefield bombardment that feels close to the outer madness. . . ." Another analysand afflicted by the archaic level unleashed somatically and emotionally in his psyche by the barraging images of Desert Storm complained, "I closed that stuff, but this war is opening up an old wound, and I have to be a hero and go back and look at intolerable pains in me as much as I have to look at the news, [because] . . . my old, buried, inner pain merges with the present fear and chaos. It gets pulled into the light as if by a magnet. . . . But I feel as helpless now as ever I did then."

The media and military attempted to erect primitive defenses of depersonalization and dissociation as they sought to make us feel we were watching a video game rather than people like ourselves under those elegantly precise, computerized, cruciform bomb sites. How often we heard not about the human deaths but only about "collateral damage." The military and the media spoke of a "turkey shoot" on the road to Basra when the fleeing armies were so easily killed. Many people were deeply disturbed by the crazy communication patterns and

---

[9] C. S. Ierodiakonou, "The Effect of the Threat of War on Neurotic Patients in Psychotherapy," *American Journal of Psychotherapy* 24, no. 4 (October, 1970): 643 ff.

weird reversals of some of the feeding media, which spoke of devastating bombing raids as if they were sport, of war actions as a video game, of missiles as "smart,"[10] and of fireworks at a baseball game weeks after the hostilities had ended as missiles in the skies over Baghdad (*The New York Times*, April 21, 1991). Such dissociation and reversals replicate magic-level and psychotic communications, which create perceptual and cognitive dissonances that were often close to schizophrenogenic. The metaphors forced a painful jarring of cognitive categories and were often felt as sadistic. One woman was reminded of her father's habit of venting his sadism by throwing his keys at his children's elbows when they rested them on the dining table while he blithely proved that he had not lost his baseball pitcher's aim.

An analysand who is also a therapist wrote about the onslaught of chaotic devastation in her own psyche that she experienced on the night of January 16, 1991, when she had inadvertently turned on the news:

> Bombs are falling in Baghdad. The ancient city of empires that once conjured up magic lanterns, jewel-colored carpets, and the attar of roses and oil is tonight devastated by modern weapons and tyranny and war. Tonight as the people slept, I have seen their city stalked from the air and suddenly prey to deadly explosives. I have seen it ringed in the light of tracer bullets and bombs. Sitting here, waiting for friends for dinner in New York, I have seen war falling from the skies onto Baghdad as if I were inside the distant city, sharing the horror of the people there. Weirdly we here could know what our forces are doing to them before our own commanders announced it and before they even knew its effects.
>
> I feel shaken in my core. Some always-assumed order has collapsed before my eyes and ears. The endangered TV crew presented the truth raw to my/our senses. No safely distancing authority censored or told us what to believe. That feels as momentous an overturning of the hierarchy of safety as reading the vernacular Bible must have felt to medieval

---

[10] This belief in the animism of tools is ancient and widespread. Celtic warriors believed their swords could even sing of the battles they had fought.

Catholic minds. I feel shattered. All rational boundaries tumble into an abyss. Time is collapsing. Effect seemed to come before cause. Space collapses. I see from within ravaged Baghdad, which I view from inside my safe Manhattan room, the immediate, cataclysmic results there/here of the enemy's enemy—ourselves. I feel fear, excitement, horror, despair, fascination, helplessness. Especially helplessness. I did not want this; I have worked all fall to avoid it, but I am now deeply part of it. Yet I am still here; safe and helpless and suffering helplessness and fear like some catastrophe inside me.Where is this going, this rough beast unleashed and horribly slouching so near to Bethlehem? I would like to pray but I have only chaotic fear and confusion to be a prayer. Evil is on all sides, and sudden, awesome destruction. I can only stare into the chaos that is over us all. Cruelty and disorder beyond justice, beyond mind.

The chaotic war images triggered catastrophic psychological upheavals in certain sensitive individuals. In such times of crisis when we cannot maintain our habitual psychological defenses and patterns of coping, we may suffer profound confusion and are thereby propelled into realizations that may otherwise have been much slower in forming. Such a transformation in order to form a new consciousness or achieve a new integration does not seem to develop without each of us going through a period of what the alchemists called dismemberment and nigredo. Periods of emotional turbulence and chaos may actually prepare the way for transformation. The Gulf War gave those of us who were intensely involved as participant observers an opportunity for a short, potent, and blessedly safe-enough descent into chaos that overwhelms or dismembers the ego. We know that such descents can take us into borderline and psychotic layers in the psyche where our own pockets of still-unworked complexes make us susceptible to dismemberment. We know that such descents may be transformative if we can work through our personal complexes and find meaningful images around which to create a new integration. As one analysand poignantly said:

The images and emotions out there pierce through me. I feel torn apart because I feel both sides are wrong. I can't flee to any fragment of this mess to hold me because there is nothing to polarize my fear against . . . to make a hated adversary and make me a whole against it. . . . I know I need to seek a higher integration, but where is an image to integrate this dark chaos?

The Mother of All Battles

Most often we think of war as conflict between opposing parties, and our concern is with power, right and wrong, winning and losing, and/or conflict resolution. We coalesce ourselves, as this analysand could not do, by pitting ourselves aggressively against an adversary. A group or nation, too, can pull itself together by facing a common enemy. By focusing attention on external threat, we may divert ourselves from domestic issues. We may also distance ourselves from the emotional impact of war by assessing combat skills, strategy, and weaponry. After the war is over we may try to explore the historical, economic, cultural, and inevitable archetypal roots of such profoundly acted-out discord. We talk in abstractions about attachment and hostility, love and death instincts, or in terms of biological drives or testosterone levels. We differentiate aggression into the libido that fuels intraspecies mating fights and that which forces combat against outsiders. We look at power, at issues of domination, and the need for outlets for power and aggression. We talk about nations playing robber and policeman/messiah and about the inflations that are inevitable as both sides proclaim that God is theirs alone. We try to manage the archetypal potency of war with rituals, war games, and strategies of conflict resolution.[11]

As Jungians, we speak of war—whether enacted or experienced between nations or experienced in the individual psyche—as a conflict between opposites. On the psychological level we are trained to use the imaginal realm and the transcendent function to find some grace of a reconciling third position. On both psychological and political levels we look at issues of the shadow and shadow projection onto the

---

[11] See Anthony Stevens, *The Roots of War: A Jungian Perspective* (New York: Paragon House, 1989) and Jerome S. Bernstein, *Power and Politics: The Psychology of Soviet-American Partnership* (Boston: Shambhala, 1989), especially pp. 79–124.

enemy. We explore how we distance from and dehumanize the other, transforming the enemy into a nonhuman demon so that we are free to vent our hate and destructiveness without empathy.[12]

Such shadow levels came up in some clients' material. One man had consciously identified with what we were told was a brainwashed POW and told me, "I [also] learned to say anything to get the brutes off my back." After this was explored with reference to his communications in therapy, he then dreamed that Saddam Hussein was sitting in his new kitchen waiting for him to come home. The dreamer initially identified the figure of the dictator with his mother saying it "represents sadism—a torturing power that does not care, that has no bounds to cruelty, destruction, and greed." I also saw the figure as related to his experience of my questioning his identification with a victim forced to appease even in his therapy. The dreamer tended to experience questions as confrontations that he felt were a sign of powerful destructiveness, and this projection had often made him feel at the mercy of his wife, girlfriends, and therapist. After the transferential implications had been discussed, the dreamer mused on the image of the Iraqi leader. He began to push out his chest. When his attention was drawn to his change in posture, he noticed how it conveyed his pleasure in raw, chthonic, dominative power—a shocking idea to him but one that he had to meet in his own personal kitchen, the psychological place of cooking and transformation. As we worked on the dream image over several weeks, he began to acknowledge his own power shadow and to realize that "such power capable of the worst horrors of war might be part of me."

The deeper existential level that the Gulf War opened in my clients and friends and in myself includes issues of inner conflict and shadow confrontation; however it has been better named in the hyperbole of the Arabs as "The Mother of All Battles." This phrase is actually an English translation of the Arabic, but it holds an image of the matrix of primary consciousness beneath polarizations and warring conflict. Thus it does indeed belong to and encompass both sides. This Terrible Mother is an ancient, archetypal image of war's chaos and destruction that we know from various mythologies. Once more its archetypal

---

[12] See Sam Keen, *Faces of the Enemy: Reflections of the Hostile Imagination* (San Francisco: Harper & Row, 1986).

meaning and powerful horror crashed into our contemporary psyches. Public figures acted to mute the dread that the phrase conveyed. It quickly became a catchword in this country after its initial impact subsided and we became confident we would decimate Iraq's forces from the air. With repetition we drained the phrase of its grim power. We reduced it to a mere slogan that proved our strength against the Terrible Mother of Death. Headlines referred to "The Mother of All Defeats." To dispel lingering terror in New York, Mayor Dinkins began to speak of the ticker-tape homecoming of U.S. troops as "The Mother of All Parades." General Schwarzkopf, who led the allied victory on the field and in his television interviews mediated both the hysteria of some newscasters and the chaos of the war itself, was named "Father of the Year." He carried the archetypal role needed to balance the terrible Mother of All Battles.

Nonetheless, the phrase and the images we were compelled to watch on television opened many of us to experiences of the Terrible Mother of Life and Death and the primal, painful, overwhelming affects of her children. For a short time she possessed us and drove many of us into states we associate with psychosis. One particularly susceptible client expressed this horror when she said she feared the end of the world. She suffered acute diarrhea in her panic throughout the weeks of combat. For her, this war held the terrible danger of apocalypse—of global annihilation, the primeval terror that underlies all our undoing and fuels the fires that overwhelm consciousness and bring on psychosis. Many people were initially scared of the realistic potential of nuclear involvement and the terrifying, boundary-violating chemical and gas weapons. This client's belief that the apocalypse was imminent exacerbated such realistic collective dangers. She felt her sense of ordered limits and security on earth eroded just as profoundly as nameless fears of annihilation undermine the psychotic's ego.

In this war, too, the use of high-tech equipment gave some of us a strange sense that something awesome and nonhuman was in charge of an unfathomable horror. At the primitive, autistic level of consciousness, there is no experience of safe human boundaries to define and protect the psyche's body ego. Things, parts of things and people, and shapes substitute for human beings and are often felt as invasively threatening. The war's unleashing of awesome inhuman power replicates early experience of parental caretakers as all-powerful, impersonal forces in charge of events we had to suffer, and it touches the numinosity of relationships between ego and Self, between human and divine or demonic.

Many people palpably experienced a fear of terrible Fate and an unknowable maw into which they expected that life might plunge. This terror exposed an underlying sense of helplessness and a felt lack of protection from giant, arbitrary forces. While this helpless fear led some people to church to seek spiritual connection, containment, and an outlet for dependency needs, it also led some to deep analytic work. The images and feelings outside provoked by the Gulf War reverberated deeply into old personal experiences of fear and helplessness before sadistic and chaotic caretakers—the terrible parent of all battles and defeats.

Inevitably, those for whom the external collective crisis touched the deepest levels of the psyche were individuals with early personal experiences of terror in the face of helplessness, annihilation, chaos, and eruptive primary emotions. They could identify with the vulnerability and impotence of both soldiers and civilians, because their own histories of childhood abuse or neglect made "the frightening images they see on television . . . resonate with their early perceptions of an unsafe world."[13] Some defended against the news, avoiding it altogether because it stirred too painfully into old traumata with which they were not ready to deal. One client, denying any "particular interest" in the war was, however, seized with asthma attacks when the war began. These replicated a long-gone, childhood problem. As we worked on the reactive somatic symptom, he realized that he was terrified that his only son, who had just turned 19, might be drafted and killed. Underneath his immediate and realistic concern, he found the old symptom of asthma also pointed his attention to his own childhood terror of annihilation now projected where there was a poignant reality hook to carry the problem.

For many of us the boundaries between group and individual, outer and inner, were stretched thin and often torn. What was manifesting collectively opened resonating wounds in personal psychology, and these reciprocally alerted us to the depth of destruction and madness in war. Conversely what was an individual and chronic "psychotic

---

13 Yudofsky, quoted in Wagner, "The Effects of War."

pocket" in personal psychology was manifesting collectively, and it was gripping. One man felt compelled to watch the news for hours even though it meant abandoning ongoing personal projects. He said, "My work, my family, life itself feels trivial in the face of the horrors out there." This was a rather common feeling—that daily life palled before such grim intensities. In his case, however, the compulsion to sit by the news and feel anxious had a magic quality: "By watching and feeling so much worry, at least I am doing something. Maybe it even helps." As we worked on his reactions, he discovered memories of his chronically sick mother, whom he began to realize he had also sat beside and watched, hating her absence from his active life and also giving her the gift of all he had then, which was his participant anguish. Defending against unspeakable helplessness, he had used anxiety magically in both the past and present situations.

Some people I know and/or work with had only passing reactions to the war, for their own lives were either in a personal chaos that dwarfed the events across the globe, or they were involved in deeply introverted processes.[14] Some of those least touched by the events of the war were preoccupied with their own creative projects. Two pregnant clients were focused on the life processes within them. One writer forced himself to stay with his novel. Each of these three felt engaged in consciously asserting an alternative to destruction.

One client was overwhelmed with gratitude for a television commentator's concern about children's fear of the war and furious at a reporter who dismissed a child's questions about his own fear to speak only about needing to perform his job well. The dismissal reminded her of how she had experienced her father's abandoning the family in wartime Europe to go off dutifully and "act the hero." She could vent fury at the reporter she had never allowed herself to feel or express against her father whose leaving was felt to be an emotional rejection. She was, however, fascinated and relieved to follow the reports of officers helping soldiers in the field discuss their fears of mutilation, gassing, and death. "The macho world of denial, even in

---

[14] That my own clients tended to have strong reactions to the war and its images may have been influenced by my own involvement in the war. It is possible that the holding environment in the transference/counter-transference field in my practice was more permeable than that of some of my colleagues, who had no immediate and personal concerns with individuals and issues on both sides of the conflict in the Gulf area.

the army, is shifting. I wish my father had lived to hear that it is all right to have feelings."

With other clients, the war's violence reverberated into their own personal, primal fears of annihilation and brought to consciousness a personal existential anguish and feelings of lack of containment in a terrifyingly vast and dangerous universe. The war re-evoked childhood terrors before experiences of boundlessness, chaos, inner and outer explosiveness, and memories of zombie-like defenses against overwhelming hate and violence. As one woman said, "If you don't feel safe on earth anyway, then this war makes life nearly impossible." She experienced the sudden re-arousal of her victimized child complex as the images of bombing replicated fears of her raging alcoholic mother, who had "invaded—like war from the skies." Lurched into parallel emotional resonance, she also began to re-experience her attempts to "play dead and numb out" to avoid being the target of her mother's violent attention.

Another client, normally a competent professional, was so fearful of terrorism he could not even make the trip to therapy. He was convinced he would be blasted by terrorists in the train station or airport. The outer reality of such a possibility was felt by several out-of-town clients, by many New Yorkers in public spaces, by commuters who bought up all the gas masks available in New York fearing terrorism in the train stations, and by those who canceled air reservations. This client was plunged unexpectedly into inchoate fear and felt ashamed of his cowardice, for it belied his persona of competence. Working in therapy by phone, we explored his terror of terrorism as an objective reaction to real threat that showed he was guarding himself as no one had cared for him as a child. Gradually we began to uncover specific memories under the nameless dread. His maternal uncle and abusive brother had blasted his body boundaries from outside when he was a boy just as his own overwhelming feelings of terror and rage had blasted his psychic boundaries from inside, because no one had mediated his emotional reactions to the early physical abuse. He began to remember how it felt to be treated inhumanly and brushed aside as if he were merely "collateral damage." He realized he never expected to be treated like a human being. He dreamed of a cockroach that lay in his bed. In his associations he recalled a television interview with one pilot who had helped to bomb the Iraqi Republican Guard. "They look," the pilot had said, "just like cockroaches." The client readily identified himself as a lowly but surviving cockroach who had lived in darkness, hiding all his life behind his persona. Nonetheless, he projected an explosive terrorism onto strangers lurking in Penn Station. The righteous ruthlessness of the Republican Guard sometimes erupted unconsciously through him. His wife complained about sudden outbursts of panicky rage with which he blasted his family when they disobeyed his somewhat fanatic requirements. The dream and his associations of the cockroach with the Republican Guard point toward a conscious potential to mediate assertion and guard himself in a way that would make cockroach hiding unnecessary. While still identified with the fragile victim of attack, this potential is still in thrall, like the Republican Guard, to an inner sadistic and tyrannical superego that substitutes for ego strength and the Self's authority. In the dream, the lowly cockroach is still in bed. But it came out of hiding to be seen as he hid himself away from the "dangerous trip" to therapy.

Fear of gas attacks roused terror in many people whose relatives had died in the Holocaust. The image of Israeli civilians and reporters in their shelters fumbling to put on their masks haunted one client as if it was her own experience of traumatic stress. The image leapt over and over into her mind to re-evoke the nameless dread that had hung over her family. She retreated to her bed, the one place of safety she remembered from childhood. Only when she could ground her current sense of fearful helplessness in her own parallel childhood experience did she find some relief. This occurred as she vividly began to remember a series of painful operations she had undergone before she was six that made her feel mutilated. She spoke of the repeated experiences of anesthesia:

> I thought I would die each time, like the relatives in the camp showers. And I would wake up hurting, but no one wanted to hear about it. They told me I was lucky, and I held onto that. I made myself believe it finally. I never wanted to look at this again, but that gas mask scene and the terror of chemical weapons are bringing it all back. . . . I know that fear. It's an attack on my body, just like on theirs. The dread then was like an evil gas that erodes me, unnames me, so I was less than nothing. [Note how the present and past are fused.] And there was no one to communicate myself with. So I was gone, like the tree in the forest [that] no one hears. And I could not speak from within my fear; I was told I was foolish. So I still think I was

bad, even evil, for having fear and hurting, when others had had it so much worse. . . . It's a relief to talk now, but scary. Then, I felt chopped up into pieces that got smaller and smaller. And I died as if there was something wrong with me like the Jews in the showers. Eventually I got myself renamed to myself as this big, coping superwoman, who can't really manage, who can't really feel. . . . But this war has undermined me again. . . . Imagine, I have collapsed with just one television scene!

Her experience of being "gone like the tree in the forest" had crept like gas through her life to create an underlying, dissociated numbness. When she first came into therapy, she was still cutting herself with nails to "feel something" and to fasten herself into reality—albeit a reality of suffering. Now, several years after she had stopped cutting herself, she was still the victim of attacks of hysterical fear that gave her a sense of aliveness and wild energy even as they incapacitated her. The war gave her another opportunity to return to the underlying, archaic dread and express more of it in a secure, empathic and contained space.

Almost everyone was appalled by Saddam Hussein's environmental terrorism—the spilling of oil onto the sea and the burning of oil fields. Images of the oil-covered, helpless cormorants (actually taken from another oil spill but epitomizing the current issue) touched viewers viscerally. As one woman said, "We look at raw evil here, the wanton use of power to destroy nature and innocent creatures that are not even party to this madness. Now I feel hate and rage." Again, the outer collective scene touched an inner personal chord. In the alchemical way that is central to analytic work, this client worked across the thin membrane from collective to personal. She felt an upsurge of identification with the helpless bird, of the helplessness and rage she had experienced as a small child. Exploring what was both a realistic and a complex reaction, she remembered

> . . . body memories of abuse to my body—caretakers who did invasive things . . . medical procedures . . . a hospital stay where children screamed and I was as silent as a stunned rabbit, alone in my bed, hiding from awful "procedures" that were supposed to be good attention.
>
> Now, I can feel enraged for the cormorants and fish and the people whose waters are spoiled. I want to kick and

scream, to kill the abusers. But again I feel so helpless and
hopeless. The war machines are rolling. As a child when I
was helpless, I learned to get quiet and retreat so far inside
I became a tiny, hard ball, and I never really knew what was
inside that. Maybe it is the rage I feel now as all those memories of frailty and fear are just like what I feel for that cor-
morant and our troops and all the people being bombed. I
wish I could erupt like a volcano to equal the violence and
horror. The rage inside me has been frozen for so long.

Reheated by the immediate experience of fury at the war's massacre of
the innocents, this woman made a dance in one therapy session that
began to mediate her rage into consciousness.[15] She later named it
"red-fire volcano against all destroyers."

Regression

Some individuals were forced to experience layers of psyche that led
them beyond shadow confrontation and the depressive position into
paranoid-schizoidal processes and primary autism. They collapsed into
what Wilfred Bion calls "psychotic crisis" where catastrophic change
arouses feelings of disaster in participants and abruptly and violently
subverts the order of things.[16] Many felt shame to find their usual
sense of identity so dismembered by uncontained, overwhelming emotions as they suffered the "nameless dread" triggered by the war
images. The reopening of aboriginal chaos, which came about through
identification with the war images, evoked archetypal emotions: rage
at overwhelming helplessness and uncontainment, anguish at abandoning loss, and terror for one's bodily integrity.[17]

The current experiences related to the war were intensified by and
restimulated affects and experiences that had been palpably present
and unmediated in very early childhood. For some clients the outer

[15] Sylvia B. Perera, "Ritual Integration of Aggression in Psychotherapy," in Murray Stein and
Nathan Schwartz-Salant, eds., *The Borderline Personality in Analysis* (Wilmette, IL: Chiron,
1988), pp. 233–266.
[16] Leon Grinberg, Dario Sor, and E. Tabak de Bianchedi, *Introduction to the Work of Bion*
(New York: Jason Aaronson, 1977), p. 41.
[17] Louis H. Stewart, "Work in Progress. Affect and Archetype: A Contribution to a
Comprehensive Theory of the Structure of the Psyche," in Murray Stein and Nathan Schwartz-
Salant, eds., *The Body in Analysis* (Wilmette, IL: Chiron, 1986), p. 200.

chaos and the powerful images of war forced a sudden, dismembering regression to what had been scarred over with primary defenses of denial, depersonalization, dissociation, projective identification, and splitting, and framed into habitual character structures. Viewing the war images returned these analysands to levels of psyche and affect that revealed traumatic stresses in the parental/child complex, stresses so severe in some cases that they had prevented adequate learning about the process of metabolization of raw affects and about the creation of an incarnation vessel or ego center of consciousness that had the strength and integrity to survive and thrive.

The induction into what is a "realistic" madness is awful, but in some cases individuals were able to wrest from it a purpose and meaning. The overwhelming power of archetypal affects and presymbolic thoughts that were aroused by and hung projectively onto video images enabled some clients to experience a chronic psychosis that they could not experience in childhood, because they lacked then a viable container in which to confront such overwhelming anxiety. Adequate caretakers were not available to validate, protect against, or dose the overwhelming anxiety. Lacking adequate consciousness of self from which to disidentify and witness without unbearable pain, they had to withdraw instead behind various autistic and paranoid-schizoidal defenses.[18] They functioned in the world with only a brittle, false self or persona. Now in therapy these analysands could use the therapeutic relationship as a container for the dismembering affects that blasted ego boundaries and opened consciousness into suffering the seemingly limitless space of chaos itself. Held within the transference and assisted by the analyst's empathy and counter-transferential awareness, they could begin to look beyond the emerging bizarre images and dismembering emotions for long-hidden personal memories. Within the constancy of analysis and by relying on the functioning aspects of their adult selves, these analysands could begin to use the regression to the psychotic part of themselves as the beginning of a healing process.[19]

---

[18] Thomas H. Ogden, *The Primitive Edge of Experience* (Northvale, NJ: Jason Aaronson, 1989), p. 102.

[19] This part is sometimes experienced as a walled-off layer into which the fragile ego collapses. But in more developed personalities, it is more often felt to be a pocket that has been disidentified from and lived around. When the pocket's chaos is experienced, the rest of the functioning personality can support this to some extent. In many creative individuals, access (via mood shifts induced by emotion, mind-altering substance, meditation, etc.) to this pocket is considered valuable as a source for imaginal work.

Often collective and/or personal situations or relationships can restimulate and then begin to release the grip of fearful, traumatic events and complexes by triggering or throwing us back into them in a different context. Most often in therapy the transference and counter-transference serves this function. It unsettles the inert, complacent structures and defenses in which we habitually and blindly dwell and forces us into psychological areas that still hold experiences of pain, fears of the unknown, and boundless primal chaos. At this depth, we must follow the guiding Self as we grope to understand our complexes and express their energies in structures that may be more appropriate for our individuation. This is slow, patient work. Sometimes as with the Gulf War, an outer event crashes through to the cellar, ripping open the central complex like the SCUD/Patriot missile debris. From this violent confrontation, we may begin to build a "new world order," but it is not a simple Bushian concept to be bandied about to quell anxiety. It is quite a perilous undertaking that involves us in a plunge into the depths of our psychic wounds, into the maternal/child archetype with its inchoate presymbolic fears of chaos, annihilation, and primary affects, into what is madness and the still remaining layers of madness that are too often part of collective human culture. "War and madness are scarcely unrelated," Michael Eigen says pointedly.[20]

Toward Healing

The relatively well functioning woman who wrote about the chaos of the first bombing of Baghdad soon recognized the analogies between outer events and her inner madness. Plunged into preverbal emotionality, she initially could not write or even express her mixed emotions. She told me her mind was taken over by the incoherence of primitive chaos. She said she had felt "blank terror and jittery, dissolving and all atremble." At first like a psychotic, she felt uncertain of boundaries and distinctions (inside/outside, animate/inanimate, subject/object, image/meaning). She therefore could not feel that she had a container for her chaotic reactions and could do nothing with them except "sob like an

---

[20] Michael Eigen, *The Psychotic Core* (Northvale, NJ and London, England: Jason Aaronson, 1986), p. 20.

infant overwhelmed." Disoriented, she hung on to her friends and was only relieved of the "pressure of the bizarre" when they could empathize with her as they were also transfixed by the television news. When her experience was thus validated, she could put her extreme reactions into the collective emotional container—much as an infant would put her anguish into the maternal-child field. Soothed by the empathic mirroring of her friends that she had rarely felt in childhood with borderline parents, this woman could begin to experience herself as a more intact and open person responding to legitimate horror. She could begin to disidentify from the outer events that reverberated into her wounded maternal/child complex and that dropped her into the pit of re-aroused experiences of raw, explosive, primary emotions. She could even recognize that only part of her was swamped. The rest of her could hold, function, wash dishes, and even begin to hope that she could sort and metabolize an experience that felt so peculiarly shattering.

Later alone, when the stress began to intensify again, she showed me that she had found another container for her reactions. She drew the chaos she felt in wild shapes and colors. Still later, she tried to describe her "horrible jumble" by writing in her journal. Human empathy, art, and verbal expression all functioned as containers in which presymbolic chaos could be shaped into symbolic forms, providing some measure of control and disidentification. Finally she brought her journal and her still frighteningly ungrounded panic into analysis, allowing another level to be held for further exploration. Supported by the analyst's knowledge of her history, she began to realize that she was particularly susceptible to "night bombing," because her infancy had been marked by the explosions of a violently loud and insecure father returning from his late night workaholism to disrupt her sleep. Her mother had been unable to deal with the abusive sounds or to mediate her daughter's fear and protect her from the onslaught of archetypal emotion. Again without shield and container as the images of Desert Storm plunged into her peaceful consciousness, her early situation was replicated precisely, and she found an opportunity to explore her early body memories and to find mediating channels for her experience. She knew *about* her early fear and its effect on problems of sleeplessness and occasional paranoia; she had worked on these issues in analysis and body therapy. But she had not had any precise and forceful life trigger to bombard her with fear comparable to that which she knew as a child. The bombs falling on Baghdad served to create an uncanny replication of her infant emotions. Her friends, her art and journal, and her analysis validated her anxiety and helped her to contain and metabolize it. None of this had happened in her infancy. As a result, she had to bury her experiences of disaster in a closet of uncontained, nameless dread that was not to be fully reopened. Because she had looked through the crack several times before, she was able to endure the replication of her early experience relatively easily when the door of the forbidden room was blasted down. With that explosion a new level of healing could begin.

Similarly the man terrified of terrorists was astonished to find that rather than forcing him to face his fear of annihilation concretely as his parents had done by leaving him with abusive caretakers, his therapist supported his staying home in safety and using painting and dancing to express or "evacuate" his painful emotions and using the telephone for frequent therapy sessions. When the war hostilities ended and he felt able to risk the journey, he expressed a feeble and ashamed wish to take a friend along for the first trip rather than to brave the terrorist's den alone. The therapist—now an ambivalent object that both "forced" and protected the trip—still supported his need for safety. By validating and containing his terror through exploring its objective rationality, its need for nonverbal and verbal containers, and its roots in personal history and the transference, his therapy supported his actual safety and provided a multiple-leveled environment in which to explore and experience his psychotic fear in a new context. In an ensuing dream he imaged himself riding in the elevator that had a floor, unlike earlier dreams in which floors were often missing. Rather than falling helplessly into an abyss of terror that he had felt and learned to deny in childhood, he discovered a safe-enough container for the human sensitivities that had been so abused. For this analysand, as for others, the war image riveted emotional attention to the psychotic pocket that was ready to open. Therapy then provided a concrete means of confronting, containing, and metabolizing the exposed chaotic elements. Previously this client had relied on sadistic superego categories to control his life and contain his emotions. He had also used denial, distancing, and dispersion of affect to manage eruptive lability and the underlying existential fear of annihilation.

As we can see in some analysands, Desert Storm unleashed a primordial sense of chaos and catastrophe, much like the chaos the Greeks imaged as the egg from which all life emerged. The alchemists called this the *prima materia*. This state is similar to the underlying sense of catastrophe that Wilfred Bion saw as the matrix of personality. For Bion, the primordial terror of this level underlies the parts of our personality: our first thoughts ("beta elements" made up of feelings of depression, persecution, guilt, envy) are indistinguishable from body sensations and float like hallucinations without a clear sense of boundaries and order. We try to expel these fragments to feel whole. Jungians would also call this primal level the *pleroma*—the primordial matrix of all that comes into existence. The pleroma is also the oblivion into which we redissolve consciousness in mystical experiences and in death. Most of our forms of awareness seem to violate this pleromatic boundlessness, because we usually know ourselves only as separate entities within containing limits we feel are relatively safe—of body, family, group, locale, species, etc. We habitually use modes of consciousness that make us feel distinctions. In the West, we tend to identify ourselves with our limits and the verbal labels that express such closed forms.

Our dominant religious traditions have mythologized what we call earthly life as a Fall into matter and limited form. But they, nonetheless, posit the existence of another more fluid realm in another dimension of time/space. Their images thus mediate the relationship between pleroma and closed forms. Modern science is closer to gnostic mystical traditions. It mythologizes an ocean of information and energy that pervades all individual forms and species. Lacking experience of new paradigms of consciousness and a more permeable ego that are congruent with this worldview, we are too often personally caught in old formulations. We may then feel our lives permeated by dread of catastrophic submergence in the boundless sea that surrounds it. The burden falls on individual human caretakers, who are given the incompleted cultural task of mediating the transitions from pleromatic to limited, from unconsciousness to waking. Individuals carrying such an immense cultural task are inevitably inadequate. But they also provide the uncomfortable seed beds of the new consciousness. Their very inadequacy forces the growth of new patterns of relationship between energy and form. Just because these early caretakers can rarely adequately and empathically mediate what the culture itself cannot bridge, vulnerable human infants are left to experience transitions from states of blissful fusion to separateness with a lurch of fear that must be managed by a primitive psyche that pulls in and away from others.

Such liminal spaces are filled with "beta-elements" and primary emotions, and we may—in our psychotic parts—dread disintegration or dissolving in them. Or we may jump across from one emotion to another in our borderline parts, or we may pull away and repress our emotions into shadow areas, if we are more neurotic. My sense is that we may do all of these, for we are formed in different layers like the snowflakes. Nonetheless, in early-childhood times of greatest vulnerability, the patterns of dissolving, separating, bonding, and limiting are set. And we live with those patterns relatively unconsciously, dealing with experience according to inertial habits we may rarely even notice. As we have seen, images of war served to break through these inertial habits and open some individuals again to the experiences of chaos that formed us as we know ourselves. Different psychological aspects were touched, but for some individuals these war images forced a return to face again the threat of death and the nameless dread that ushered them into life. The images opened awareness to the possibility of vastly enlarged and less rigidly fearful consciousness and even of transformation. They forced all of us back to the fearsome matrix of life and consciousness from which any regeneration must come.

The Morrigan—
Archetypal Images behind War and Madness

Seeking an image of the matrix as the Mother of All Battles that could help to structure and hold my own consciousness as I worked with my own emotions about the war and my clients' chaos, I thought of the various battling goddesses of heaven and earth. Many of these seemed too identified with active, yang force, the energy of fighting itself. The patterns of energy that are made conscious in the archetypal images of Anath, Durga, Kali, Innana, Maeve, Sekhmet, and Scathach did not mirror my clients' experiences or my own. The reactions I heard and felt to this war went to a more primeval level, one I associate to the raw images of the triad that the Irish called the Morrigan, the Mother of Life and of Death. She does not take part in battle as do many other goddesses, for the archaic culture out of which her stories grew has deeper roots than the heroic period.

One man's dream triggered by his experience of the Gulf War presents an image that replicates one that we find in the ancient Irish tale of "The Cattle Raid of Regamna or Cu Chulainn and the Morrigan." The dream image is, in Bion's terms, a "bizarre object":[21]

> I am in my childhood house watching the war news on CNN. I suddenly see on the screen two people with a hobby horse monster. It's a pole with a head on it. Somehow I know that it is a person destroyed, without skin or flesh, just a pole and a red, bloody disk head. I scream with terror because it is also in the room.

This analysand's childhood psychosomatic symptoms of intestinal cramps and diarrhea had reappeared with the onset of the war. Every morning he awoke seized with painful spasms. While investigating the symptom medically, he also began to realize its psychological import: he felt unable to stomach or contain the stream of destructive and painful emotions by which he felt barraged. After affirming the horror of the war news and his somatic reactions, we also looked reductively for the circumstances in childhood that had initially elicited such symptoms. He began to perceive the degree of underlying existential fear that had gripped him all his life in reaction to which he had heroically proven himself by becoming a leader in his profession.

The skewered puppet-like animal shows us the carrier of the life process as a monstrous, suffering distortion. In Jungian work we also look for amplificatory material, which the Irish tale of "The Cattle Raid of Regamna or Cu Chulainn and the Morrigan" provides. With it we will now consider the archetype behind chaos and our defenses against it, behind the catastrophic experiences and images of psychosis and war, and behind the wisdom of suffering and bountiful life that may help to take us beyond madness and war.

In the beginning of that tale:

> When Cu Chulainn lay asleep in Dum Imrith, he heard a cry sounding out of the north, a cry terrible and fearful to his

---

21 Grinberg, et al., *Introduction to the Work of Bion*, pp. 29 ff.

ears. Out of a deep slumber he was aroused by it so suddenly, that he fell out of his bed upon the ground like a sack, in the east wing of the house.

He rushed forth without weapons, until he gained the open air, his wife following him with his armor and garments. He perceived Loeg in his harnessed chariot coming towards him from . . . the North.

"What brings thee here?" said Cu Chulainn.

"A cry that I heard sounding across the plain," said Loeg. . . .

"Let us follow the sound," said Cu Chulainn.

They went as far as Ath da Ferta (Ford of the Two Chariot Poles). When they arrived there, they heard the rattle of a chariot from the loamy district of Culgaire. They saw before them a chariot harnessed with a *chestnut horse. The horse had but one leg, and the pole of the chariot passed through its body so that the peg in front met the halter passing across its forehead.* Within the chariot sat a woman [the Morrigan], her eyebrows red and a crimson mantle around her. Her mantle fell behind her between the wheels so that it swept along the ground. A big man went along beside the chariot. He also wore a coat of crimson, and on his back he carried a forked staff of hazel wood, while he drove a cow before him [italics added].

The skewered, living hobby-horse represents the motive power of the terrible goddess. The tale continues to reveal more about her:

"The cow is not pleased to be driven on by thee," said Cu Chulainn.

"She does not belong to thee," said the woman; "the cow is not owned by any of thy friends or associates."

"The cows of Ulster belong to me," said Cu Chulainn.

"Thou wouldst give a decision about the cow!" said the woman. "Thou art taking too much upon thyself, O Cu Chulainn!"

The mightiest of Ulster's warriors is made helpless before the Morrigan, and Cu Chulainn, himself, feels confused and ashamed. He then "made a leap into the chariot. He put his two feet upon her two shoulders and his spear on the parting of her hair." Undisturbed, the woman orders him to move further off and recites a poem that only further frustrates him. When the warrior is about to spring again into the chariot, he finds that

> [H]orse, woman, chariot, man and cow, all had disappeared. Then he perceived that she had been transformed into a black bird on a branch close by him. "A dangerous enchanted woman you are!" said Cu Chulainn. . . .
>
> "If I had only known that it was thou," said Cu Chulainn, " we should not have parted thus."
>
> "Whatever thou hast done," said she, "will bring thee ill-luck."
>
> "Thou canst not harm me," said he.
>
> "Certainly I can," said the woman. "I am guarding thy deathbed, and I shall be guarding it henceforth."

The Morrigan tells him that the cow she leads came out of a fairy mound and that she is taking it to breed with the Bull of Cooley. She prophesies: "As long as her calf shall be a yearling, so long shall thy life be; and it is this that shall cause the Cattle-Raid of Cooley." The hero boasts of all the feats he will accomplish and the honor he will gain in that battle, and she reminds him that she will come against him

> ". . .when thou art engaged in combat with a man as strong, as victorious, as dextrous, as terrible, as untiring, as noble, as brave, as great as thyself. I will become an eel, and I will throw a noose round thy feet in the ford so that heavy odds will be against thee."
>
> "I swear by the god by whom the Ulstermen swear," said Cu Chulainn, "that I will bruise thee against a green stone of the ford; and thou shalt never have any remedy from me. . . ."

The Morrigan foretells that she will also attack the hero in the shape of a gray wolf that "will take strength from thy right hand, as far as to thy left arm." Cu Chulainn swears he will spear out her eye. Undeterred, the goddess promises she will then become a white, red-eared heifer who will lead a rush of otherworldly cows to trample him. He swears to break her legs.[22]

In another tale, we learn the outcome of the story. Then, the hero is exhausted after his successful battle against his adversary and the animal shapes of the goddess. The Morrigan, in the shape of an old woman milking a cow with three teats, gives the exhausted hero milk. He blesses her and unknowingly heals the wounds he has inflicted on her when she shape-shifted into eel, wolf, and heifer.[23] Although the hero and the death goddess are adversaries, they are also related in another way, forever linked by mutual need.[24]

We know the Morrigan best in milder guises. Morgana le Fay of Avalon, King Arthur's sister and lover and a witch, is a later and tamer version. So is the elderly Lady Morgane who tested Sir Gawain through her son-in-law, the Green Knight. Older mythological evidence of the ancient Morrigan as a Great Goddess of the Irish is scattered throughout various medieval texts and in stories about parallel figures in Scotland, Gaul, and Wales. Her likeness is also represented in some Celtic relief sculptures. Gathering these bits, we can build a picture of this archetypal figure.

Old material tells of the Morrigan as a beautiful woman, with nine loose tresses, washing herself on Samain, the beginning of the winter year, at the fording place of the river. She has one foot on each side of the broad rushing torrent, straddling the waters of life. There she meets with the father god of the tribe when he comes to her for the destined sacred marriage rite of the New Year. The Morrigan was a pre-Celtic goddess of nature, representing the inexhaustible process of life, death, and transformation. We can surmise that she was originally celebrated as the flowing rivers and bountiful and withholding earth. Mountains in Ireland are called her paps (breasts). She is often represented by cows. She is also depicted in stories by those most ancient of animal forms connected with the Great Goddess. We find her as snake, bird, mare, and wolf, as well as feisty heifer and bountiful cow.

---

22 T. P. Cross and C. H. Slover, *Ancient Irish Tales* (New York: Henry Holt, 1936), pp. 211–214.

23 Thomas Kinsella, ed., *The Tain*, translated from the Irish epic *Tain Bo Cuailnge* (London: Oxford University Press/Dublin: The Dolmen Press, 1970), pp. 135–137.

24 Erich Neumann, *The Great Mother: An Analysis of the Archetype* (Princeton: Princeton University Press, 1955), pp. 301 *ff.*

We find her presence manifest in myth on Samain (our Halloween), the Neolithic feast marking the end of the summer year, the end of the year king's life, and the beginning of the winter year. This goddess appears at liminal times—not only on Samain but also on the days of battle, death, or birth, and places like the fording shallows of the river when and where the boundaries between supernatural and natural worlds are thinnest, and the dead and living may pass readily to show the interpenetration of realms. The goddess represents the fated crossing from one realm to another as well as the fear, courage, and wisdom that know such crossings. Thus, she is the psychopomp of an ineluctable process.

The later lore of the Iron age was patriarchal. In Celtic aristocratic warrior stories written down by Christian scribes, such as the one above, the triune Nature Goddess was redefined and cast in a totally negative light. The name Morrigan came to connote both an individual goddess and the collective term to designate any of the "sinister, powerful and clearly ancient" triad of sisters or supernatural beings who haunt the battlefields.[25] As death and battle goddesses, these were said to influence events by magic and by inspiring terror in the hearts of warriors. They are associated with various destructive animals and made into hags. Nonetheless, they retained their marked sexual and fertility characteristics. The Morrigan in the chariot with her red eyebrows and sweeping red cloak is served by a herdsman, who drives her cow. Although she is ruler of death and fate, she remains the nurturing cow goddess. In this story, she chides Cu Chulainn, the heroic guardian of the Ulster tribe and its herds, for taking too much upon himself by claiming her cow.

Many ancient goddesses appear in triune form. Sometimes these were differentiated as maiden, mother, and hag. The Morrigan, however, is a more primordial triad, one interwoven and relating to her shape-shifts between different levels of consciousness. She is differentiated into the Morrigan, Nemain, Badb, and sometimes Macha instead of Nemain. The first of the triad, and the name of the whole group is The Morrigan. It is a title meaning Great Queen, or later, Queen of Demons. She appears in various animal and human shapes including that of a beautiful seductress who lures the hero to herself. More often

---

25 Anne Ross, *Pagan Celtic Britain: Studies in Iconography and Tradition* (London: Routledge and Kegan Paul, 1967), p. 223.

she appears as a nurturing or loathsome hag. In our story, she is not as visibly ugly as in some others, but when the warrior Cu Chulainn asks for her own and her companion's identities, she pours out a string of nearly unintelligible nonsense words interspersed with more threatening names: "cold wind," "cutting," and "terror."[26]

The Morrigan appears again in a story of "The Destruction of Da Derga's Hostel" as huge and hideous. It is Samain, the night of an inevitable terrible raid and the king's death. She arrives first with a henchman who is carrying a roasted pig that is still squealing—another one of the bizarre images that the Celts used to convey the paradox of death in life and fertile life in death. She is described as "huge, black, gloomy, big-mouthed, [and] ill-favored" with a snout that a branch might support and lower lips [or pudenda] extending to her knees. Later

> in the hostel, [this] woman appeared at the entrance, after sunset, and sought to be let in. As long as a weaver's beam, and as black, her two shins. She wore a very fleecy, striped mantle. Her beard reached her knees, and her mouth was on one side of her head. She put one shoulder against the door-post and cast a baleful eye upon the king and the youths about him, and Conare [the king] said to her from inside the house, "Well then, woman, what do you see for us, if you are a seer?"
>
> "Indeed, I see that neither hide nor hair of you will escape from this house, save what the birds carry off in their claws," the woman replied.
>
> "It is not ill fortune that we prophesied, woman," said Conare. "Neither do you usually prophesy for us. What is your name?"
>
> "Cailb," she replied.
>
> "A name with nothing to spare that," said Conare.
>
> "Indeed, I have many other names," she said. . . . [and she] recited [31 of] these in one breath, and standing on one foot, at the entrance of the house."[27]

---

[26] Marie-Louise Sjoestedt, *Gods and Heroes of the Celts* (Berkeley: Turtle Island Foundation, 1982), p. 48.

[27] Jeffrey Gantz, *Early Irish Myths and Sagas* (London and New York: Penguin Books, 1981), p. 76.

The names include the festival, Samain, the river, Shannon, the Irish words for "panic," "horror," and "scald crow" as well as many non-sense words—perhaps remnants of a magical invocation and/or sugges-tions of the bewildering cognitive chaos this goddess brings with her. Again, in the tale of "Da Choca's Hostel," she is described with comparable hideousness as a

. . . big-mouthed black swift sooty woman, lame and squint-ing with her left eye. She wore a threadbare dingy cloak. Dark as the back of a stag-beetle was every joint of her, from the top of her head to the ground. Her filleted gray hair fell back over her shoulder. She leant her shoulder against the door-post and began prophesying evil to the host, and to utter ill-words.[28]

Her hideous anthropomorphic form evokes the horror of violent destruction to come. Unlike the hag in other Celtic (and Vedic) myths who can be disenchanted by a brave partner's kiss, the Morrigan stands apart and seems to bring only "ill fortune" or "evil" to her heroic partners. In only one tale does she bring help and favorable advice.[29] This is after a sexual encounter with her primary divine part-ner, the father god of the Tuatha pantheon who is her equal and treats her with loving respect.

Usually she foretells and initiates mortals into the unknown state that we call death, and it is our ego's fear of annihilation that is pro-jected into her as loathsomeness. To the individual identified only with present consciousness, the experience of change seems only malefic and monstrous, a deathly crossing into what is unknown and still unconscious. The Morrigan is thus hag-like and monstrous because her power over our inevitable and destined end is seen only negatively as the finality of death in a world that has lost connection to the cyclic and transformative process the goddess represents.[30] Yet, today we are again redefining our relationship to the unknown and unconscious by

---

[28] Ross, *Pagan Celtic Britain*, p. 248.

[29] Cross and Slover, *Ancient Irish Tales*, pp. 38–39.

[30] Transformation in this realm does not connote development as it tends to when we use the term today. Rather it connotes the changes of shape or form that the underlying essence under-goes throughout the life, death, and regenerative cycles. It is closer to shape-shifting and the psy-choidal levels of psyche, not to the development of consciousness.

revaluing many forms of awareness that render them more accessible to us.[31] Our sense of identity and consciousness is expanding to include forms of awareness that render "ego" more permeable and closer to the Self, just as the ego's tightly-edged boundaries are being stretched to include the experienced reality of more process-oriented modalities and even of the dissolutions and reformings that feel like death and regeneration. We are finding that it is only by overcoming our fear of going through the many changes in our development demanded by the Self that the new ego—one in tune with the Self's guidance—can emerge. Like the shamanic warriors of old who had to learn to live with death as a constant companion, we need to practice and struggle to overcome the fears that make us shrink back into defensive securities that render us inert. Through time and the many deaths we experience in our development, we may then gain a transformative sense of the "me" that is able to flow or lurch or scramble, even kicking and screaming, to serve the Self's intent.

Fate and Destiny

Typically, the Morrigan is a figure of Fate and the female wisdom of serpent, raven, flowing waters, and blood. As birthing, destroying, and regenerating aspects of the whole life process, she represents sight from the pleromatic perspective—the cosmic eye, which sees from the matrix underlying and beyond opposites uniting what is below and above, past and future, the snake's and bird's-eye views. Like the triple Norns who "rise out of the ground with the spring of living water, knowing both Life and Death,"[32] she is thus the prophet of destiny. She can foretell the outcome of the battles of life to those who ask. Even today, rites of divination take place at Samain, the night on which the mythic Celtic rulers were fated to die and the new cycle begin.

Sometimes the Morrigan is depicted at the crossing of the water, washing the armor and weapons of those about to be slain in battle. In the story of "Da Choca's Hostel," King Cormac and his men see a red

---

[31] These forms include extrasensory perception, participation mystique, out-of-body, and near death experiences, dreaming and imaginal and subtle body mentation, and awareness of synchronicity. Neumann already in 1952 pointed to the need to explore such "extrane psychic systems" of awareness (or "field knowledge") that lie beyond ego-consciousness and that we therefore have tended to call "unconscious." (Erich Neumann, "The Psyche and the Transformation of the Reality Planes," *Spring*, [1956]: 81–111.)

[32] Edgar Herzog, *Psyche and Death*, (New York: G. P. Putnam and Sons, 1966), p. 97.

woman standing in the water of the ford, washing the cushions and harness of a chariot. When she lowers her hand, the river bed becomes red with blood and gore. When she raises it, the water also rises and leaves the river bed dry so an army might cross easily. Repulsed by the sight of her, the king asks one of his men to approach the hag and ask what she is doing there. Standing in the magician's ritual posture—on one foot, with one hand raised, and one eye open, to represent the unity of the cosmic perspective, she chants that she is washing the arms of the doomed king.[33] With such foreknowledge, he must still carry on bravely—as we all must. The magician's pose in which the goddess stands is typical in Irish tradition. It conveys the idea of energy roused to the pitch of focused intensity that can support magical intent. Monocular, single-pointed, pre-ambivalent energy holds an orgiastic potential that has effective power in the magic dimension of consciousness to focus emotion and compel events. Such focused energy provides a powerful tool of magic in the occult traditions. The posture gives us an apt image for the seemingly magical compulsion of split affect states that we may experience—often by induction—generated from borderline levels of the psyche.

In the myth of The Tain Bo Cuailnge (The Cattle Raid of Cooley), the Morrigan again foretells the outcome of events, but she also acts to rouse the bull force to participate in the destined events of battle. The text says she "settled in bird shape on a standing stone" and sang to the Brown Bull—the totem of the armies of the north. She describes the anxiety that will mount before the fight and the beautiful land in its prosperous bounty that is doomed to destruction. As the sinister force behind life and·death, she sings the stark contrast of bounty and death (good breast and bad) in a poem that expresses how many of us felt during the winter of 1990-1991 as war preparations in the Persian Gulf intensified:

Dark one are you restless
  do you guess they gather
to certain slaughter
  the wise raven
groans aloud
  that enemies infest

---

33 Ross, *Pagan Celtic Britain*, p. 245.

the fair fields
  ravaging in packs
learn I discern
  rich plains
softly wavelike
  baring their necks
greenness of grass
  beauty of blossoms
on the plains war
  grinding heroic
hosts to dust
  cattle groans the Badb
the raven ravenous
  among corpses of men
affliction and outcry
  and war everlasting
raging over Cuailnge
  death of sons
death of kinsmen
  death death![34]

With this terrible dirge, the Morrigan rouses the bull to participate in the process that returns all that thrives to the abyss through grinding, devouring death.

Before the famous second battle of Moyatura, which is part of the mythic history of Ireland, the Morrigan trysts with the Father god of the Tuatha De Danann. Then she helps him by providing information of the enemy landings and a present of two handfuls of her own sacred blood, which streams forth in birth and battle to deprive the foe of "the blood of his heart, and the kidneys of his valor."[35] As the spirit of war, she "heartened the Tuatha De to fight the battle fiercely and fervently" until the battle becomes a rout. Then

---

[34] Kinsella, *The Tain*, p. 98.

[35] This gift is similar to Athena's gift to Asklepios of two phials of Medusa's blood—one to raise the dead and one to destroy. Similar also to the moon blood of women which brings life or death. (Barbara G. Walker, *The Women's Encyclopedia of Myths and Secrets* [San Francisco: Harper and Row, 1983], p. 629.)

... after the battle was won and the corpses cleared away, the Morrig[an], proceeded to proclaim that battle and mighty victory which had taken place, to the royal heights of Ireland and to its fairy hosts and its chief waters and its river-mouths. And hence it is that Badb (i.e., one of the Morrigan) also describes high deeds.[36]

The Morrigan is one singer of the gods, the voice of fate in which we may find our own stories. And these stories inevitably express alternations and ambivalence—moments of triumph followed by collapse, moments of order followed by chaos, and vice versa. The Morrigan sings one song that is redolent with the bounty of life and the process by which things attain their peaceful order. She sings to celebrate the end of a war:

> *Peace up to heaven,*
> *Heaven down to earth,*
> *Earth beneath heaven,*
> *Strength in every one,*
> *A cup very full,*
> *Full of Honey:*
> *Mead in abundance.*
> *Summer in winter. . . .*
> *Peace up to heaven.*[37]

The images lure us to relax just as we did after the fighting in the Persian Gulf seemed to bring peace. But our experience of Desert Storm is echoed in the Morrigan's song. The old text immediately shatters our comfort and unsettles any security we might crave. It continues:

She also prophesied the end of the world, foretelling every evil that would occur then, and every disease and every vengeance; and she chanted the following poem:

> *"I shall not see a world*
> *Which will be dear to me:*

---

36 Cross and Slover, *Ancient Irish Tales*, p. 45.
37 Elizabeth A. Gray, *Cath Maige Tuired: The Second Battle of Mag Tuired*, vol. 52 (London: Irish Texts Society, 1982–1983), p. 71.

Summer without blossoms,
Cattle will be without milk,
Women without modesty,
Men without valor,
Captures without a king...
Woods without mast,
Sea without produce....
False judgments of old men,
False precedents of lawyers,
Every man a betrayer,
Every boy a reaver.
The son will go into the bed of his father,
The father will go into the bed of his son.
Each [will be] his brother's brother-in-law.
He will not seek any woman outside his house....
An evil time,
Son will deceive his father,
Daughter will deceive...."[38]

The new world order seemingly established by victory is destroyed by the turbulence that inevitably follows. Peaceful bounty gives way to infertility; social stability gives way to chaos in society and incest in the family. Disruption overturns the previously ordered forms to force life forward in an endless rhythmic process. So after our momentary victory in Iraq, children and Kurds were dying, more refugees were fleeing, oil wells were seething black flames and soot across the sky, mysterious plagues affected both the allied soldiers and the civilian survivors. Initially, there was more starvation, more homelessness, more pollution, and more disillusionment. Now, 10 years later, we know that the embargo has wreaked untold suffering on a whole generation born since the war. Like the river whose force she represents, the Morrigan warns us in this poem that human life appears to be a series of chaotic, rapid drops in the flow. In her grim view, stasis, triumph, and peace appear as only little pools of momentary safety and/or inertia in the currents that rise and fall with the seasons and the processes of the matrix of life and death that the goddess represents. War, chaos,

---

38 Gray, *Cath Maige Tuired*, p. 73.

and abrupt flux between the pools predominate. Such is the sight and song of the Morrigan's vision. It challenges us to find ways other than those of war's upheavals to create and sustain change.

Shapeshifter

Moving from one perspective to the other as a seer and singer of the life process, the Morrigan is also a shapeshifter. In our story of Cu Chulainn and the Morrigan, the red-browed hag shape-shifts into a raven, a bird form with which she is often associated. Then she is called by the name of the second goddess in the triad, Badb, the raven or scald crow of battle. Sometimes the goddess Morrigan, or Badb, is also represented as a devouring wolf. Raven and wolf are viscerally gripping images of the matrix that dissolves or, more aptly here, devours all life forms back into itself.

When the storytellers of the warrior aristocracy want to suggest that the goddess' powers are unimportant to the real hero, they sing of the mighty Mac Cecht, who "was among the wounded on the field of slaughter." This great warrior complains with typically heroic bravado that something like a fly or midge is nipping at his fatal wound. A woman, passing through the slaughter field (and she may even be another form of the Morrigan herself) honors the old powers with her deeper and wider view. With empathic "fear and horror" at the carnage around her, she renames what the stoic hero calls a little midge telling him that it is the wolf that is already gnawing his bloodied body. She calls the wolf an "ant of the ancient earth."[39] With this metaphor, she evokes the Morrigan's powers to clean up the carrion left from battle. She calls on the goddess as eater of the dead, who buries broken forms back into her bowels and re-earths the fallen hero. In Irish tales the battlefield itself is called "the garden of Badb,"[40] for the dead are both the harvest of the dark goddess and her seed food, dying into the earth for regeneration.

Thus when Badb appears in human form, she has a marked sexual character—a huge vulva like the Sheila-na-gig's—and she is associated with rites of childbirth. Badb, the raven, was also considered a psychopomp, carrying off the dead in her claws to the otherworld, like

---

[39] Gantz, *Early Irish Myths and Sagas*, p. 105.
[40] Sjoestedt, *Gods and Heroes of the Celts*, p. 45.

the Norse Valkyries and Indian dakinis who were said to claim the final breath of the dying with a kiss of peace. An old pagan song contains these words:

> Fear not, the raven's red eye,
> Her sight all aflaming will shine on our hearts.
> Fear not, the raven's black wing,
> The light of her feathers will carry us home. . . .

Sometimes the third of the Morrigan triad is Nemain. From the wider, pleromatic perspective, she represents the ritualized shamanic possession that the Celts sought in order to experience predifferentiated atonement with all forms of life. This totally open state of participation mystique allows us to experience ecstatic fusion with the underlying matrix of life and attain intimate perception of the essence of discrete life forms. It provides a wisdom that is beyond mental cognitive modes and most science as it is currently practiced. This ecstatic and mystical vision is related to the "radical presence" of ecological consciousness that we are struggling to reawaken in our culture.[41] It is an affect-based correlate of what Jung calls "absolute knowledge."

But from the perspective of the combative warriors, Nemain is the frenzy of battle madness that sweeps them into combat with violent excitement, a state the Romans identified with the Celts and called the "furor Gallicus." Nemain literally means frenzy or panic. Such ecstatic possession by Nemain's rage made the Celts intrepid and fearsome adversaries, who rushed headlong into battle, naked except for the neck torc that bound them to their deity. They were filled with the inebriation of the war goddess as raging frenzy, like the psychotic rage that can totally possess those seized by it. Panic is the other side of such frenzy. It represents a mad seizure by terror in response to the uncontrollable emotions that can possess us. In contrast to the passion to fight that represents the drive to defend our more coherent sense of self, Nemain's panic makes us go mad, dissociate, or even die. Instead of fighting wildly, we flee. One story tells us that Nemain once used her power to rouse panic in the enemy "and confusion in the army so

---

[41] Joanna Macy, interview in *New Age Journal* (January/February, 1991): 36.

that the four provinces of Ireland massacred each other with their own spears and their own weapons, and that a hundred warriors died of terror and heart-failure that night."[42]

This primordial aspect of the Morrigan is similar to the wild and nameless dread that assails us when we are confronted by our own helplessness before the vast forces of life and death. It may be the terror we endure as we are buffeted through the birth canal to confront life outside the womb, lacking strength, coordination, and even adequate myelin sheathing for still-raw nerves. We may meet this dread again many times in life before the onslaught of any severe trauma. Some people found such dread stirred by images of the Desert Storm. The nearly inchoate and threatening words by which the Morrigan names herself aptly evoke this sense of primordial terror that we suffer in the grip of catastrophe—nonsense words (like Bion's beta-elements) interspersed with threatening allusions to "cold wind," "cutting," and "terror." Nemain represents the nearly imageless, dread-filled emptiness or chaos of the *prima materia*—an experience we flee when we have felt overwhelming pains in infancy before we have coalesced a constant sense of other to trust and/or before we have coalesced a constant sense of ourselves to defend. It is in the face of this overwhelming terror that we are sometimes reduced to psychotic processes, which may safeguard us from our experience of fear through primitive hallucinations, mindlessness, dissolution or rigidity, denial, hate, chaotic ideation, and reversals.

In our story, it is Nemain's dissolving cry that, like a nightmare, rouses the fearless Ulster warrior Cu Chulainn and sends him rushing out, unclothed. The sound from the pleromatic abyss threatens to dissolve all boundaries that permit life forms to manifest. From the perspective of the pleroma, these forms are only illusions (like *Maya* in India), but they nonetheless give shape and substance to life on earth. It is their valued discreteness that the hero leaps out of unconsciousness to defend. As guardian of the Ulster tribe, his task is to preserve the sacred structures and boundaries that permit social discourse and cultural order. Fear and disciplined responsibility can stimulate heroic aggression to defend those forms.

---

[42] Kinsella, *The Tain*, p. 223.

Comparable dread of the terrible matrix is what my analysand, who dreamed of the hobby horse, felt when he erupted into his childhood mornings with his stomach skewered in knots. In life he had become a hero defending the boundaries and structures of conscious life. Similarly, when we have known only horror within a terrible matrix, family container, or maternal relationship, we are frightened by the seeming threat of returning to any relationship in which we might feel dependent. Because we expect a repetition of early suffering, we use all our creativity to erect defenses against the presumed threat of such agony. The prospect of lowering habitual defensive consciousness and fusing with another may fascinate us, but it also propels us to flee and rigidify our grip on the defensive structures to which we cling. We try to stay vigilant. We may feel paranoid. We may leap eruptively into the intoxicating thrill of rage and battle, letting the excitement hold us like a surrogate mother.

We could also say that, to the woman who feared the gas threat, the television images served her as Nemain's cry. They roused her out of mute and relatively peaceful denial to restimulate her inchoate terror of early entanglement in a destructively dissolving matrix. They aroused panicky flight reactions. Whether defended by fight or flight, the underlying fear of too early, too negative experience of the pleroma opened the psychotic pockets that many people experienced under bombardment by the images of war. Such dread itself has no image, for we originally felt it before we could manage our relation to images or hold even parts of them constant in memory. Such dread grips the gut. It seizes us from inside, like Nemain's penetrating horrible scream, and makes us feel we are going to pieces. We feel we will fall forever, without relationship to the containing mother or body, and without orientation. These states call up what Donald Winnicott named "unthinkable anxiety."[43] They are Nemain's realm. Only by returning regressively to experience these states as deeply wounded aspects of our infant/maternal bonding, and by re-experiencing our fear of them in a different context, can we even begin to heal and to find our creativity freed. Whether such healing is at all possible and to what extent, often seems more a matter of grace and destiny than clinical fit and skill. But in this image-

---

[43] Donald W. Winnicott, *The Maturational Processes and the Facilitating Environment: Studies in the Theory of Emotional Development* (New York: International Universities Press, 1965), p. 58.

less area of "unthinkable anxiety," the figure of Nemain herself gives us the gift of an image that can help immeasurably when dealing with our psychotic parts and their processes.

Sometimes the third of the Morrigan trio is Macha, the mare goddess of life, agricultural prosperity, battle, and death. In Irish tales, she brings bounty to her chosen partners and tribespeople, sovereignty to her chosen kings, and glory to her warriors. The heads of the battle dead are like the heads of grain to the mare goddess. They are called "the mast [seed food] of Macha." In our story of Cu Chulainn and the Morrigan, the goddess' agricultural and battle steed is a bizarre, monstrous apparition like the weird, bloody hobby horse in the analysand's dream. Its appearance in Celtic lore is reminiscent of royal burial rites in several cultures. In Scythian royal funerals, Herodotus tells us, the finest horses were killed, disemboweled, stuffed with chaff, and stitched up with stakes run through them from neck to tail.[44] Sacrificed to be literal psychopomps, they went into the tomb to carry their royal masters to the other world. Comparable impalements are found in Gallic sacrificial customs and myths. In Britain, one witness describes Queen Boudicca's sacrifice of women before her tribe's victorious battle with the Romans who had raped her daughters and stolen her lands. He tells us that the women dedicated to the goddess Andraste had "their breasts cut off and stuffed in their mouths, so that they seemed to be eating them, then their bodies were skewered lengthwise on sharp stakes."[45] Andraste, like the Morrigan, represented the paradox of bounty and milk, war and destruction. Thus women sacrificed to her to arouse war energy had their breasts removed, indicating that nurturant energy was to be reassimilated to become available as (oral) aggression. As Lady Macbeth wished metaphorically to be, the women dedicated to the goddess were "unsexed" literally, mutilated to be rendered incapable of nurture and forced to assume a horrifying, aggressive form.

Usually we feel safe from the magic consciousness of such concretistic terrors. But when we are seized on the archaic level of the Morrigan, our dreams are as full of such gory stuff as were the ancient rites. How are we to process the "bizarre image" of the skewered, one-

---

[44] Ross, *Pagan Celtic Britain*, p. 222.
[45] Cassius Dio, quoted in Ross, *Pagan Celtic Britain*, p. 222.

legged horse and the images of war? Are we to defend against their impact by distancing our consciousness from their horror, by labeling it as "collateral damage?" Are we to say such images are "psychotic," pretending they are Other, denying that we all have roots into this layer of the psyche? Are we to frame them as "interesting archetypes" or name them "witchy" and "a witch's hobby horse" to drain their potency? Then we can deny and avoid any visceral empathy with the sadistically tortured, gruesome animal and war victims that represent a part of human experience.

This hideous form of the skewered horse suggests that the ongoing process of life energy has been maimed, rigidly impaled, and staggers on only one leg. It is an image like that of the crucifixion but borne by the instinctual form of the mother who carries all life. Uncannily in the myth, the horse moves on—like the cooked pig that squeals. Realistically, it should be dead. This image aptly suggests the horror of maimed, rigidly impaled, and suffering life that underlies both war and psychosis. And if, like the man who dreamed of a similar horse, we have met such horror in our childhood house, it is no wonder his young body used diarrhea to lessen its grip, and frantic masturbation to find some rigidly automatic, self-sufficient, heroic holding for himself. Too early and too personally he had to face the unmediated experience of the suffering earth spirit in a monstrous revelation of life in death and/or destructive sadism in life.

Serpent

The analysand who was terrified of the chemical weapon's threat dreamed:

> I have taken a bottle marked with spiral-coiled snakes from the [therapist's] office. Somehow it was able to contain the [deathly] gas.

Working on the dream image, she began to recognize that there was a holding environment in therapy that could mitigate her fears of dissolving into vapor. She associated the snakes to the medical sign of healing, but they were not wound around a caduceus. I recognized the far older motif of the spirals of energy that mark many ancient sites and artifacts to suggest life's endless transformations. The snakes coiled around her dream bottle mark it as a vessel of the goddess' powers over life, death, and regeneration—a serpent power commensurate with the all-potent destructiveness that had been the terrorizing ruler of this woman's life—a ruler which she described as "Death, the familiar air of my childhood." Such power was originally associated with the Great Goddess of the serpent rivers, the earth's energy lines, and the snake. The Morrigan, like the river's winding flow, was one of the primordial serpent goddesses of Neolithic Ireland.[46] Sometimes even called "Lamia" in text and on sculptures,[47] the triple Morrigan resembles Middle Eastern serpent and bird goddesses like the pre-Hellenic, Medusa/Athena.[48] Indeed, there are two tales linking the Morrigan to the ancient serpent goddess of the Celts. In one, her serpent form is changed to that of a water eel, which twines itself three times around Cu Chulainn's legs during one of his battles and drags him under the water to make him suffer defeat for spurning her.[49] In the other, the Morrigan's serpent power is more totally negated, for the story expresses Christian repugnance for the ancient cult and shows us clearly what happened to pagan images of power and of the ecstatic interconnection of life and death in the fullness of human experience.

In a legend connected with the Morrigan's son Meiche that explains the name of the River Berbha (Barrow), we read how the goddess' original power is projected and negated. Seen only as destructive, it still cannot be destroyed. The place-name legend asks "Whence Berbha, [Barrow]?" and then answers the question by telling us how the river got its name:

> Into this river were thrown the three snakes that were [found] in the heart of the Morrigan's son Meiche after he was slain by Diancecht [the healer god of the later and more patriarchal Tuatha pantheon] on Magh Meichi; which plain's name at first was Magh Fertaighe. The three hearts that were in Meiche bore the shape of three serpent's heads and, had not

[46] Cf. Marija Gimbutas, *The Language of the Goddess* (San Francisco: Harper and Row, 1989), pp. 121–124.
[47] Ross, *Pagan Celtic Britain*, p. 223.
[48] Barbara G. Walker, *The Women's Encyclopedia of Myths and Secrets* (San Francisco: Harper and Row, 1983), p. 629.
[49] Kinsella, *The Tain*, p. 135.

the killing of him come to pass, those snakes would have grown in his belly and eventually left no animals alive in Ireland. When he had slain Meiche, Diancecht burned the snakes and their ashes he committed to that current, with the effect that it seethed and boiled to rags all living things that were therein.[50]

We know the triple goddess as a triple spiral of snake forms from the carving deepest inside the great fourth-millennium B.C. mound temple at New Grange. The serpent power of the waters of life and the spring river's warming was connected to many Celtic river goddesses and their healing cults. Here, it is deprived of its connection to the feminine and to healing. In this variant of the place-name tale, the snakes are projected into the Great Goddess' son and denigrated as his three evil hearts. In another version, the son is represented by the three coils of a single devouring snake that was intent upon "wasting worse than any wolf-pack, [and] consuming utterly."[51] The serpent power is thus reversed and negated, made into a one-sided power to destroy, leaving "no animals alive in Ireland." The story suggests that the priests hoped that by teaching that their power was evil, the snakes of the old religion might be driven out of Ireland and cut out of human hearts. Meiche, son of the Morrigan, becomes a killing dragon monster and devil. Severed from its place in the whole process of life's flow and even burned to ash, the serpent power cannot be destroyed. Projected, reversed, denigrated, corrupted, and one-sided, it is still indestructible. Burnt and dissolved, it maintains its potency, albeit now only destructively, by making the water seethe and turning the living to rags. The pagan healer-god Diancecht, like the later snake-banisher, Saint Patrick, cannot fully repress what he brands as evil. His actions merely focus and potentize it. He cannot even destroy the remnants of the old religion, for the name of the Morrigan's son, although now identified only with destructive power, becomes the name of a grassy plain. And the river where the ash of his heart snakes was strewn is called Barrow. This name reminds us of the transformative process that reduces and carries away forms of life as if they were rags—just as the barrow mound raised as a tomb in

---

[50] Ross, *Pagan Celtic Britain*, pp. 345-346.
[51] Edward Gwynn, *The Metrical Dindsenchas*, vol. 2, 1903 (Dublin: Institute for Advanced Studies, 1941), p. 63.

Neolithic times carries us to dust and the otherworld, just as the barrow cart moves earth and its harvests and compost. The ancient potency of the spiral marked the jar of the analysand's dream. We may experience its more one-sided, negative and destructive form when we feel only the loss that any death brings. Then, if we identify with the structure that is dissolving to rags, we fear the serpent power, because we cannot yet see the whole transformative process that it symbolizes. In therapy, the chaos-making and corrosive powers of destruction appear as an alchemical *nigredo* to dissolve forms and/or relationships. Images of such negating powers may coincide with a phase of depression or negative transference, or with a descent into chaos in order to free space and energy for new forms to emerge. Inevitably, even images of good-enough containments and relationships may become negative to the analysand or child in order to make space for separation to discover new patterns more congruent with current developmental needs. During such inevitable phases (which sometimes feel like personal destruction) therapist and parent are forced to suffer and abide through the destruction of the old bonds while seeking for trust in the larger process.

Raven

The Morrigan sometimes appears in raven form. As a black, noisy, ever-alert bird, the raven sounds nature's alarm with her raucous cries, and she lives on in poetry as a foreboding voice. She struts on the ground, displacing smaller birds, a match even for small animals. Large and omnivorous, she sweeps down on the fields to eat both the grain of their harvest and any unburied carrion.[52] We read in an old text of the "longing" of the Irish crow or raven goddess for war, chaos, dismemberment:

> *For the fire of combat;*
> *The warrior's sides slashed open,*
> *Blood, bodies heaped upon bodies;*
> *Eyes without life, sundered heads,*
> *these are pleasing . . . to her.*[53]

---

[52] Valkyries, too, took the form of ravens to drink the blood of the slain, which was called "the raven's drink" (Walker, *Women's Encyclopedia of Myths and Secrets*, p. 847).

[53] H. D. D'Arbois de Jubainville, *The Irish Mythological Cycle and Celtic Mythology*, R. I. Best, trans., 1903 (New York: Lemma Publishing, 1970), p. 110.

Later folksongs of the three ravens that sat in a tree over a dead
knight harken back to this triple goddess and her harvest. In the
Celtic cult of the raven goddesses, black-robed women flapping like
crows raced among the warriors to stir up their war frenzy before
battle just as the raven's song roused the Brown Bull. We know that
the presence of these wild raven women among the Welsh at
Anglesey in A.D. 62 roused tremendous fear among the Roman soldiers opposing them.

In this cult, the three-fold raven goddess was honored by sacrifice.
A description "imperfectly understood by those who committed the
old oral tale to writing" in the early Middle Ages tells us of

> . . . a trio, naked, on the ridge-pole of the house: their jets of
> blood coming through them, and the ropes of slaughter on
> their necks. "Those I know" says [the speaker], "three of
> awful boding. Those are the three that are slaughtered at
> every time."[54]

The presence of the goddesses on the ridge-pole implies that they are
in their bird form. The blood and hanging represent the sacrifice of
birds in the cult—the goddess sacrificing to herself much as the Celtic-
influenced raven god Odin did when he hung on his tree "given to
Odin, myself to myself."

Just as she had predicted when she told him she was "guarding"
his deathbed, "the battle goddess Morrig[an] and her sisters" came in
raven shape to sit on the shoulders of the mortally wounded Cu
Chulainn. Their presence informs his enemies that they had nothing
more to fear from the quintessential hero, for his fated death had come
upon him. As one of his thus heartened enemies said laconically before
the hero was finally beheaded, "That pillar is not wont to be under
birds."[55] Indeed, all through his short life, until he broke all his taboos
and lost his strength, Cu Chulainn fended off the death the Morrigan
had in store for him. Then she flew to his shoulder and claimed him
finally as hers. Celtic heroes are termed those "who know the way of
the black ravens," for those old warriors, like shamans, inevitably live
closely with death, building their courage, power, and fame by defend-

---

[54] Ross, *Pagan Celtic Britain*, p. 248.
[55] Cross and Slover, *Ancient Irish Tales*, p. 338.

ing their lives against its presence and their own foreknowledge of its inevitable claim on them.

The raven often appears in analysands' material to symbolize the dark energies and far-sightedness of the triple goddess. Representing the spirit-devouring and/or carrying primordial libido, it usually signifies a transitional phase marking the process whereby, for example, manic defenses are opening into depression, depression is moving toward rage and curiosity, or rage-defended fear is shifting toward dependency. Representing the ideation of a dark vision of the otherworld, the raven destines and supports our crossing through such transitions. To make them, we inevitably return to the matrix that is both feared and needed in order to develop our integrity and capacity for relatedness. The image of the Morrigan represents annihilation, rage, death, birth, and regeneration in one whole that presents a nearly unbearable challenge to our consciousness. Thus, the Morrigan is connected to regression to the psychotic parts of us and to the terrible upheavals in the collective that we call war.

Conclusion

The Gulf War and its aftermath has been traumatic on many levels. The images of war opened chaotic pockets even in those who were fortunate enough to be only participant observers. We find similar images in the mythologems surrounding the Celtic deity called the Morrigan. These horrific images hold up mirrors of the dread, dissolution, dismemberment, and rage that we may have experienced in the grip of unmediated primary affects. On the one hand, they are the projection of that misery discovered and created by the primary caretaker experienced as destroyer. On the other hand, they are the mirrors of what is always beyond us and threatening our sense of secure boundaries and secure identities. They provide images of the unknown that we dread, forcing us to "the great and ultimate task [that] is to understand fear in all its forms as an instrument of the Self."[56] Such images provide terrifying and ravishing experiences of the pleromatic source. To individuate, these experiences of fear must be lived through—sometimes as

---

[56] Erich Neumann, "Fear of the Feminine," *Quadrant* 19, no. 1 (1986): 28.

psychotic episodes in which the adult can metabolize and transform what the infant could not bear and had to eject and/or deny. At other times such experiences form the basis of spiritual crises in which the adult is forced to confront the Mother of All Battles, the matrix of chaos, fear, grief, rage, birth, bounty and mystic atonement with the macrocosm. Such working through is analogous to facing the fearful reality of the unconscious, and coming to terms with what comes through the battles of life and the destruction of life forms and is also beyond these battles and destructions. As we struggle to work out new relationships to such seemingly chaotic and painful paradoxes—life in death and death in life—we may regain access to the polyvalent matrix that supports us. Subsequently from that ground of renewal, we may discover and create a new heroic stance, the wisdom of emphatic consciousness, and a capacity for blessing the very matrix from which we arise and in which we surrender.[57]

---

[57] This lysis is reminiscent of the ending of the poem of Innana's descent to and return from her dark sister: "Holy Ereshkigal, sweet is your praise!" (Perera, p. 92).

Kali—The Dark Goddess

Ashok Bedi, M.D.

Ashok Bedi, M.D., is a diplomate Jungian analyst and a board-certified psychiatrist both in Britain and the USA. He is a member of the Royal College of Psychiatrists of Great Britain, a diplomate in Psychological Medicine at the Royal College of Physicians and Surgeons of England, and a fellow of the American Psychiatric Association. He is a clinical professor in psychiatry at the Medical College of Wisconsin in Milwaukee and on the faculty of the Analyst Training Program at the C. G. Jung Institute of Chicago. His interests lie in the emerging frontiers of spirituality and healing and the synapses of the mind, body, soul, and spirit. He is author of *Path to the Soul* (Weiser, 2000). He has been a guest lecturer in India, Great Britain, and the USA and practices in the Milwaukee, Wisconsin area.

When we break down our hang-ups at the altar of terrible, dark, mother goddess Kali, we permit the depths of our soul to break through into our life.

Kali is the fierce, dark Hindu goddess who amputates the darkness of our soul and makes room for the light. Whenever our life is out of balance, our darker, or shadow, aspects get into the driver's seat. The archetype of the dark goddess Kali incarnates in our life drama to destroy the darkness of personality and make room for new consciousness to emerge. While new consciousness emerges within the realm of Aditi, the Grandmother Goddess of Void and new creation, this can only occur once Kali cleanses the consciousness of its darkness. Both Kali and Aditi are nonrelational goddesses in that they mediate our relationship with the transpersonal Self instead of specific individuals; they maintain the rhythm of destruction and creation, respectively, within individual personality and in collective human consciousness. The wisdom of the Kali archetype stops us in our tracks and forces us to take note of aspects of our personality that remain in the shadow so that our soul-making may proceed. Kali frightens and fascinates us. Kali renders our old attitudes and adaptations powerless, yet empowers us to undertake new ways of perceiving and managing life and its traumas. We experience her as a paradox within our psyche. She is the bloodthirsty goddess, yet she infuses new passion and hope for change in our life. She is dark, yet she paves the way for the light in our personality to shine through the dark clouds of difficult situations. She embodies the *complexio oppositorum*—the union of the opposites in our personality. Join me now in honoring the realm of Kali.

Kali's Myth

Kali most often appears in the context of the destruction of evil in battle. Kali's warrior aspect is the goddess Durga, who is summoned by the gods to battle the demons. Early in the battle, the demons approach Durga, threatening her with their weapons. Under this provocation, Durga becomes angry, and suddenly the goddess Kali springs forth from her forehead, ready for battle. She tears and crushes the demons. Later in the battle, Durga summons Kali to help defeat the demon Raktabija. He has the ability to clone himself instantly whenever a drop of his blood falls to the ground, so wounding him only multiplies him. Kali destroys Raktabija by sucking his blood away.

In these two Durga episodes, Kali embodies Durga's rage. Kali plays a similar role in her association with Parvati, Shiva's gentle spouse. When Shiva is threatened by the demon Daruka, who can only be destroyed by a woman, Shiva summons Parvati's assistance. Parvati then enters Shiva's body and transforms herself into Kali via the poison that is stored in Shiva's throat. Kali now destroys Daruka, fulfilling the role of Parvati's dark, ferocious aspect.

Kali also appears in the myth of Sati, Shiva's first wife. When Sati's father, Daksa, infuriates his daughter by not inviting Shiva to the great sacrificial rite and later insulting Shiva *in absentia*, Sati immolates herself in protest. But before she does so, Sati rubs her nose in anger and transforms herself into ten goddesses, the *Dasamahavidyas* (*dasa,* meaning "ten," *maha*, meaning "great," and *vidyas*, meaning "goddesses' wisdom"). The first of these ten goddesses is Kali.

Kali is of central importance in Tantra, particularly the left-hand path of Kundalini Yoga. In tantric rituals, both physical and spiritual, the seeker or *sadhaka* seeks to gain *moksha*, freedom from opposites in human nature and the psyche. The crucial theme in this endeavor is uniting the opposites: masculine and feminine, spiritual and physical, microcosm and macrocosm, sacred and profane, life and death, order and chaos, Shiva and Shakti.

The seeker practices spiritual enterprise to achieve moksha. The seeker must undertake the ritual of the five forbidden things, or truths. This supervised ritual includes the partaking of wine, meat, fish, parched hallucinogenic grain, and illicit sexual intercourse. This helps the seeker experience, master, and then transcend the dark side in order to establish wholeness of consciousness. In this context, Kali—the patron goddess of tantric rituals—not only symbolizes the dark side of human psyche but is, herself, a symbol of its experience and mastery. This paves the way for integration of the shadow into the totality of one's being.

Kali's Attributes

Kali crushes, tramples, breaks, or burns the enemy. She is described as having a terrible, frightening appearance: she is black, naked, and has long, disheveled hair. She has four or more arms and wears a necklace of freshly-cut heads. Children's corpses serve as her earrings, and serpents as her bracelets. Her fangs are long and sharp. She has claw-like hands with long nails and fresh blood drips from her lips. When Kali is shown on the battlefield, she is often portrayed as a furious combatant, drunk on the hot blood of her victims. She resides in cremation grounds where she sits on a corpse surrounded by jackals and goblins. Kali is usually depicted as an independent deity. However, when she is depicted with a god, it is with Shiva, her consort and companion. Kali dominates Shiva who is portrayed as passive or dead in her presence. While Parvati tames, socializes, and domesticates Shiva, Kali incites him to wildness and disorder.

Kali is the feminine aspect of *kala*, or time. She is the origin and the end. She represents the energy of time and stands on the corpse of the cosmos, Shiva himself. Since she represents time, she wears a necklace of skulls, signifying her sway over life and death. She is black, the ultimate color that assimilates all other colors. Like Shiva, she frequents lonely places at the outskirts of towns. Symbolically, she gives voice to the marginalized aspects of society and personality—the shadow and the inferior functions of both individual and collective consciousness. She embodies the fury of the dishonored Feminine.

Kali provides a worldview of the shadow. She gives context to why we have disease, disorder, and anarchy—why we have childhood cancer, why the dark side prevails over the light forces of the numinous. She imparts a view of asserting that existence is about death as well as life; chaos along with order; illness as well as health; and vice along with virtue. These polar opposites create the tension that we call life. When Kali connects us with the dark side, she opens up the possibility of wholeness.

In Tantric Yoga, where spirituality is attained via sexuality, Kali is described as garbed in space, or sky-clad. In her nakedness, she is free from all coverings of *maya*, or illusion about attainment of power, material success or attachments. Her garland of 50 human heads, recalling the 50 letters of the Sanskrit alphabet, symbolizes the repository of knowledge and wisdom, and represents the 50 fundamental vibrations of human consciousness. She wears a girdle of human hands, the principal instruments of work that signify the action of accumulated *karma* (actions and their consequences); this reminds us that we have the potential to accumulate tremendous positive and negative karma in this lifetime. We also have considerable opportunity to retire this karma.

Kali's three eyes represent the past, present, and future. Her white teeth symbolize the *albedo* (whiteness), or purity of soul, her red tongue represents the *rubedo* (redness), or passion for life. Kali has four hands: one left hand holds a severed head, symbolizing the sacrifice of our shadow, and the other hand carries the sword that cuts the threads of pathological relationships or codependences; one right hand gestures to dispel fear while the other exhorts spiritual strength. In this form she is changeless, limitless, primordial power acting in the great drama, awakening the Shiva (unconscious masculine principle) beneath her feet.

How Goddess Kali Guides Our Path to the Soul

The archetype of Kali is the guiding principle in our management of our life's traumas. Whenever we face crisis with which our ego or existing consciousness cannot cope, we become overwhelmed and the crisis becomes traumatic, that is, it leaves permanent scars on our psyche. When the trauma first occurs, we may regress to a survival mode of adaptation. Goddess Kali presides over this emergency operation. If we can honor Kali's appearance, our soul can move from survival to mastery of the trauma and this results in a quantum growth in our personality.

If the trauma occurs very early in life, before we develop our verbal function, the trauma and its memory tends to be stored in the body on a cellular level. This leads to a host of somatic problems mediated via the psychoid space (the hypothetical space between the body, psyche, soul, and the spirit), contributing to the evolution of the psychosomatic problems. Such trauma occurs before the ego is firmly established. When trauma is severe, it overwhelms the existing ego. Archetypal defenses of the Self are thus constellated activating an archetypal rescue. In Donald Kalsched's view, the goal of such a rescue is survival rather than growth.[1] This subhuman or superhuman trauma calls for a corresponding divine or archetypal defense.

In the Hindu view, however, when an archetypal defense is activated, the goal is to surpass individual survival to attain the potential growth of the entire human consciousness, or what the Hindus call the *dharmic* consciousness (living in the soul). In this view, the individual life and personal interests are sacrificed to enhance collective consciousness and serve collective growth. The individual who is called to this sacrifice lives out his or her highest potential for community good. It is as if the trauma recruits the individual to serve in the realm of collective welfare. This raises the threshold of our culture onto a higher plateau. When Mahatma Gandhi was abused and traumatized by the racist regime in South Africa, he was deeply wounded and traumatized. This trauma led him to call upon his deepest potential to love his enemy's divine core, in spite of their outer dark side.

---

[1] See Donald Kalsched, *The Inner World of Trauma: Archetypal Defenses of the Personal Spirit* (London and New York: Routledge, 1996).

This was the beginning of *ahimsa*, or nonviolent civil protest, and moved human civilization to its higher potential. His personal trauma was a gift to humanity. An angry response to abuse and trauma is understandable and human. However, if we can rise above the personal hurt and respond to trauma soulfully, we raise the rest of human civilization up to a higher threshold of culture and consciousness. The trauma is a catastrophe for our ego but an opportunity for our soul to serve the spirit.

I have had the opportunity to work with a very courageous woman named Helen. Her grandfather sexually abused her when she was a child. This led to deep trauma and subsequent emotional and relationship problems for her. She could easily have stayed wounded for the rest of her life. Instead, she saw her personal trauma as a calling to understand and assist abused men and women, and is now an expert psychotherapist in trauma treatment and a fierce advocate for the rights and treatment of abused women and children. Like Gandhi, she has turned personal adversity into a soulful opportunity to serve her fellow human beings. I deeply admire her.

In my clinical work with trauma victims and survivors, I have found the template of the Kali archetype a very useful framework to comprehend and work through the trauma experience. These patients include war veterans, sexual abuse survivors, and survivors of catastrophic medical illnesses like cancer and life-threatening surgery. When these traumatic experiences are seen as encounters with goddess Kali that can overwhelm the ego and protect the archaic Self, then we get a framework within which the work of rekindling the journey on the path to our soul or spiritual potential can begin. Activation of the Kali archetype in trauma survivors leads to survival-based adaptation at the expense of personal growth, but by honoring and working through the Kali archetype experience, we can ensure survival and then rekindle our soul-making.

Archetypal defenses may be inflationary, as in narcissism and mania, or negative, as in depression and schizophrenia. When archetypal defenses are activated, they have archaic, primitive qualities— demonic or angelic, black-or-white consciousness—and they are disrespectful of and even destructive toward the ego, with the sole aim of protecting the archaic, rudimentary Self. Spurred by this inner conflict, the soul seeks a relationship or experience that reflects its core qualities to feel lovable and competent. The downside is this search often results in a dependency relationship in which one gets a good feeling about oneself from an outer source, rather than building upon a core sense of one's self-worth. Some people seek kinship within a group to feel good or viable as individuals, but this may render them susceptible to gang or cult memberships. Yet another group of people may seek refuge in the strength of a powerful, parental teacher, guru, or guide, thus divesting themselves of their sense of their own strength and power.

These archaic, relational needs are likewise activated in the transference matrix in the analytic container. Here, the patient may depend on the therapist to mirror his or her self-worth, provide friendship, or become a source of strength and comfort.

Kali's Guidance in the Survival of Trauma

When life crises push us into survival mode, our ego steps aside and our soul takes over the management of our life and relationships. The soul has a numinous side, which guides our growth, and a dark side, which manages emergency survival. This dynamic is akin to civilian administration during peacetime, and martial law during wartime. The martial law over the demonic aspect of our soul suspends growth and soulfulness and focuses on mere survival of personality. This is the realm of goddess Kali. Under the auspices of Kali, the archaic defenses are activated. When trauma is absorbed and the crisis over, Kali refuses to relinquish control. It is the task of the individual to gradually reclaim management of personality from Kali. Once wartime is over, the military must retreat and defer to civilian rule. The following therapeutic approach outlined by Kalsched amplifies this method:

1. In the early stages of analysis, the emphasis is on restoration of the ego complex (conscious personality) and disengagement from possession by the archetype (Kali energy). However, the personality may resist relinquishing its romance with the dark side of the soul (deeper, unconscious center of the personality), which depletes total personality through identification with archaic, archetypal survival defenses, such as splitting, projective identification, paranoia, etc. When the ego complex gains the strength to stand against the dark Kali, the split-off, positive, numinous aspect of the soul (the civilian authority of the soul

rather than its martial law aspect), gradually starts to cooperate with the ego and personality growth resumes. Now Kali can bestow her gifts of passion for new life and discernment of reality on the individual as the resuscitated ego complex takes back the steering wheel from the dark, demonic side of Kali. This involves honoring and making appropriate sacrifices to propitiate Kali. The ego must also relinquish its identification with the power of the Kali archetype in order to take on the responsibility of consciousness. The personality now moves from Kali's cruise control to our conscious personality taking responsibility of the steering wheel of our life and its challenges. It is only then that the ego can come into a mutual and true relationship to the Self (soul). The ego-soul partnership can then replace the dark side of the soul as director of the emerging personality.

2. The dark, demonic aspect of the soul as imaged in Kali is always a perfectionist tyrant. In analysis with trauma victims, it is essential to maintain the analytic stance so that the very frustrations that arise from maintaining analytic boundaries create a "little bit of trauma." This is like a psychological immunization from the bigger trauma. The Kohutian school of psychologists calls this "optimal frustration." This forces the individual to modify the experience of the other, or the therapist, as limit-setting, yet loving. Such a new, composite image of the other is mature and mutual, transforming and transmuting the relationship and making it relevant to one's own life. The composite image is then internalized as a new role model in a process called "transmuting internalization." This then helps the creation of new, mature self-structures that gradually replace the archaic self-defenses and the need for primitive, self-esteem sustaining relationships. The little bit of trauma inherent in the frustrations of the analytic situation acts as a vaccine that helps the ego separate from its identification with Kali in order to evolve adaptive ways of managing life, relationships, and growth potential. The dreams in the trauma victims reveal this battle between the emerging ego and the dark, demonic Kali. In this matrix, a *third position*, a new synthesis, constellates, in which the individual's personality comes up with a novel way of dealing with life. For example, in Rose's dream discussed later in this chapter, the third position emerged when she decapitated a rapist and protected her child, a symbol of her emerging Self.

3. Transference issues in trauma patients in the grip of the Kali archetype need particular attention. While the demonic Kali is in control of
the personality, the individual continues to re-experience trauma. The
neurosis is not only in the past, but continues in the present as a persecutory Kali, with the patient responding to what he or she perceives
as inner and outer threats. Analysis itself may be perceived as a traumatic threat, with the analyst as a tyrannical traumatizer. It is important that the analyst see the analysand's dreams as not only
transferential but also as indicative of the Kali's archetypal forces operating in the interactive field of the analytic relationship. In the analytic
working-through, the ego must insist on the soul's numinous potential,
in spite of its apparent darkness; in other words, the analyst has to
keep in mind the *Answer to Job* paradigm.[2] In Jung's rendering of this
biblical incident, Job is put through very traumatic trials by Yahweh,
the God of the Old Testament, to test his loyalty. In spite of this
trauma, Job continues to treat Yahweh with love, respect, loyalty, and
expectation of fair treatment. Eventually, this forces Yahweh to abandon his trial and treat Job with kindness and fairness. Job's trust in
God and insistence on fair treatment eventually forced Yahweh to rise
to the occasion. According to Jung, this is akin to our fragile ego's
insistence on a fair and mutually respectful treatment by the soul, even
when the dark aspects of the soul have temporarily taken control of
the personality in a crisis situation. This is like martial law. In a civilized and advanced nation, the civilian law would always have domain
over the military, however uneven the power dynamic may seem in
times of crisis. This differentiates a civilized nation from a primitive
one and a soulful life from an archaic personality.

4. Optimal violation of the therapeutic neutrality is essential at times
so that (a) the ego complex is reinforced in the form of support of
higher adaptive defenses; (b) the demonic, dark pole of the Self is confronted; (c) the light, numinous pole of the Self is reinforced. In other
words, in working with trauma victims, the therapist must be prepared
to be flexible and sometimes violate therapeutic neutrality to support
the conscious personality against its own dark side. For instance, on

[2] C. G. Jung, *Psychology and Religion: West and East, Collected Works of C. G. Jung*, vol. 11,
R. F. C. Hull, trans. Bollingen Series XX (New York: Pantheon Books, 1963), pp. 355–470.
Further references to this work will be cited as CW 11.

occasions, I have encouraged patients to break their workaholic routine and make room to play and take vacations. While this violates my neutrality, it encourages the playful aspects of my patient to stand up to their repressive, dark, hard-driving, perfectionist, all–work-and-no-play side of their personality.

5. In working with trauma victims, the analyst must consider several additional points: the appropriate management of affect (permitting neither too much nor too little expression by either party), the attunement to the meaning as well as the mystery of personal growth, working through loss and grief over the lost, unlived childhood.

It is important to prepare patients in the grip of the Kali archetype for breaks, vacations, absences, and separations. This preparation permits the ego to maintain an evocative memory of the numinous aspects of the soul as well as of the analyst in order to not succumb to the demonic Kali experience during such vulnerable periods. Perhaps one of the crucial healing interventions in the treatment of trauma victims is for the analyst to admit to "counter-transference errors and feelings," what Racker terms counter resistance.[3] The analyst's emotional honesty with the patient constitutes a corrective experience that influences working through, not just in transference, but also to a retroactive correction and reconfiguration of the images and the memories of the primary family relationships.

Finally, the patient and analyst must honor the emerging new myth of the patient and be prepared to dialogue with it. The analytic task is to incubate the emergence of a new creation myth for the patient—to honor "not knowing." "Knowing" may impede the emergence of a new creation myth from the patient's psyche. If we stay respectful of the void that the Kali experience leaves in our life, we make room for new beginnings in our personal growth. Goddess Aditi presides over this experience of void and new beginnings.

Trauma is divine suffering as it activates the deepest layers of the Self under the auspices of the Kali archetype, and may individuate not just the person but also the collective, thus redeeming one's dharmic potential: one's highest duty to Self and the collective consciousness.

---

[3] Heinrich Racker, *Transference and Countertransference* (New York: International Universities Press, 1968), pp. 186–192.

The Sacred Union of Our Masculine and Feminine Potentials under the Auspices of Goddess Kali

Kali is the embodiment of the negative, dynamic feminine *par excellence* as compensation to the negative, static, masculine order. When the patriarchal order becomes rigid, dehumanizing, inauthentic, complacent, and petty, with rigid expectations, organized for its own sake, the great Kali archetype is activated to behead it. In this bloody initiation, Kali decapitates and dissolves the existing dysfunction and the despotic masculine order.[4] Kali accomplishes this transition by invoking the apparently negative, dynamic feminine.

Clinically, such a bloody or watery initiation may be perceived as an altered state of consciousness, as emptiness, depression, substance abuse, hysteria, and borderline psychosis. These clinical experiences may lead to despair, even suicide and death. If patient and analyst can hold on to residual ego and establish a connection with a deeper layer of psyche, the source, the Self, with or without therapeutic intervention, then transformation of personality or culture becomes possible.

However, the experience of the inner madwoman is a disorienting experience, for both therapist and patient alike. Yet, goal-directed exploration of the psyche modifies and transforms the personality into new awareness and a new state of being. To accomplish this goal, the individual must deal with the archaic, dark Self-care system, transform it, and reassimilate the transformed substance into a higher *conuinctio* with the personality. An alchemical perspective facilitates this assimilation of the darkness, of the sacred essence of Kali in one's wholeness.

Worldview from the Perspective of Goddess Kali

In the Hindu goddess pantheon, Kali is the singular archetype that imparts a structural worldview to individuals and cultures. Hers is the realm of clarity of facts and purpose. She is the "No Nonsense" goddess. Kali does not get caught in undirected feelings or possibilities, but is firmly grounded on relevant facts and how they impact life experience. Her general attitudinal vector is extroverted and her presence is felt as that of a very solid handshake with an iron-fisted individual.

---

[4] Gareth Hill calls this dissolving action a "watery initiation." See Gareth Hill, *The Masculine and the Feminine* (Boston: Shambhala, 1995).

Images of Kali depict the dark goddess holding the severed heads of her victims. She decapitates the existing thinking function, making room for new logic to adapt to the crisis and the developmental challenge at hand. Individuals embedded in the Kali structural worldview excel in applied sciences, business, administration, banking, law enforcement, military service, production, construction, etc.

Comparative Mythology: The Innana-Erezkegal Split

Innana-Ishtar, the Sumerian goddess of heaven and earth, journeys into the underworld to Erezkegal, her dark sister, and returns.[5] Innana is the queen of heaven, goddess of the radiant, erratic morning and evening stars. She is the queen of the land and its fertility. Like Durga, she is the goddess of war. As the goddess of sexual love, she is passionate.

When Innana descends into the underworld to visit her dark sister Erezkegal, she is gradually disrobed, humiliated, flagellated, killed, and hung on a meat hook for several days before being resurrected and rescued by her loyal servant with the help of god Enki and his deputies. However, she is much the wiser for having encountered Erezkegal. Now she has a wholistic view of reality, being informed of the dark side through encounter with her Erezkegal nature.

Erezkegal is the queen of the Netherworld and the dead. Her name means "Lady of the Great Place Below." She symbolizes the Great Round of nature, growth and grain above and below, seed dying to sprout again. Her husband, Enil, in his various disguises, repeatedly raped her, yet out of love for him she followed him into the underworld when the gods punished him. Like Kali, Erezkegal is the root of all potential energy—inert, but ready to sprout into action upon the battlefield of birth and life. Erezkegal, like Kali, is enraged when Innana invades her realm. In anger, her face turns yellow and her lips, black. She is full of fury, greed, and the fear of loss. She symbolizes raw instinct, split off from consciousness. She unleashes the animus, similar to Kali's unleashing of Shiva's destructiveness. Like Kali, she symbolizes an energy we begin to recognize through the

---

[5] See Diane Wolkestein and Samuel Noah Kramer, *Innana: Queen of Heaven and Earth; Her Stories and Hymns for Sumer* (New York: Harper and Row Publishers, 1983).

study of death, disease, and destruction—of nuclear bombs, the AIDS virus, the feuds between nations and peoples, and the dark side of human psyche.

An Alchemical Perspective of the Kali Archetype

Alchemy is the medieval art of transforming lead into gold. Carl Jung was fascinated by alchemy as a metaphor for understanding the transformation of personality from its base to its higher potential. There are essentially four stages of alchemy. These are black, white, gold, and red. The black, or *negrado*, implies confronting the darkness of our personality. Once this has been accomplished, we encounter the white, or *albedo*, aspects of our personality. This is the experience of the purity of our soul after cleansing or baptizing of the psyche. After the *albedo* stage, we experience the yellow or golden stage of alchemy. This is the spiritual phase of our life. It is called the *citrinatio* (citrine—yellow) stage when we are grooved in our spiritual moorings. However, the highest stage of alchemy is red, or *rubedo*—the color of blood and the passion. All of our soul work and personal growth is academic unless we are willing to put our sweat and blood into what we believe in. This is the stage of sacrifice as Christ did in his crucifixion, to lay down one's life for what one believes in.

The *nigredo* (darkness), *putreficatio* (rotting) and *mortificatio* (death-like) are the sub-aspects of the *negrado* stage of alchemy. These are necessary Kali experiences that form a bridge to our dark, neglected aspects of personality and thus establishing wholeness of the soul.

The alchemists thought that in order for a given substance to be transformed, it must first be reduced or returned to its original, undifferentiated state, to its *prima materia*. Kali mediates this experience of the primary substance of our personality. She strips our personality of all its rigid, dysfunctional, superfluous trappings and gives us a sense of who we really are and what we are about.

This procedure corresponds to what takes place in psychotherapy under the auspices of the Kali archetype. The fixed, habitual aspects of personality lead back to their original, undifferentiated condition as part of the process of psychic transformation by Kali. This formless state of pure potentiality is necessary in order for a new structure of personality to emerge. Fixed, developed aspects of the personality allow no change. They are solid, established, and sure of their rightness. Only the indefinite, fresh, and vital, but vulnerable and insecure, original condition symbolized by the child is open to development and hence is alive. We must experience the naïve, vulnerable child within from which we can start growing again. We must find our innocent, playful, creative, child nature to rekindle our soul.

Shiva promised the lesser gods that he and his consort Parvati would not procreate so that their offspring would not compete with the lesser gods and cause a power imbalance. This was not acceptable to Parvati and she created a divine child by rubbing her skin. When Shiva met this divine child, Ganesha, he beheaded him. Later however, he adopted Ganesha after transplanting an elephant's head onto him. Similarly, when we deny our creative potential for political or relational expediency rather than confront the envy and competition of others, our anima, the inner feminine, the creative life force urges us to find the divine child within in spite of our ego or outer consciousness. The child is the symbol of emerging consciousness.

We consider the image of a child in dreams as one of the symbols of the emerging soul, but it can also symbolize the *prima materia* of the personality, the building blocks of our potential. Rose's dream, presented in this chapter, contains an image of her child as a symbol of her emerging Self, rescued under the auspices of goddess Kali.

The problem of finding the *prima materia* corresponds to the problem of finding what to work on in psychotherapy. Under the guidance of Kali, we may find this *prima materia* in a number of places. Although of great inner value, the *prima materia* is vile in outer appearance and therefore despised, rejected, and thrown on the dung heap. Psychologically, this means that the *prima materia* is found in the shadow, that part of the personality that is considered most despicable. Those aspects of us that are most painful and humiliating are the very ones to be brought forward and worked on.

The *prima materia* is without definite boundaries, limits, or form. This corresponds to those experiences of the unconscious that expose the ego to the spiritual dimension. It may evoke the terror of dissolution of our consciousness or the awe of experience of unconscious eternity. The Kali encounter is both.

Mortificatio and Kali

Mortificatio and *putrefactio* are overlapping terms that refer to different aspects of the same operation. *Mortificatio* means "killing" and refers to the experience of death of a certain aspect of our consciousness. It is like pruning the psyche to permit the rest of the personality to grow and blossom. *Putreficatio* means "rotting," decomposition that breaks down dead, organic bodies. Kali destroys the rotting personal complexes or hang-ups, and the shadow or the dark aspects of our personality and culture.

Mortificatio has to do with darkness, defeat, torture, mutilation, and death. Patients dealing with depression and borderline disorders often struggle with these images, and unfortunately sometimes act them out rather than reflect upon them as transitional, alchemical images. However, these dark images can often lead to highly positive ones: growth, resurrection, and rebirth. The hallmark of *mortificatio* is the color black—the symbol of Kali.

Putrefaction blots out our habitual, old nature and transforms our personality into realizing its spiritual potential. This is akin to transforming the complexes that impede personality into bearing new potentialities to enrich the spectrum of personality.

In psychological terms blackness refers to the shadow. Awareness of our own shadow permits us greater consciousness of our dark side. This awareness illuminates our self-knowledge, giving us a better map of our own personality. Paradoxically, the darkness lights the way. On the archetypal level it is also desirable to be aware of evil because blackness is the beginning of whiteness. By the law of opposites, an intense awareness of one side constellates its other. Out of darkness is born the light. Out of night is born the day. Experience of the Kali archetype through the dark leads to experience of the light of one's personality.

Kali and the *Rubedo* Dimension

While the primary experience of Kali archetype is *nigredo*, if one successfully holds the tension of this experience, it leads to *rubedo*, or redness, the color of blood, passion, and sacrifice. This also symbolizes our feeling or value function, and leads to re-animation of life

informed by our feeling function where we factor in what is of value
to our soul in resetting the priorities of our life.

The four stages of alchemy—*nigredo, albedo, citrinatio and
rubedo*—symbolize the parts, qualities, and aspects of the One, the
totality of our personality.[6] When an individual has assimilated Kali's
nigredo experience and experienced the guidance of Aditi, the Kali
dimension now takes on a new significance. The Aditi experience is the
void, the *albedo* that heralds the rising sun or emerging new consciousness. The growing redness *(rubedo)* that now follows denotes an
increase of warmth and light coming from the sun. When we recom-
mence feeling warmth and passion, we are in our soul groove. Our
conscious and unconscious now start doing a dance together. We
establish a rhythm of personal growth to the music of our soul.

Red and rose-red are the color of blood, our passion about life.
While Kali confronts us with what is dead or what must die in our personality, when we make these necessary sacrifices, she reanimates life
with feelings and passion for what really counts—our soul experience,
or true calling. When we are willing to be crucified on the altar of life,
when we are prepared to shed our sweat and blood for the calling of
our soul, we resurrect our highest Christ potential.

Perils and Promise of the Kali Archetype

In analytic experience, the encounter with Kali consciousness is the
confrontation with the shadow and the demonic aspects of Self.[7] We
must descend into our inner Kali realm, encounter and honor her to
achieve wholeness. Kali consciousness puts us in touch with the death
of our complexes or hang-ups, so that the deeper potential of the Self
can emerge. Anticipation of the possibility of fire leads us to build fire
escapes. Acceptance of the possibility of disease leads to discovery and
the use of immunizations and vaccines. Factoring in the possibility of
war leads to peace via strength. An individual who has encountered
Kali in life experiences can anticipate and build the necessary ego
structures in order to confront the dark side of reality, which in turn
can activate the experience of the numinous aspects of the Soul.

---

[6] C. G. Jung, *CW* 11, § 98.
[7] Kalsched, *The Inner World of Trauma.*

I have encountered Kali several times in my life journey. Three such encounters occurred during my immigration from India to Britain, migrating from Britain to the USA, and my analytic training. In each of these Kali experiences, my previous ego adaptation was beheaded, and new connection with deeper layers of Self became necessary. These were initially painful transitions, though in time they made room for new beginnings and fresh attitudes about my world, my future and myself. In the initial stages of these transitions, my goal was survival, though later it made room for the possibility of individuation.

Rose's Story—Empowered by the Goddess Kali

Rose was in her third year of analysis when she had an important dream. She was then in her mid-forties. When she started analysis, Rose had resumed her college education, which had been interrupted in her early 20s. The oldest of five siblings, she lived in a family with an alcoholic father and untreated manic-depressive mother. Rose was the caretaker of her younger siblings and her father's confidante. Since Rose was five, her parents had slept in separate bedrooms. Until age nine or ten, she would go into her father's bedroom and sleep with him for comfort. Whether there was any sexual abuse committed by her father has remained an unanswered question in the analysis. She had an idealized transference to me, but embedded in it were seeds of anger and rage that only gradually emerged within the safe container of the analytic vessel. In this context, Rose reported the following dream, which she titled "Rage":

> I am back in college, climbing a sheer rock wall with my friends. It is very dangerous, but we do it quite often. I don't like it. Now I am at a party in a house with all young men. They open the door to a larger room where many naked young men are lying in beds. I am told the only exit is through the window on the opposite side of the room. I have to make it past the men. I wonder briefly if it would be enjoyable to have sex with all these men but decide it would not. I run in the other direction and am chased and caught. I scream as I am carried down the hall.
>
> Next, it is night, and I'm walking back down the hall carrying the head of a man. His hair is long and I'm holding the head by it. I enter the room of naked men. They are asleep

now. I jump onto the window ledge, facing the room. I throw the head to the floor in the center of the room. I say in a loud and chilling voice, "This is the head of the man that raped me. For each woman raped, another head will fall." I see my son on the ledge next to me. He is a baby sleeping in his Superman outfit. I scoop him up and climb out. I climb the brick wall of the building to a tall bell tower. I climb into the belfry and let out a loud, shrill scream. I awake with the scream still in my head.

Here are some of Rose's associations to some of the dream images: Her son is her vulnerable Self, the superman outfit is compensation for her feelings of vulnerability. College and climbing the sheer rock wall signify the dangerous, vertical path she has to climb in reclaiming her inner worth. As for the element of men being a danger, Rose said, "I was in an all-girls high school, guys just wanted sex. I quit college as a senior. I went to a frat party with a young man in my freshman year. It was horrible; the focus was to get drunk. The scream was inhuman, like an animal cry of intense rage. It expressed the pain—uncork the wine bottle, get this out of me, this pain, you are pissing me off." The tall bell tower reminded Rose of "a sacred place," as well as of "the movie *Vertigo*, where the hero is betrayed by a woman." She felt "betrayal by my father," she said. "Something was breached, a line crossed, he moves into my space and crosses my boundary; he is laughing ignorantly as he does it, poking at me, invades me then teases me about it."

Archetypically, I see in Rose's dream the incarnation of the Kali archetype to empower and renew her. When her vulnerable, core Self was feeling threatened and in danger of fragmentation, the Kali archetype was activated to empower her to confront the intrusion of the Masculine, with a sense of her own voice and rage at the injustice of the father's encroachment upon her space and her soul. Like the great Kali, she decapitates the rapist and protects her son, a symbol of her emerging Self. Then she lets out the battle cry of Kali as she asserts her arrival and presence from the top of her church, atop Mother Church, the great Kali incarnate.

This dream had a tremendously empowering impact on Rose as she worked on the dream in analysis. The dream imaged her ego capacity to confront the shadow of the masculine, the negative animus that dominated her internal world. Kali helped her in this confrontation as the dream ego embodied the goddess capacity to behead this negative masculine force. Through this activation of the Kali archetype, Rose began to cut through her identity as a victim and begin to reclaim her soul and her journey toward mastery over the academic, creative, professional, and relational sectors of her life.

Edward's Story—Reclaiming the Kali Within

Edward was in his early 40s when he consulted me to explore his ambivalence about his marriage. He and his wife, Mandy, had been married over 10 years, and Edward was a professional, while Mandy was a homemaker and a socialite. Because of infertility problems the couple could not have any children. At a superficial level, the couple had accepted this loss, but latently it continued to fester as a bone of contention in the marriage. Edward presented as a polished, mellow, sophisticated professional, while Mandy was an exotic, wild, flirtatious, hot-tempered woman. Over the years, Edward assumed the role of a kindly, caretaking, indulgent father, and Mandy regressed to the role of a rebellious, teenaged daughter to replace the void for the missing child. While initially this was endearing, eventually it became a major flash point for dispute in the marriage. Mandy ran up Edward's debt liability over a quarter of a million dollars in compulsive spending, nearly driving them to financial ruin. Edward managed to pull them out of crisis by cashing in his retirement plan, only to see Mandy repeat the spending cycle over the next three years. Moreover, Mandy had taken to drinking, drug abuse, and an excessive party life, while Edward slugged away at his professional grind. All attempts on his part to confront, cajole, and contain his wife and her problems were unsuccessful. She refused to get any professional help. Reluctantly, Edward moved out of their home and filed for divorce. At this point, he had the following dream, which invoked the goddess Kali and turned his life around.

> I am a passive observer. The famous singer Madonna (with blonde hair) is in a new, luxurious private suite at the baseball stadium. The room looks like the living room of a modern expensive home . . . or perhaps a high-rise penthouse.

She is on the floor conducting business with her agent. He is standing. I see her but never get a clear image of the agent. She is making big demands and walking a fine line between arguing and throwing a tantrum. She is rude, vocal, and watching the baseball game that is being played.

I observe a woman dressed just like Madonna distributing flower petals everywhere—pleasing the crowd. She is sweet and pretty . . . nothing like the woman negotiating upstairs in the suite. . . .

This dream was a turning point in Edward's analysis and soul work. All his adult life, Edward had been a kind, sophisticated, soft-spoken man, raised in a pious, Catholic family. However, he was in denial of his shadow, his dark side, the tough, and ruthless professional in him. This tough side manifested occasionally in his work and his leadership qualities, but mostly he suppressed this dark side. This was his dark anima, the Kali within. Over the years, this Kali aspect of his inner life was projected onto Mandy. Mandy's own inner dynamic was susceptible to getting hooked by this Kali projection as it was consistent with her rebellious daughter dynamic; an unfinished business from her own family of origin issues. This collusion of mutual dynamic got their marriage in the stranglehold of the dark goddess Kali.

Clearly, Edward was living out the persona of the public Madonna. The dark Madonna—the Kali within—was projected onto Mandy. Over time, Edward reclaimed this dark, powerful anima energy in his professional and personal life. It revived his soul. He was revitalized, and became more assertive, communicating his needs and feelings in a timely manner. Professionally, he reclaimed his leadership and played out his fuller potential. While his marriage was beyond repair, he established a new relationship on a firmer platform of mutuality. He became able to live out both the Madonnas—the public, polished one and the private assertive one. The split in the Kali energy was healed. Edward felt healed and whole. The darkness of Kali lit his path to the soul.

Helen's Encounter with Kali—Let the Darkness Light the Way

Helen is a survivor of sexual abuse committed by her grandfather when she was six. Later in life, her husband betrayed her and ditched her for a younger woman. In her mid-fifties, Helen found herself hit-

ting the dating scene. Unprepared, she felt out of her league in negotiating this relationship challenge. She felt further compromised
because of her history of abuse by her grandfather and betrayal by her
ex-husband. Then she reported the following dream:

> I am in my condominium and see this black woman making
> out with this white man.

Helen was raised in a white, upper-class family in the eastern U.S. She
felt ashamed of her legacy as a great grandchild of former slave own-
ers. In her conscious life, she had deep empathy and respect for black
people and devoted considerable time and resources toward volunteer
work in the inner city. However, her first response to the dream was
one of prejudice in that she considered the black woman's behavior
blatantly promiscuous behavior.

Upon deeper association with this dream, Helen acknowledged a
sense of envy and admiration for the black woman in her dream and
her freedom to joyfully and spontaneously express her sexuality. She
wished she could be like her! In the past, she had considered erotic self-
expression as disgusting and unladylike. It seems that the black
woman—the shadow aspects of her own personality—appeared in her
dream to guide her into the way of the Eros and relationship. The
darkness in her soul lit the way to the possibility of relationship. It is
as if Kali, herself, appeared in her dream to guide her path.
Subsequently, Helen felt freer to express herself and this opened up the
relationship scene for her.

Cultivating and Honoring Kali

Two interventions on behalf of one's individuation best honor the Kali
potential in psyche's deliberations: honoring the shadow, and making
necessary sacrifices to receive Kali's grace.

Honoring the Shadow

We must acknowledge and honor the descent into our dark side to
honor the goddess Kali. This may involve dealing with the blackness
of depression (*nigredo*), the deadness in one's personality and situation
(*mortificatio*), and the rotting aspects of one's personality, relationships, and life situation (*putreficatio*). We may need to recognize the

complexes that darken our personality or that we project onto significant relationships. In the analytic matrix, the early stages of analysis may constitute this process when shadow must be acknowledged, complexes confronted, and ego "beheaded" to make room for the Self (soul) and the deeper layers of psyche and rekindle personal growth. The defeat of our ego is the victory of our soul.

Sacrifice

Once we have confronted our dark side, we must make the sacrifice. *Sacrifice* means to make sacred, as in the act of worshipping the goddess Kali. Sacrifice, in my conception, is a symbolic relinquishment of a certain aspect of one's psychic life. When we are skewed either in the instinctual or the spiritual pole of life, Kali restores the balance by forcing us to stay in optimal balance between the instinctual and the spiritual pole of the experience. Where the optimal point of balance lies for each of us is the mystery of our individual souls. When an old viewpoint is obsolete and not adaptive to deal with an inner or outer reality, an inner tension develops. At this point, we are forced to challenge our perceptions and views of others, the world, and ourselves.

Sometimes this tension or conflict is projected onto someone, usually an adversary. I once had a partner who I really despised for his concern for financial reimbursement, which seemed to supercede his attentiveness to quality patient care. On closer assessment and self-reflection, it became clear to me that I was making this person carry my dark side. I had to confront my own shadow and unconscious greed. Paradoxically, this got me more into my soul and my mission to serve my patients. The greed was now conscious, subject to my conscious monitoring and therefore more regulated. A known enemy is easier to fight than an invisible one. For the soul journey to continue and the personality to grow, we must recognize this projection and dissolve it. This calls for a sacrifice of our personal myth or philosophy of life, to make room for a new personal myth. My old myth was that I was a superior, soulful psychiatrist. My new myth was realistic. I was a regular human being, who had to constantly struggle to balance my altruism and professional calling with my legitimate self-care and self-interests.

Such dissolution of projection is mediated by Kali consciousness. Our path to the soul calls for breaking up the unity of personality with the archaic, shadow aspects of our unconsciousness and assimilating these shadow and other unexplored potentials of the unconscious to relate to the consciousness. Such dissolution is painful, although freeing, and occurs under the auspices of Kali.

Sacrifice is accompanied with psychic and emotional suffering, and both have to be experienced to move our emotional, psychological, and spiritual development forward. Kali demands sacrifice to usher in our soul-making. An inner pruning of the plant of our life is necessary for our potential to blossom and achieve its full flowering. These sacrifices lead to awareness of the successively higher dimensions of the soul and eventually connection with our soul's code. At times, Kali overrides our individual well-being in the service of collective consciousness. This permits us to move from serving our soul to service of the spirit. Jung calls this a development of Self from "individuation" to "divination," from self-focus to service of the collective goals and community welfare. In the Hindu framework, this is akin to moving from sva dharma (selfhood) to reta dharma (devotion to higher consciousness), which is the zenith of an individual's psychic and spiritual development in the Hindu roadmap of individuation. Analyst David Rosen calls this process egocide,[8] a viable alternative to suicide.

Just as the darkness of the night heralds the dawn of a new day, encounter with the dark goddess Kali paves the way for new beginnings in our life. When we engage Kali to behead the existing consciousness, we make room for the new consciousness, and the soul can emerge on the stage of our life and consciousness. New beginnings become possible. Kali paves the way for Aditi. A new creation myth then emerges for us as individuals and for societies under the auspices of Aditi, the great Grandmother Goddess of Void and new beginnings.

---

8 David H. Rosen, *Transforming Depression: Healing the Soul through Creativity* (Berwick, ME: Nicolas-Hays, 2002).

Guadalupe Is a Girl
Gang Leader in Heaven

Clarissa Pinkola Estés

Clarissa Pinkola Estés, Ph.D., and diplomate Jungian analyst, has a doctorate in multi-cultural studies and clinical studies from The Union Institute. She is an award-winning author and, as a *cantadora*, an artist-in-residence for the state of Colorado. She has created several audio tapes including The Jungian Storyteller Series: *The Wild Woman Archetype; Warming the Stone Child; In the House of the Riddle Mother; The Creative Fire;* and *The Radiant Coat*. She is the author of the acclaimed *Women Who Run with the Wolves*. "Gaudalupe Is a Girl Gang Leader in Heaven" is from *La Pasionaria*, forthcoming from Alfred A. Knopf.

"Guadalupe Is a Girl Gang Leader in Heaven" is part of a long chant in praise of our Lady of Guadalupe. In the family tradition—as in some parts of the Hebrew tradition, and in the street-Christian tradition—there is an old legacy of speaking of and to the holy people as though one has a brother-sister relationship with them rather than a vassal-serf or a lord-subject relationship. This is a resistance poem at heart, saying in many different ways that others and outsiders, no matter who they are, are not allowed to define or distort, for political reasons, the people's personal experiences with the belovedly holy.

Guadalupe, La Nuestra Señora, *Our Holy Mother,*
is a girl gang leader in heaven.

I know for a fact she is Pachuca
and wears the sign of La Loca on her hand.

Guadalupe is a girl gang leader in Heaven,
this I know for I come from people who eat
with knives—no forks—just knives.

I come from people who sit on curbs to talk—
and stare down cars that want to park there.

I come from people who drag a chair
into the middle of the sidewalk
and sit all day staring straight into the sun
without blinking,

They say this is good medicine for their eyes.

The Virgin Mary is a girl gang leader in heaven.

She is a Hell's Angel and she rides a Harley.

This I know for I come from people
who think axle grease is holy water.

They hold Mass out in the driveway
under the hood on Saturdays.

The engine is their altar.

They genuflect and say prayers all day,
and baptize themselves in crankcase oil.

The soles of their shoes
always smell like gasoline.

I come from people who think Confession
is a necessity only the moment before a head-on-collision.

Guadalupe is a girl gang leader in heaven,
and I know this for certain
because I come from people who
have the kind of Abuelita who,
when you tell her about the musical Grease,
she runs around like a squirrel in snagged stockings
yelling that her grand-daughter told her
about this great new movie called El Vaselino.

I come from the kind of grandfather
whose eyes are a thousand years old,
but his teeth are brand new,
less than two years old those dentures.

They make all his teeth the same length and size.

His face from the nose up is old,
his face from the mouth down is young.

I come from the kind of old people
who can sit on the edge of straight back chairs
without touching their backs to the slats,
and who can sit there without moving for a long time.

They just sit straight-backed and proud
breathing in and out like frail paper bags.

I come from people who in the night,
call the old ones down the dream chute
into our bedrooms so we can hear the old truths.

They tell us that story the Spaniards told
is a great slander against our people, that part the gringos
love to tell about our habit of human sacrifice
is false. We have always valued life.

The conquistadores *mistook our greatest story*
about the great spirit warrior who was killed
by those who could not stand his loving radiance.

In the story his heart is cut out

His murderers threw his body into a cenote,
a sacred well. He died and was buried or burned.

In the great myth he was resurrected
three days later, and as the old ones say,
who cares what side he was on, he was God.

The Spaniards had no understanding of our God,
and they were so enraged by the "witches"
they thought they saw in the Aztec healers, singers
and poets that they were forced to extend their Inquisition
to the New World there and then, and these foreigners forced
the priests and the storytellers and the old people
up onto the stairs of the stone towers, they forced the
people to kill their own in the most heinous of crimes against
the soul. And this is what the old ones say, the ones who
were there and come down on Dia de los Muertos.

I come from people who hunt in the winter for their food,
and are always arrested for poaching.

They try to get arrested together
so they can sit around in jail
telling the old stories,
crying together and singing
at the tops of their lungs.

I come from people who were and are crammed
into immigration and deportation shelters,
sitting there with shivering silver price tags
shot through their ear lobes like the cattle
in the slaughter house.

200 dollars to go back or come here,
either way, to the coyote, it makes no difference.

I am Mexican by nature, a Magyar,
a Romany, a Rom by nurture.

And Guadalupe is the one who looks after
fools such as we.

Guadalupe is a girl gang leader in heaven.

I know for a fact that she is Pachuca
and wears the sign of La Loca on her hand,
drives a four on the floor with a bonnet
and blue dot tail lights.

And I pray to her, mio Dio, Dio mio,
because she is the strongest woman I know.

Dark Bride: Magdalene as Mystic

Annette M. Hulefeld

Annette M. Hulefeld, L.C.S.W., A.C.S.W., is a psychotherapist, shamanic practitioner, consultant, ritualist, writer, and artist. She integrates the traditions of shamanism, mysticism, the tarot and the Dreamtime, and practices in the Chicago, Illinois area. She is currently a D.Min. candidate at the University of Creation Spirituality, Oakland, California.

Mary, the Mother of God appears, gently announcing she is leaving me. I begin to weep, begging her not to go. She says: "It's time for you to bring forth another Mary." As the Mother disappears, Magdalene crystallizes into form, dancing in the hot, desert sand. Her skin is exquisitely dark, smooth as polished onyx. She is clothed in swirling veils of orange, red, and gold tones. In her hand is a chalice-shaped jar. Her eyes pierce my heart, breaking open the dark wounds of womanhood too long repressed. I scream out my ignorance and unworthiness in accepting this task.

A new consciousness is emerging from the darkness of the Cosmic Soul, from the incredibly sumptuous, devouring belly of the Dark Cosmic Mother: Magdalene as Dark Bride and Mystic. For centuries, certain religious and cultural sects have perpetuated the myth of Magdalene as prostitute, a woman possessed of demons. This myopic viewpoint serves not only to dismiss her dignity as a woman, but also to eliminate the possibility for a radically different story to emerge. What if the truth were that Magdalene as Bride and Jesus as Bridegroom were destined to complete parallel journeys in order to bring forth a new planetary consciousness? Consider the following message I received from Christ in a vision in 1994:

... from the fire of my love and the tears of my Mother's womb, so will my woman arise. ... I died to let you know my passion for my woman, for all women. She is destroyed for her silence, humiliated in her submissions, ridiculed for her service, whipped for her loyalty to Truth—the truth of listening only to the voice of her Beloved. The pain of this knowing broke my body, pierced my heart. I atoned for the rape of her spirit, the rape of her body. I came from woman and I return to woman. ... As I was born in a stable, so she was born from the Cross.

I believe that Magdalene completed this path by undertaking a mystic's journey, a cosmic, deconstructive process that was necessary to clear the barnacles of accumulated religious and cultural distortions about the feminine spirit. I also believe that the time has come to reconstruct the essence of Magdalene as incarnate mystic and co-creator with the universe story and to restore her image as bride, lover, partner, friend, and Beloved of Christ.

The story I present is not an attempt to prove anything about the historical Mary Magdalene. The knowing and memory I have of her as bride and mystic was awakened and unfolded through life experiences and dreams, culminating in two spiritual quests: one to the Basilica of Our Lady of Guadalupe in Mexico City, the other to the Village of Dano in Burkina Faso, West Africa.

Although the details of my journey are unique, my intent in sharing them is to uncover universal aspects that connect us all. I believe we are all born with an unquenchable thirst for divine union, and it is our life's path to become insanely courageous enough to surrender and dissolve into the heart of the divine. At times, the path is blinding, lonely, confusing, chaotic, and downright devastating. I've come to the conclusion that living from the heart of the mystical Magdalene demands a dissolution of personal victim consciousness and, beyond that, a transformation of the darkness of dispossession and of the not-good-enough mentality. Only when we strip away the layers of personal drama, religious dogma, and cultural history are we able to authentically and directly experience divine union. Only then can we live from the memory of who we are as beings of the universe story, a story that is simultaneously beyond and within our biological selves. The possibility of birthing the consciousness of the

Divine Feminine in this fashion was presented to me in a dream I had
in December, 1999:

> *I'm observing a scene in the night sky; the figures appear
> larger than normal. There is a giant wheelchair in which an
> unidentified person is restrained with beautiful leather straps.
> A plush, black velvet blanket is draped over the legs and the
> edges of the blanket are bound in gold. The individual in the
> wheelchair wears black leather gloves, which are cut to reveal
> fingers. The person is desperate and determined to push the
> wheelchair away from a black vortex, which threatens to suck
> it in. I remember saying in the dream that I am looking at the
> black hole of the universe. The vortex is stronger than the per-
> son is and the immersion is gentle, and without sound. A few
> minutes later, a burst of light shoots out like a fireworks dis-
> play, revealing a huge baby, lying in a transparent womb,
> draped in pink silk.*

I'm not sure how many people manage to surrender to God with finesse
and grace, but I knew from the dream that it was time to re-examine
whatever childhood belief systems were keeping me a spiritual cripple. I
was raised Catholic and was incredibly hooked on the traditions of
being pure enough and good enough to get approval from a Father God.
Although I believed in a personal relationship with Jesus and Mary, I
never told anyone that the Blessed Mother Mary appeared in my room
at night, nor did I ever breathe a word about my conversations with the
dead. One of my best-kept secrets was traveling out of body at night to
the giant cottonwood tree behind my bedroom window. There I met my
best friend, Jesus, and we'd talk or be silent for hours.

At a very young age, however, a demon named Betrayal decided to
take up residence in my home, seriously disrupting the image I developed of myself as a pure, translucent, buttercup child of God. The
demon dimmed the lights, scattering my hopes for God's love like bird-
seed in a windstorm. Yes, life reflected a not-so-fairy-tale ending I had
dreamed around the age of four:

> *I wake up every morning, knowing I can swing from the stars,
> play with the moon and the sun, paint rainbows for God
> across the skies. One day I realize no one cares, no one
> notices. In fact, someone is messing with my paints. I shut the*

*paint box and slowly dissolve into the centers of the dried up
colors.*

At a tender age, I entered a dark night of pain and invisibility. God certainly would have no use for a used child. I became the mysterious girl, dressed in crystal tears, a girl who lived in the moment of death, hoping that each breath would shorten her stay on Earth. I had an exquisite longing for the ultimate bonding with God, flesh without skin, wind without fire, and sky wrapped in earth, God without form. Crippled with wounding, I succumbed to a path of physical and emotional pain, a desperate attempt to keep in the good graces of the almighty God. This gave me the illusion of being redeemed in spite of others' transgressions on my body and mind. I was caught in a powerful dilemma: to the outside world I pretended to be a Magda-Lily, yet inwardly I was tortured with an identity of the disgraced Magdalene.

This pattern was deeply ingrained in my numbed psyche and was revealed years later in a near-death experience following the birth of my first son. I kept asking the doctor why my belly was so distended, why I was feeling so weak. My complaints were dismissed as simply the fears of a new, young mother. When I began passing clots that were bigger than my newborn, it was clear I was hemorrhaging to death from a burst artery. Part of me was distressed but the larger part was incredibly euphoric. Finally, there was hope for a permanent release from a very pained body. And then came the moment of leaving the body, entering the tunnel where the Beloved appeared in splendor, Light unto Light, Love beyond Love. Surrounded by ancestors, celestial sounds and over-the-rainbow colors, a brilliant, iridescent Christ appeared, reached to touch my fingertips, and whispered my name. In that moment, I was temporarily blind, drunk with the insanity of love. My hope for death, however, was short-lived. He spoke: "Annette, it is not your time, you must go back."

I know that in that moment Christ sealed my heart with life but I sizzled with silent rage, branding the lining of my heart with death. I couldn't die and I didn't want to live. There I was, a dried-up garment with unfixable static cling. The wounded child heard Christ's words as rejection and was crushed by the belief that she was not even good enough for God. These feelings of worthlessness and disposability plunged me into deep wells of despair that soon manifested in battering pain in my head, body, and spirit. From the eyes of a betrayed child, I could not fathom my best friend inflicting this ultimate betrayal.

I had no perception at that time of the spiritual significance of this encounter. I didn't have the insight to know that to hold the energy of the divine, I would first have to claim my humanity in the body, embrace the passion of womanhood, and accept my placement in the grid of life. What separated me from the Christ was not his directive but layers of childhood terrors and disenfranchisement from humanity. I had no idea that in sending me to earth, Christ was challenging me to enter the path of the mystic, the path of the shaman. The challenge was to leave him behind as childhood friend and become an incarnate, passionate woman. I had to surrender the safety of the prostitute-Magdalene mentality, which for me was a woman imprisoned within her own body, a woman crucified by her victim mind.

It took 16 more years to awaken my soul, years of severe migraines and undiagnosed, mysterious illnesses. Through divorce and separation from my children, I lost my health, my job, friends, and anything I was attached to. Wedged in there was what the medical professional labeled a psychotic breakdown, what a shaman labeled as an initiation into the workings of the spirit world. Throughout this dark night of the soul, every vestige of patriarchal lies, lies gathered through the institutions of religion, psychology, culture, and family dysfunction, had to disintegrate, burn into ash, and be sifted through. Years later, I became aware that the day of my collapse occurred on July 22nd, the feast day of Mary Magdalene. It was not until my second marriage, to a man who lives the compassion and unconditional love of the Christ, that I awakened to a conscious path to find, to experience the Divine Feminine. I never dreamed that the Mary, the Mother of God would lead me to find the Dark Bride in Mexico City, in Egypt, in Africa, in me.

ॐ

In 1994, I had a dream directing me to visit the shrine of Our Lady of Guadalupe, in Mexico City, by myself. At first, I was delighted, and like Little Red Riding Hood happily going to visit her grandmother, I packed my bags with the bare necessities—a journal, two pens, black knit pants, two cotton shirts, Imodium for diarrhea and one pair of walking shoes. In essence, I was prepared for nothing!

For several years I kept the details of this trip resting in the back of my heart, a sunken treasure never revealed. And yet, ripples of mystic fires have slowly burned away the spider web veins of fear that motivated me to hide the mystery. I thought I was sent for a deepening of my relationship with the Virgin Mother. I now believe I was sent to begin unwrapping an incarnational memory of mysticism and divine union, a union housed within flesh and blood, a reclaiming of the Dark Bride of Christ.

In accepting the call of the Mother, I innocently anticipated spiritual wonder and miracles but instead encountered scenarios scripted out of a horror movie. It all began with my attempt to cross the street while hundreds of beetle bug Volkswagens appeared around corners like cockroaches when the lights suddenly go on. At any moment, a random "bug" could suddenly drive up my leg, over my back, across my head to the next stoplight. My body shifted into instant Raggedy Ann position, thinking that if I relaxed, the tire marks wouldn't leave me permanently disabled! Somehow I managed to get across the street, to be faced with political demonstrations that were peppered with staccato drumming, organ grinders, and standing guards with aimed rifles and bayonets. I ran down the stairs to the train, primarily to catch my heart that had catapulted from its cavity. Sometimes it is best to let fear run in front of you so you can walk and appear normal. In the subway, I was an abandoned hamster looking for the safety of its Habitrail. No one spoke English, or if they did, I was not about to be let in on the secret. And I thought my charming smile and hand language would get me anywhere! I gulped down my tears, which turned into loud hiccoughing. I was so disoriented that at first I didn't feel the tap, tap on my right shoulder. A very lovely young woman, dressed in tight black leather, hair tinged with bright fuchsia dye, sweetly asked if I needed help. Hysteria radar had worked! In perfect English, she gave me directions to Guadalupe's shrine and then vanished into the crowd before I could say "thank you." I thought to myself: "Holy Mary, you sure have changed!" Once again, the Mother had rescued her naïve daughter, or was it the Magdalene looking after me? Who cares? I was bound for the glory of the Basilica.

While riding the train, all the images from the streets I'd just left returned with a power that threatened my emotional circuitry. I wasn't prepared to deal with a noisy city bulging with haunting women, wasting away on the sidewalks like the mounds of garbage rotting in the alleys. Magdalene ghosts appearing as alley rats. The peasant women with gaunt, filthy faces, swayed their mechanical arms in the dusty air, begging for loose change. Like whimpering stray dogs, they waited for crumbs to feed their hungry broods. They nursed their bone babies on the sidewalks, hiding their faces under darkened blankets, stiff with urine and sweat. I imagined placing myself in one mother's lap, a lap so rice paper thin, it risked shredding with one unexpected jolt. I could hardly breathe wondering what it was like to be sucking for life with hundreds of feet trampling over your head, any moment someone might accidentally squash out your existence. Surely these women and children were endangered species. My naivete did not fare well in these streets. I shivered and muttered anxious prayers to the Blessed Mother, wondering if I had misinterpreted the intent of the dream.

One of the women I stumbled across was particularly dismaying. She was on a second story landing, propped against some iron rails. Something about her gray milk eyes and toothless, dribbling mouth brought me back to memories of my grandmother during her times in the insane asylum. There was a sickening similarity between the foreign peasant imprisoned in the open air and grandma in solitary confinement, restrained in leather straps. Both appeared deranged, wearing the anguish of despised women, a face often projected onto Magdalene. Somehow I knew that the real craziness wasn't in these dazed, inwardly and outwardly incarcerated women. My guts twisted with a knowing that both grandma and these women were society's scapegoats, bearing society's hatred and fear of the feminine spirit. The face of insanity was perhaps their way to cope with helplessness, poverty, and rage.

The pathos of the women's shrunken bodies and wasted minds sent me reeling with the memory of the separation from my children after divorce and illness. My head began to split with pain, the beginnings of a crown-of-thorns migraine. I was terrorized that I was disintegrating into the universal world of the dispossessed, insane woman. I didn't want to enter that space again; I'd already suffered that humiliation.

And then, in great peace, as if a ray of sunlight had slipped into my heart, I knew the truth of human connectedness. These women and

I were One Woman, tragically bound to a false blueprint of Magdalene.

Entering the courtyard of the Basilica, I opened a pamphlet and read these words:

> *I am your merciful Mother, the Mother of all who love me, of those who cry to me . . . here I will hear their weeping and their sorrow . . . their necessities and misfortunes. . . . do not be troubled or weighed down with grief. Do not fear any illness or vexation, anxiety or pain. Am I not here who am your Mother? Are you not under my shadow and protection? Is there anything else you need?* (Words of the Virgin spoken to Juan Diego, December 9, 12, 1531.)

Just then, an impish young boy, with black ringlets bouncing like uncoiled springs, began to dance the tarantella around my legs. He tugged at my shirt, giggling, his eyes beacons of rocket fire that short-circuited my heart. As I clumsily looked for coins, he rapidly waved one arm, a windshield wiper with no contact. Reaching for his hand, I recoiled, noticing he had no fingers, merely a sharp fingernail jutting out of his third knuckle. I shut my eyes for a moment, trying to hide my reaction but in that moment, he vanished like smoke into the polluted air. Had I just met a miniature Captain Hook bedeviling Peter Pan? Was this a coyote spirit trying to unplug my sanity? In retrospect, it was just one of many distressing events that scrubbed me raw in preparation for a birth my consciousness was dreading.

Inwardly I screamed "Holy Mother, where are you?" but outwardly I hissed, "Why?" A gust of wind rustled through my hair, speaking this message:

> *The woman is starving, she begs for her children, she seeks entrance into the kingdom. She has submitted and said yes to the king, yet he dismisses her, sending her begging, making her children dance and steal for their mothers. The king is the no-man. Annette, know that the time has come to set the Woman free. Listen to me. Look into my eyes. Do not dance in the dark man's eye. Come dance with me. Now you are wrapped in the cloak of the Mother, a cloak of blue and gold. She will bring you to Truth. You will dance with me.*

At first I was startled, wondering who the dancing woman could be. A second reaction bubbled up as the doors opened to reveal a forgotten woman within me, a stumbling, dark spirit that yearned for equality, dignity, and internal freedom from the power of the no-man. I was intimately aware of the no-man within me that congratulated my mute desperado spirit for finding ways to buy, sell, manipulate, and entice Christ to see me, hear me, touch me. I had listened to his voice when I began roaming the midnight hours, hunting the Christ who had sealed me with a death penalty of life. What an impressive spiritual, whoring imposter of a woman I'd become, begging for the Beloved's return, determined to be a suffering servant as reparation for being a failed, inadequate woman.

The next morning I visited Teotihuacan, site of the famous Sun and Moon Pyramids. The bus ride was nearly hallucinogenic. The speed of the bus made the tires float above layers of sweltering heat. The overall effect was that acres of shacks and roadside beggars blended into a lackluster aura of haze and fumes. In the Plaza of Quetzalcoatl, the local male vendors swarmed around selling their wares, annoying me more than horseflies on a muggy day. Perhaps the migraine from the bus trip influenced my demeanor, but, after several aborted attempts to stop their hawking in my face, I lost all propriety and screamed like a banshee! To say the least, the vendors were startled and retreated. I sprinted ahead to the first level of the Sun pyramid. Although I felt incredibly weak, drained by my fears, there was an urgency that propelled my feet to the top of the pyramid, where a person was laying face down, dead center. I waited, intuitively knowing that I had been taken to the center for some unknown reason. Without warning, the wind shifted, sending a Popsicle cold chill through my body. At the bridge of my nose was a black butterfly, dazzling with wings edged in liquid sunlight. Then there were two. Then there were three. My knees genuflected, sinking in adoration. Three butterflies swirled around in a circle, coming together in oneness, separating out, forming a cross, coming back together into one body, one wing. Other people gathered, stunned as the butterflies vibrated, dancing in ecstasy for several seconds around my head. Later, as I wobbled down the stairs, two white butterflies flitted around me, whispers of angel lace, delicately praising Life. Looking back, had the Black Madonna manifested to her daughter a new paradigm of spirituality, an ecstatic dance of creative, cosmic partnership versus a path of dualism and suffering?

I spent the following days in the Basilica, filled with images of humble peasants crawling on their knees to the altar, clutching black, brown, yellow, red, or white rosary beads in their weathered hands, praying fervently with quivering lips. The men labored under the weight of gigantic, rainbow-colored bouquets while the women offered their babies to the untouchable Virgin, suspended above their heads, protected behind bulletproof glass. To see the beloved mantle, you stepped onto a conveyor belt and craned your neck in a position that guaranteed the need of chiropractic services! The priests said Mass and distributed communion like robots with rusty hinges. Never before had the Body of Christ tasted like stale, discarded straw. Later, that straw ignited unexpectedly inside the Chapel of Tepeyac, the site of the first apparition of Our Lady of Guadalupe to Juan Diego in 1531. I was making my way up the stairs, being bumped by bodies hungry to receive sustenance from their Mother. In spite of the discomfort, I, like the local peasants, would not miss the opportunity to place a devotional candle in front of the Virgin. Once I was inside the chapel, a short, disgruntled priest wearing the face of an injured stray dog, came from behind a closed door, holding a rather large piece of stiff cardboard. With no hesitation, he fanned out all the candles on the long, narrow table that was set up to hold the lighted intentions of all those seeking favors from the Holy Mother. With no hesitation, I yelled out, "You cannot do that. These people have sacrificed so much to even buy these candles. How dare you?" Although I was shaking like strawberry Jell-O, I placed the discarded candles back onto the table. The priest's eyes registered gunfire, yet, he walked away with the smoldering heat of the day.

Later that afternoon, I returned to the main Basilica to contemplate the Icon of Our Lady of Guadalupe. I was spellbound as her robes came alive, blood pouring out of her heart onto her right side, shaping the opening of a womb. The Shroud of Jesus appeared on her left knee, her left shoulder turned deep blue. She smiled at me, saying she had much to tell me. I was too frightened to do anything but run to the bathroom, which, of course, was out of order!

My anxiety drove me out of the Basilica into the back courtyard where I was greeted with racks of pornographic magazines to the right and overflowing tables of tacky, gold, plastic images of Mother and Son to the left. Inwardly I felt trapped, wondering if I'd ever get out of this seemingly divinely-ordained labyrinth! Milling about the courtyard were young men sporting white T-shirts that glaringly depicted a nude couple making love. It was interesting that inside the Church the Lady was concealed and untouchable, revealing only her hands and face, while outside, images of her disowned and disrespected daughters were totally exposed, daring free hands to explore and enjoy and eyes to gawk over.

Right in my face was the devastating religious paradigm I'd been fed since childhood. Sanctity meant being unavailable to human touch, a body under glass. Sinfulness meant sexuality, exposed flesh, human passion. I'd worshipped a sexless Virgin Mother and followed a divine, suffering son who had no genitals. This dualism left me spiritually full, humanly withered, no different from the exiled, emaciated daughters of the Mother begging on the sidewalks, cloaked in sweaty, tattered cloth. I had flashbacks of the onset of my own spiritual prostitution, the hours spent creating schemes that would bring me back into God's good graces. I honestly thought that asceticism and disconnection from the body were the way, the truth, and salvation.

I was beginning to think the Mother brought me to her Shrine to surrender the smelly, dualistic beliefs I still lived regarding body image and the repressed feminine. I felt a bit humiliated admitting that in terms of being fully human, I was still more dead than alive. Uncovering Magdalene was not a simple process of unwrapping a package and taking out the contents. It swirled around, now seen, now unseen, understanding now shifting into total bafflement.

About one year after visiting the Shrine of Our Lady in Mexico City, I found myself in Egypt, doing ceremony in the Great Pyramid while presenting at a conference on near-death experiences. One particular incident stunned me then and still evokes unease in my belly. One morning, I went with two conference attendees to a nearby stable to rent horses for a ride in the desert. I was intimidated not only by the ghostly hour, 5:30 A.M., but also by seeing the Sphinx looming over the back fence of the stable. Not to mention, I was and am terrified of raw animal power. I prayed to God to get a demure, well-behaved

Arabian stallion (!)—along with an equally gentle guide. The angels definitely were on my side that cool, pristine, blue-sky morning. The owner of the stable appeared first, dressed in a simple, dark brown linen robe, followed by his robust, dimple-eyed wife. She came over to me and wrapped my head and neck with a soft white scarf. A mother wrapping her child in swaddling clothes could not have been more tender. I stumbled over my words like a skittish colt, determined that my request for a quiet horse be honored. The husband smiled, semitoothless, and motioned for me to look over his shoulder. Out stepped his twelve-year-old daughter, dressed in a blue serge gown, a white veil, pulling a white donkey for herself, and a white horse for me. My Catholic scripts came alive as I thought of Mary on the donkey, going to birth her son, Jesus. The father gave strict instructions to the daughter not to make the horse go "chi-chi"—her signal for "let's go—full speed ahead until you get swallowed up in the dust!" Her body slumped in obedience but her eyes flashed "we'll see . . . we'll have some fun." The other women galloped off on their supercharged black stallions, while I on my horse, she on her donkey, did the shifting-sand shuffle, barely disrupting the top layer of moist sand. At times, the girl would stop, twirl on the back of her donkey, and twitter "chi-chi." I pretended to be praying to the rising sun. Just when my tolerance reached saturation level, the father appeared behind us, saying that he'd been told to "give me a gift from the Pyramids." What passed through my mind was "What will this cost me?" so I froze in place. However, he placed two raw pieces of white alabaster in my hands, communicating that at the right time, I would understand this gesture of the gods. He then took my hand, leading me back, in silence, to the stable. My mind and heart rattled and bumped against each other like tin pots and pans. The stirrings of the relationship I had with Jesus washed over me with such intensity that I was swooning. My mouth would not open, so my eyes said thank you. As I walked away, the young girl ran up to me, grabbed my face, riveted her deep velvet eyes into mine, and began to sob uncontrollably. I tried to comfort her but she would not loosen her gaze until I too burst into tears. She was awakening something and I was in a semicoma. I gave her my blue crystal bracelet with the Blessed Mother medal and we parted. Her wailing pierced the sunrise, leaving me shivering from more than the crisp air.

A few years later, as I was cleaning my desk, I crumpled and threw into the wastebasket a flyer that had blown past my foot. Three times it popped out. In exasperation, I unfolded it to see staring in my face the title of a new book, *The Woman with the Alabaster Jar*, about the story of Magdalene and Christ, by Margaret Starbird.

§▲

In January, 2000, I was one of a group of spiritual initiates visiting the village of Dano, located in Burkina Faso, home of Malidoma Patrice Some, a Daguara medicine man. The ostensible purpose of the trip was to receive divination readings by the local shamans, visit the sacred cave of the Kontomble (beings from the Other World), and experience village life. The agenda of unseen forces was quite different! What happened to me during those 12 days fulfilled the prophecy of the wheelchair dream: I was sucked into the vortex of the Void where my life as I knew it was shattered. I was brought directly into force of the Dark Magdalene, through and in the form of a Black Kontomble.

Nothing can erase the memory of the suffocating heat, the indelible mark of dusty, red earth on your clothes, the sparseness of food, the dried-earth homes, the lack of water, and the absence of almost all material goods. In the village, bonding to the divine was a simple matter of breathing in the red dust that clung to your cells like static electricity. Without a doubt, the all and nothing environment provided the space to open the eyes of the soul, the eternal vision of the heart.

The silence in the village compound was haunting, a seductive invitation to enter the heart of the Universe by directly aligning with God. I rarely heard a baby cry (and there were many children); I heard no harsh, angry, or elevated tones. Granted, the pigs snorted irreverently at four o'clock in the morning, while the rooster crowed the song of the new day. The vultures, scanning for carcasses of sacrificed animals, soared elegantly overhead, then landed with resounding thuds on the rooftops. Their presence created a heavy, breathing stillness. Even the children giggled without sound as they pulled defeathered chickens from the fire. Against the backdrop of stillness, the most compelling sound came from the heavy wooden mallets held by women pounding the millet. Their rhythmic beat traveled through the heat, settling into the crevices of my heart, into the marrow of my bones. The silence, the pounding, all contained the invisible yet immanent African Momma.

One morning, I withdrew to a field in the back of the village compound to face what was troubling me. On the surface, I was panicked
that I'd collapse from the suffocating heat. Yet, on a deeper level, I was
heartsick about the animal sacrifices and the dominance, as I perceived
it, of the male shamans. Just the day before, as part of the divination
rituals, I had to lead and take certain animals to be sacrificed on my
behalf. As I stood there, drenched in perspiration, I saw again the little red goat that hid between my legs waiting its turn to die. I wanted
nothing more than to stretch my heart into its heart. How I wanted
that goat to know I loved him and was grateful! I felt again the pulse
of the soft, warm hen, submissively hanging from the palm of my
hand. I was stunned by their dumb surrender, spilling their life force,
so that the veils of cultural and religious curses, the lies and traumas
could be lifted from generations of crippled women like myself.
Chicken feathers floated before my eyes, dried blood was barely visible in the red earth. I could not help thinking of the sacrificed Jesus,
the lost women of my generation who had sacrificed their lives through
drugs, suicide, and mental illness. My God, is that what happened? In
the oneness of animal and human, had we participated in the collective
healing of violence against the feminine spirit?

I was so wrapped up in my head that I did not hear the invisible
African Momma touching my pain. A wind arose from nothingness,
wrapping me as tight as the village women wrap their babies in batique
cloth. Before I could even exhale, I knew there was nothing, No Thing,
between me and the Divine. The Wind of the red earth Mother was letting me know that in that moment all my questions were irrelevant.
My fears unraveled like ribbons falling out of a baby's soft curls. What
mattered was that nothing mattered but being One in Love. What mattered was the brilliance of cosmic chaos and the knowing that all is
inter-related, all is inter-connected. My puny little brain would never
grasp the power and mystery at work in this tiny village.

Soon after, we were taken to the space where one of the shamans
had made talismans for several of us from the sacrificed goats. I never
told anyone the overwhelming vision I had that day. As I was waiting
for my turn to participate in the ritual, I looked over the roofs of the
homes in the compound to see a very dark, amorphous spirit, something like a dust cloud, rise up from the horizon. It was as if the sun
had a dark twin climbing out of the earth's womb to say "good morn-

ing." She, the African Momma, settled into form and I met her eyes and she touched my heart. This profound embrace of the Dark Mother was the last preparation before meeting the Kontomble, the midwife in birthing the Magdalene Bride.

The following day we journeyed to a mountain in the region to visit a sacred cave, a place of initiation rites, holy ground to meet the Kontomble. Part of the protocol for meeting the Kontomble was to prepare a question, which was translated by the shamans and returned back to you. Depending on the needs of the individual, certain rituals or sacrifices might also be included. My questions were clear: How best to serve the planet at my age? What ancestors would help me fulfill my soul's path? What was needed to regain and protect my health? Although my spiritual self knew that entering the cave was surrender to the unknown and a commitment of trust without expectation, my human self repeated the intention over and over for several hours. I was obsessed with a fear that I would either not see the Kontomble or I would do something stupid or ruin the whole experience. Or worse, what if they didn't like white women?

When the "boom, boom" sound announced the arrival of these beings, my soul shivered with delight. On entering the cave, I sucked in my breath, trying very hard to be inconspicuous as I gagged from the wretched, pungent odors of decay, stale dust, and blood. The darkness was a bit intimidating, yet my heart pounded, anticipating a leap into the womb of God. Waves of energy pushed me toward the opening where the Kontomble sat, bursting open an incredible, repressed passion to be alive. As I knelt down on one knee, the Kontomble grasped my hand with an electrifying power that was the pure, generative, galactic energy of Spirit. I was smitten with a love and compassion unsurpassed in my finite mind. I'd had near-death experiences, but this was different. This was a physical/divine being, not merely a spiritual presence. In that moment of being plugged into Source, I was annihilated into Oneness and birthed into existence.

Words betray the holiness of encountering this very dark, small being, sitting yogi style. As I looked into the face I saw infinite, crystal eyes rolling into the back of the head, exploding into a brilliant halo. Not far behind, the other world glowed with a blinding light. I swallowed fiercely so as not to cry, not to be inelegant and throw up! Like a supernova star, I exploded into ecstasy, experiencing simultaneously the presence of both Christ and the Buddha united. The touch of this being was so intense I literally gasped YES! YES! YES! In saying YES! I acknowledged I was a woman with an indigenous heart, united with universal Truth, not bound by tradition or cultural beliefs.

The Kontomble, in extending the right hand, blessed me with the power of creation, the power of purpose and bliss. My holy-innocent victim mentality belly-flopped into the furnace of Divine fire and instantaneously I had knowing of being a human/divine woman, of being Kontomble. The Indian mystic and poet, Kabir, captures the scene perfectly when he says: "Meeting with Him, my own courtyard became the Universe."[1]

I walked away from the space like a drunkard, my legs wobbly as a dying chicken's. As I stood on the rocks outside the entrance of the cave, I swayed with the wind, inebriated with love, stunned by the power of compassion. The Dark Mother had brought me to this sacred space that could resurrect her dark daughter from the ashes of a white virgin. The cosmic heart of the Mother had pounded away at me for years until this moment of release. Now I would be sent into the world with the passion of a woman, wild about her divinity, wild about her Lover, in love with the Universe. The 12th century mystic, Hildegard of Bingen, exquisitely captures what I felt deep within my heart: "With an embrace and a kiss the human being is released from the depth of God's heart and sent into the womb of the world."[2] In saying "Yes," I could not escape the knowing that I was called to awaken the Feminine in others. I wanted to do nothing in life but to hold humanity and electrify everyone with the compassion of the Source.

In all honesty, I may never fully grasp the significance of the events of Africa—or any other spiritual experiences for that matter. I do know that every cell of my being, perhaps even my DNA, was altered. In addition to the extraordinary events, there were ordinary times that served to remind me of the interconnectedness of all human beings. For example: how could I ever forget the Eddie Murphy poster that hung in the ritual space of one of the shamans? Or the young mother descending a ladder, wearing a native cloth wrap and a silver lamé

---

[1] Matthew Fox, *The Reinvention of Work* (San Francisco: HarperSanFrancisco, 1995), p. 74.
[2] Renata Craine, *Hildegard of Bingen: Prophet of the Cosmic Christ* (New York: Crossword, 1957), p. 74.

camisole top? The most outrageous moment, however, occurred following a particularly intense ritual in which dead chickens landed at
my feet, splattering blood onto my white T-shirt, and I had witnessed
the sacrifice of a four-legged—about three feet from me. When I left
this particular cave, a fellow traveler and I plopped down on an inviting piece of wood, barely able to contain the barrels of nervous anxiety trapped in our bodies. As we started to giggle, an enormous gust of
wind escaped from my butt, making the children of the village squeal
with laughter. They gathered other children around and it was clear
they wanted a repeat performance from the silly white lady!

There was also the appearance of three village women whom I've
never spoken about, women of silence, laughter, and mysterious
strength. Months before traveling to Burkina Faso, several people had
dreams about me encountering the women of the village. As I waited
to visit with the Kontomble, I noticed a tiny, toothless woman, in a
light blue flowered dress, climb up the side of the hill, and sit very close
to the mouth of the cave. Although her intent was hidden from us, I
had that feeling in my bones that her presence was absolutely necessary. I was told later by another traveler that the old woman walked
away once I came out of the cave. I burst into tears, honoring her witness, awed by a manifested dream.

The second woman was tall, very slim, with eyes that danced with
the rhythm of the bats in the cave. She would walk past all of us, grab-
bing our hands, laughing uproariously. For some reason, she would
repeatedly come back to me, shaking my hand and arm as if priming
a pump! Her hyena-like voice unwrapped layers of childhood giggles
and I responded to her with joy!

I encountered the third woman on the day of my departure. The
men, women, and children of the village compound gathered to watch
the men dancers. I was barely surviving the 100-degree heat and had
wrapped a towel, very unceremoniously, around my throbbing head.
At one point, I left the gathering to find a "cool" spot next to a building wall. As I poured another bottle of water over my head, I felt a
warm, calloused hand on my shoulder. Not to be disrespectful, I
sprung up to greet the woman, promptly tripping over my feet, and
landing on my knees. As she raised me up, the necklace I'd been wearing unraveled, each bead scampering away like a freed mouse. As I felt
the compassion, warmth, and love of this old woman, I thought: "Am

I about to die?" She had better plans and began to show me dance steps. I love to dance and, yet, on that day I truly had rubber chicken legs and two left feet and a body filled with sand bags! We all laughed, for the harder I tried, the clumsier I got. It was something like watching an old Red Skelton drunk routine! Certainly I was honored by being brought into the circle. Now I suspect the women were vessels of the Dark Mother, once more reaching in, pulling the Dark Bride into the light of day.

The mystical aspects made me realize that, in some ways, my life paralleled the myth I subscribed to regarding Magdalene as a whore and a woman possessed by evil spirits, a woman not quite worthy to be in the Beloved's presence. I can humbly admit that in the beginning of the journey, I was a victim who desired nothing more than to live a life of ascetic sacrifice, a life of physical and emotional deprivation. That was my understanding of what was necessary to be accepted by God and to be loved by my best friend, Jesus. At the near-death experience, what I perceived as betrayal and abandonment was nothing more than a kick off the Cross, a catapult into the universal, chaotic abyss—the place where biological drama, cultural blueprints, and religious imprints get pulverized, then polished into translucent artifacts. Only then can we be restored to memory as divine beings of the cosmos. Throughout the years of the dark night of the soul, the Blessed Mother consistently led me to places, situations, and dreams that demanded the stripping of victim consciousness. Having released that, I could then be ignited into mystic consciousness, a state of being that sings of divine union, co-creation, alignment with the mysteries of the universe. I believe this is a universal process that can burst open cellular memory of creation and help all of us remember who we truly are from deep within the heart of the cosmos.

There will be many faces, many stories of the Magdalene. The image I've been given is Magdalene as embodied mystic, a woman who can dance with chaos and ecstasy, both in the human and other world dimensions. Truly, she rekindles the concept of the direct path to God, to the Universe. My heart leapt with this truth after having the following dream, May, 2000:

> I am aware of being an ancient woman, a Magdalene, dressed in a dark cape. I am observing an idyllic scene in which the Tree of Life is in full bloom and the River of Life is flowing

with the purity of liquid glass. Jesus appears, radiant as a star. I'm aware that he is walking effortlessly with a swirling galaxy in front of him that never touches the ground. It looks like the Milky Way. Jesus and the energy are perfectly attuned to each other, each dancing with unsurpassed grace and elegance. His finger points to the center of the galaxy and telepathically invites me to step in. I look for a way to cross the River, not sufficiently awakened to notice the beautifully arranged stones under the surface. I believe I see a newly-constructed wooden bridge to my right but it is an illusion.

The call to step into a galactic energy that holds immeasurable mystery is almost unfathomable. And yet, I believe, this is the essence of the restored Magdalene, the integrated path of beingness and active mysticism. Neither personally nor collectively can we afford to live from lies of unworthiness, from debilitating stories of not being good enough human beings, from separatist thinking that disconnects us from other sentient beings. Discarding these outmoded rags demands that we choose to live responsibly from a planetary consciousness that contributes to evolution versus the destruction of the planet.

Given the events of September 11, 2001, in New York City, what greater imperative is there than to awaken the Dark Bride from within the cosmic belly of the Dark Mother so that the Feminine can burst into the Divine Flame of Light in the world? Looking back on the experiences of Guadalupe, of Egypt, and of Africa, I perceive them to be microparticles of the deconstructing death and restructuring birth processes we are called to enter at this point in time. How many of us prostitute our lives to false beliefs and created structures to support the lies of dualism and survival of the rich and healthy? Have not our various cultures prostituted themselves to the power of competition, superiority, domination, and pride? Collectively, we are enmeshed in a victim consciousness of "you did this to me, I am right, you are wrong, and I will destroy you because you are evil." This kind of myopic, arrogant thinking will serve only to continue the reign of control that suppresses and denies the existence of the feminine and a co-creative rebirth for the planet.

The patriarchal system erected the World Trade Center's twin towers, brilliant slabs of architectural splendor, shimmering lines of perfection. And yet, how distant from the lives of the ordinary people, how removed from the co-creative processes with Life. The smoldering rubble of twisted steel and flesh has returned to Ground Zero, the heart and belly of the Cosmic Mother. She now holds our folly, our ignorance, our wounding, our sorrow—and rebirth. This time we cannot afford to return to the masculine design of "square one." Consider the following message from the Dark Mother I received in a shamanic journey, on September 11, 2001:

> *If you look closely, you'll see that I am descending into the space that you call the planet. I am catching and holding the fragments of destruction and forming new circles of creation. Towers dominate. Circles contain, form, and move with the rhythms of the Universe. Don't think for a moment that I am blind to your situation. I have unseen eyes that connect to dimensions beyond your human comprehension. My heart knows all. Yes, I see a cosmic explosion and I see an expansion of the global heart. Now is the time for the planetary Soul to evolve. Divinity is breaking through the human spirit, birthing consciousness. Terrorism cannot destroy Spirit—it cannot split a soul that is wrapped in my Truth, my Compassion, and my Love. Continue to take on the wings of Life, breathe my Life. Stay awake and be my breath.*

What will the new world look like, a world in which earthlings receive and accept the kiss of the Divine within their beingness? Perhaps the following dream about 9/11 can offer some insight:

> *There is a large, blimp-sized turd flying in the air. It is shedding a layer of white ash, revealing a huge vein of fresh, living blood wrapped around it. I am asked by Spirit to be the driver of this turd and am taken to New York, Ground Zero. The turd descends into the center of the Twin Towers rubble, dissolving into the earth, bringing me to a new city—a lost city. There are many souls to be released that I am guided to take care of. Suddenly, the Dark Mother appears, an apparition of smoke and light. She tells me to step aside as she magnetically raises the transformed turd/city above Ground Zero. The turd is now a beautiful, golden-brown city, where all the buildings are the same size, where all is peaceful, where all greenery*

begins to flourish, where all rivers shine with sunlight parti-
cles, where everyone is part of a community that supplies the
needs of every member.

Certainly, this dream goes beyond a personal perspective and is the culmination of the message in the May, 2000 dream in which the
Magdalene woman is asked to remember and become one with Life.
Once birthed, once we are awakened to the authenticity of our nuclear
self, then all that we are, all the fertilizer that has been produced from
our false self, is returned to the earth—our commitment to be interde-
pendent with all elements of the Earth and the universe. New forms
arise from turds if we are willing to be formed by them, willing to
believe in the power of living, willing to take the ride, rather than
attempt to control destiny. I believe we are at a critical point in evolution and we, as humans, have the key to transform the dynamics if we
return to the knowing of the original flaring forth of our existence fifteen billion years ago. We are the stardust of that stupendous ball of
fire and, if we are to remember this, we have to surrender, in humility,
to the rhythm of the universe. The creativity we have used for personal
gain and status would become manure that nourishes the greater
earthly community: conservation issues; redistribution of wealth;
organic living and altering life styles, to name a few. To remember
Source is also to live a spirituality that breathes with dreams, absorbs
silence, and commits to life. In other words, the key is returning to the
memory of planetary consciousness, a perspective that calls and honors the power of the mystic, the power of the Dark Bride who says
"Yes" to the dance from within the Dark Mother and dances in the
world as Light.

At First:
A Journey with the Black Madonna
into Her Initiatory Playground
—The Unconscious Mind

Toni G. Boehm

Rev. Toni G. Boehm, Ph.D., is an author, nurse, minister, and teacher on spirituality and mysticism. She is the Dean of Administration for Unity School of Religious Studies at the world headquarters of Unity School of Christianity, Unity Village, Missouri. She is the author of numerous articles and books: *The Spiritual Intrapreneur* (Dorrance, 1996); *One Day My Mouth Just Opened: Reverie, Reflections and Rapturous Musings on the Cycles of a Woman's Life* (Inner Visioning Press, 2000); and *Embracing the Feminine Nature of the Divine: Integrative Spirituality Heralds the Next Phase of Conscious Evolution* (Inner Visioning Press, 2001).

Collectively, we are embarking upon an exploration of the archetypal guardians we know as the Black Madonnas. The ideas and experiences that are related to the Black Madonna and Her feminine nature tend to be very subtle at times. Sometimes while reading, praying, or meditating, a person may experience body sensations of hot or cold, or a rapidly beating heart, or just feeling anxious or disturbed.

There are reasons for this. For example, a person may be connecting on a cellular level with what I like to call Living Ancestral History. There was a time in ancient history when God or the Divine was revered as a feminine image. This history lives on a cellular level. Such memories are alive within our collective unconscious and are a living part of our ancestral cellular history. The subtle messages, then, that come to us in our private moments may be awakening these repressed memories.

It is accepted now that long ago, in a place far away, the Divine was wrapped in a feminine mantle. She exuded fecundity, roundness, and a largeness of body that was exemplified by Her pendulous breasts whose sacred liquid was believed to feed the mortals. This sacred female portrait of the Divine offered the people of Her time protection, comfort, simple love, heartfelt compassion, a listening ear, and a sense of equality for all who entered Her domain. Her chronometers were said to be moon cycles and menstrual cycles along with seasonal turnings.

The richness inherent in the blackness and darkness of the soil, caves, and night, as well as women's bodies, were held sacred since they were recognized as womb-like places where growth and life began. Hallowed images of the goddess who bore many names abounded. They could be found everywhere one looked since Her domain was Earth, itself. Her symbols were images from nature, snakes, leopards, birds, cows, and many more. Hers was an earth-based sense of spirituality. A spirit of mutual cooperation was at the core of Her feminine-dominated thought forms.

The awareness of this kind of ancestral history can challenge and disturb our deepest beliefs that have been shaped by those who have had the greatest impact on our lives such as family, minister, priest, rabbi, friends, teachers, as well as the prevailing cultural values. We are now in a time of re-examining these prevailing beliefs alongside the new understanding of our past and then facing the difficult questions our belief systems will present.

To understand the significance of the re-emergence of the Black Madonna and the feminine nature of the Divine, we need an historical perspective on humanity's approach to the religious life and spirituality in the past.

Human history over the last 50,000 years has been one of vast pendulum swings. The feminine image of God evolved into consciousness about 50,000 years ago, with the inception of the Paleolithic era. This perception of God as feminine continued on throughout the Neolithic period (10,000–4,000 B.C.E.). Goddess worship corresponded to a relatively peaceful and cooperative era during which little advance was made scientifically, culturally, or technologically. However, within the Neolithic era there was a shift in thinking that began to bring about more masculine and feminine images as seen in multiple governing deities. With the dawn of the Bronze Age around 4,000 B.C.E., divinities of war and conquest began to supplant the Goddess. The Bronze Age brought the ability to create weapons of much greater destruction, and along with that ability came the intention and desire to use those weapons to conquer and gain power over others. This new consciousness that was being forged around weapons and warfare replaced the existing cooperatively-spirited society. The older society that was based on the feminine-dominated thought forms of equality, interrelatedness, nature, sharing, and cooperation gave way to the masculine-dominated thought forms of power, building, owning, having, and doing. The countenance of the Goddess who was known by many names would now give way to and be conditioned by the masculine archetype. With this shift in consciousness, both the Sacred Feminine and women lost their standing in the community. Woman was reduced to a state of being a possession rather than an equal with whom to share life.

This enormous shift in viewing the world eventually came to be reflected to an even greater extent within the doctrines of the religious institutions. The invention of writing corresponded to the shift in thinking that the Bronze Age brought. This new ability as it was refined and honed helped to create a mode of communication that would influence greatly the development of a new religion that was soon to be born. It might be said that the ability to write and to give form to thoughts on paper/papyrus, was the final nudge that helped to give God a masculine face.

I believe that as a species, we are ready to evolve to a higher level of consciousness. To do this we first must recognize the gifts that the Black Madonna—the feminine nature of the Divine—has to offer to the masculine-oriented spirituality of the world. This process will require a new paradigm of thinking, which I call "Integrative Spirituality."

Integrative Spirituality is the next major step on the path of consciousness evolution. It engenders a balance of the masculine and feminine aspects of the Divine within the psyche of humankind. From this state of consciousness, physical survival and spiritual growth take place simultaneously. In order to find this internal place of balance, we must first be willing to enter the sacred darkness of the unconscious mind. Here we can find the opportunity for our own integration of the masculine and feminine and thus lay the ground for its integration in the world itself.

Often an awareness of the Divine Feminine or an interest in the idea of learning to live in the world from the wisdom of the heart is a signal that the psyche is prepared for a purification process that will ultimately conceive the newborn Self. This purification process or "burning" begins to rend the shadow sides of the personality, the veils of illusion, that have been used to conceal the ancient indigenous wisdom of the soul. Once manifested, the Dark Feminine wisdom will birth an understanding and awareness of the fullness of the Truth of who one is at their deepest core. This is so because Integrative Spirituality expresses the wisdom behind any notion of the Black Madonna.

My Journey

Inherent in the qualities of the archetype of The Black Madonna
is the ability to light blazing fires of change,
to move status quo and to bring death to the old
in order that new may be birthed through you.
However, these shifts in awareness
do not come without a price. The question is;
"Are you willing to pay it?"

I was introduced to the idea of the Black Madonna in the early 1990s. The moment Her name was mentioned to me, my heart leapt. I went on a search to find out more about Her and what it was that She had to offer me. At first, it was a purely intellectual pursuit. I read everything I could find about Her. I reflected on these findings and placed pictures of Her on my altar. I questioned Her reality. "Who are you?" I lamented. "I feel you have something to teach me. What is it?"

On August 4th, 1996, the Black Madonna whispered these words in my heart. In a flash, She became a "living reality" for me. Her spark became a flame, and my life began to change dramatically. These are the words that She spoke to me on that day:

We are One, You and I, not two but One,
Remember Me, return to Me.

Let Me strip away all that is not who you are.
Be willing to be vulnerable, be willing to live in My Mystery.
Let Me lift the veils of illusion from your eyes,
For I have come to awaken you to the depths of your hidden
glory.

From this heart-filled experience, She began to make Herself known to me. She began to pour Herself through me in the form of poems, articles, plays, songs, and more. Consciously, I had never considered myself a creative individual. I had thought, rather, that my skills were more of an administrative character. Now, however, She was soon to turn my world inside-out and upside-down.

From the moment that Her flame began to blaze within my heart, life took on a whole new expression. Unbeknownst to me, I was being prepared to be "burned" in Her sacred fires. With each of the burning-experiences that She graciously brought to me, I was changed at depth, and simultaneously a new layer of Truth about myself was revealed to me. At the end of one of these burning experiences, I wrote imaginatively about entering the realm of the Black Madonna.

At first, I thought that the journey into this realm, the subconscious mind, the Black Madonna's playground, would be fun. I thought it would provide a new thrill of traversing unknown territory and uncharted courses within my being. "Who would be afraid to look at themselves?" I piously inquired. "I will go into your hinterland," I announced smugly. "Take me, I am yours!"

The Black Madonna smiled, took my hand and said, "Come hither then, my sister." Oh, what surprises She had hidden in the depths of the darkness of my unconscious mind. I knew that the underworld of the unconscious was not a territory for one to traverse alone if one is weak of heart, but I knew that I was strong. After all, I was a "power-woman," a "rock" for those around me. I could be counted on.

Dark-skinned Wise Women, members of the Black Madonna's troupe, awaited my arrival as I began to take the first steps into their homeland. Kali, Hecate, Isis, Mary Magdalene, and others, each one, stood waiting in the wings for their turn to share their graces and gifts with me.

How they must have chuckled, for they knew what I would meet as I smugly took my first steps into their sacred terrain. I can hear them now, saying, "She thinks that she understands. She thinks that she is ready. Well, let us help her see who she really is."

Into the darkness I went, arms open. "Here I am. Show me my stuff!" Little did I know how those words would reverberate throughout the universe and be returned to me heaped up, pressed down, and overflowing with my own negative thoughts and emotions and uncomplimentary feelings about myself.

Into the dark, hidden recesses of my mind I went guided by these Dark-skinned Wise Women. They introduced me to new aspects of myself—picture after picture. Like reels of film produced just for me, they revealed how I was living life. I saw how my ego had subtly tricked me into believing that my actions were for the "greater good" or for the good of others when, in reality, they were for my own enhancement and aggrandizement.

Feeling like I always had to be the one in control, Miss Efficiency, always looking good, feeling self-righteous, taking no time to rest because "they" needed me were just a few of the tricks my ego had used to divert me from my true purpose.

That Trickster, the adverse ego, had successfully woven a web of subtle distractions. I was drawn into the web of material attachment, attached unknowingly to the glory that my so-called "success" appeared to bring.

Before me, the Black Madonnas, the Wise Dark Ones, paraded all my "attachments" and "dependencies" for my review. I was stricken with grief and screamed, "No! No! This can't be me! Honestly, I have worked my stuff. I'm good. We must be in someone else's dark inner world." I cried like a baby as I saw all the shadow areas that still lived within me.

As each layer of thick, sticky, murky memories, negative beliefs, hidden emotions, and old, worn-out thoughts were uncovered, waves of anguish undulated throughout my body. "How could this be? I thought I was so far along the path. After years of study and living Truth Principles, this is what I have to show for it?" The realization stabbed at me like a hot poker branding a little calf.

I realized that my ego had subtly built me a faulty pedestal upon which I had installed myself. Now it was crumbling and I was crashing to the ground. Sadness filled me. Tears exploded from my eyes like pellets from a shotgun. Deeper and deeper I spiraled into the abyss of sadness. I felt sadness as I realized how shallow my foundation had been. I grieved for who I thought I was and all the sky-castles I had built. I felt despair because I was afraid it was too late to start over. These thoughts and emotions consumed me. They tugged at me like a child desperate to be held and would not let go. I spiraled inward, deeper than I had ever ventured to go before. Outwardly, I felt as if I was a walking shell. The smug girl in me was gone and, in her place, was one whom I nicknamed, "She Who Cries Easily."

I knew I had to grieve the loss of the "girl" or the "insecure one," in order for the Wise Woman to be born through me. So, cry I did—at home, at work, in meetings, at lunch, talking to my grandchildren on the telephone.

There was no place where tears were not permitted. Besides, I had no choice; the tears were part of the purification and cleansing process. Through this experience, I learned to honor the liquid droplets and to honor my feelings as well.

The stark awareness of my "stupidity" blinded me. For such a long time, I had put my feelings and needs aside so that I could be strong and ready to serve when others beckoned. But this was my time, and it felt good in a painful sort of way.

For weeks I lived like this, immersed in the tension as myriad feelings welled up inside of me. As I began to trust my feelings, I began to desire to get to know them and to recognize what it was that they had come to teach me. Gradually, I understood that I had to make friends with them. I knew that "what you resist persists," so I stopped resisting. I surrendered to the experience.

I did not know my destination, but I knew I was learning. I learned more deeply about my own boundaries, how to say, "No," to my control freak and "Yes" to taking care of myself.

My doctor had told me that I could be nominated or, better yet, that I had attained full-status membership in the "Overachiever Women's Syndrome Club." Oh, how I had laughed when he had said that. Now, looking back over my life, I ponder how true this statement was. I was always trying to prove how good and efficient I was, how I could be counted on. I was not like some of the men who had been in my early life, men who left me to fend for myself, and neither was I like the one who had "hurt" me when I was ten. No, I was not like them. I could be counted on. Suddenly, I realized that this was what I had unconsciously chosen to prove to myself and to the world, namely, that I was willing to be accountable for everything and everyone whether it was required of me or not.

In this state of hurt, my outer wrappings of success, confidence, being a good girl, and more started to come undone. In many ways, these facades had been holding me together, but now it was time to live from another level of awareness.

This shift in consciousness did not happen slowly. Rather, it erupted like a volcanic explosion of awareness. Here were revealed all the tears and lack of energy I felt. They were a part of the release of the pent-up pressure. It was a relief to cast off the outer wrapping. In the uncovering, I discovered that I was free. I was free to be a new version of the real me.

No longer having to be in control of the world, I now invite all of the Black Madonnas and their gifts of the mystery of life and of the unknown to eat at my table and to be my constant companions. From the depths of my heart, I have learned to call forth unconditional Love and to extend it to all I meet. I am no longer afraid of what will happen if I am not orchestrating the band. The depths of the darkness of the unconscious felt cold at first, but it was only because the false coverings, my "old ego friends," that I had been wearing and living really did not provide as much "warmth" as I thought they would.

What I now know is that the *spiritual path is a dynamic energy that comes from beyond and prepares us for the sacrifice of our own soul.* It is a sacrifice that is ultimately a small price to pay for what I received, namely, freedom from the imprisonment of the illusion that I had created about who I thought I was. What I gained was the Truth about my deeper self. I learned about the importance of the dance of the opposites and how to view them in the everyday experiences of life.

What a smug girl I was when I willingly entered the sacred abyss of the unconscious mind, the initiatory playground of the Black Madonna and Her Wise Women! What I found upon my return was that through Her willingness to love me enough and to help me peel away the illusions and the facades about who I thought I was, I found the Truth of who I really am! I recognized my imprisoned splendor and I released it! I found Freedom!

Raise Up Those Held Down: A Pilgrimage to the Black Madonna, Mother of the Excluded, Aparecida, Brazil

China Galland

China Galland, Ph.D., is an author, teacher, activist, public speaker, student of Buddhism and Christianity, and was a wilderness guide. She is the author of *The Bond Between Women, a Journey to Fierce Compassion* (Riverhead Penguin, 1999), *Longing for Darkness, Tara and the Black Madonna* (Penguin, 1991) and *Women in the Wilderness* (Harper and Row, 1980). She is the founder and director of the Images of Divinity Research Project, a work sponsored by the Center for the Arts, Religion, and Education at the Graduate Theological Union in Berkeley, California. Readers may contact her through her website, *www.imagesofdivinity.org*.

> *. . . as black*
> *as the black Madonna,*
> *who answers all prayers from the heart . . .*
> —KATHLEEN NORRIS, *Little Girls in Church*[1]

According to legend, in October 1717, a poor fisherman, Joao Alves, and two companions had been unable to catch any fish in the Paraiba River of Brazil. On the last cast of the day, the fishermen pulled up a net empty but for the broken body of a statue of a Black Virgin Mary. They cast again, and pulled up her head. They named the statue *Aparecida*, which means "appeared." They rejoiced

---

[1] Excerpt from "A Letter to Paul Carroll, Who Said I Must Become a Catholic so that I Can Pray for Him," Kathleen Norris, *Little Girls in Church* (Pittsburgh: University of Pittsburgh Press, 1995). Used by permission.

in finding the Virgin and resolved to keep her, and thereafter their nets were filled with fish. This was the first "miracle" attributed to this Madonna.[2]

This small statue of the Virgin, little more than two feet high, was passed from house to house in procession after this event. More miracles were reported, especially among the poor, and the fame of this Black Virgin began to spread. The devotion to her became so strong that she was declared the Patron of all Brazil.

How a statue of Our Lady of the Immaculate Conception came to be at the bottom of the Paraiba River is the subject of many stories. One of the best-known legends is that she was thrown there to chase away a water serpent who was terrorizing the people. The serpent fled, the Virgin protected her people.

Ivone Gebara, the indomitable, esteemed Brazilian feminist theologian of liberation who writes of this story, notes that the Virgin whom the people threw into the river was white, like the Portuguese colonizers who brought her. Legend holds that the river turned the Virgin black. In the river she lay broken, on the bottom, like the people whom the Portuguese had enslaved and colonized, until the fishermen found her and made her their own.[3]

Aparecida became beloved by those shackled by poverty and slavery for the miracles she performed for them. An 18th-century story credited with helping spread her devotion in Brazil follows:

One day, a slave was traveling with his master near the small shrine that had been constructed for Aparecida. The man entreated his master to stop the wagons and let him pray at the door of the shrine. As soon as he knelt down in the doorway, the heavy chains he wore fell off his hands and feet, and the wide iron collar around his neck broke apart. His master declared him free: the Virgin herself seemed to command it. Word of this event spread rapidly. Though it did little to end slavery, the telling and retelling of the story gained this Virgin an

---

[2] There are numerous tellings of this famous legend. I draw primarily on Ivone Gebara and Maria Clara Bingemer's *Mary: Mother of God, Mother of the Poor* (Maryknoll, NY: Orbis Books, 1989), pp. 154–158.

[3] Gebara, an Augustinian nun who lived with the poor in Recife in the northeast of Brazil, was also a professor of theology, philosophy, and anthropology with a doctorate from the Louvain, in Belgium. She was silenced by the Vatican for two years in the summer of 1995 for her outspoken views on women and the poor. See Gebara and Bingemer, *Mary: Mother of God* for more on the Madonna of Aparecida in the context of liberation theology.

even stronger following as a symbol of liberation among the disen-
franchised and the poor.[4]

In the 20th century, Aparecida became the patron of the black
intellectual movement in Brazil. Bishop-poet Pedro Casaldaliga and
composer-musician Milton Nascimento sing, in their "Praise to
Mariama," of the struggle of black Brazilians in the Mass of the
Quilombos, the settlements formed by runaway and freed slaves in
Brazil. Gebra points out that *ama*, to black Brazilians, means "wet
nurse." Thus "Mariama" is the black woman who nurses and cares for
not only her own children but also the whites, for she is mother to all.
She does not discriminate. It is to Mariama that Brazilians sing this
song from Mary's Magnificat in the Gospel of Luke from the New
Testament, when they say:

Sing on the mountaintop your prophecy
That overthrows the rich and powerful, O Mary,
Raise up those held down, mark the renegades,
Dance the samba in the joy of many feet.

....

Give strength to our Shouts,
Raise our sights,
Gather the slaves in the new Palmares,
Come down once more to the nets of life
Of your black people, black Aparecida.[5]

࿐

The whir of hundreds of doves taking flight echoes in the cavernous
basilica of Aparecida, Brazil's national shrine. It is a basilica reportedly
larger than St. Peter's in Rome, larger even than the Cathedral of St.
John the Divine in New York. Handbells ring out from the altar while
the thick smoke of incense rises in the air. There is a great stir. Seventy
thousand people rise to their feet, waving tiny green Brazilian flags and

---

[4] Slavery was abolished in Brazil in 1888.

[5] Palmares, a city of twenty thousand people in the mountains, was the largest of the *quilombos*, communities of freed and runaway slaves; hence Palmares is like Zion, the promised land
where all are free.

shouting, "*Viva Aparecida! Viva Aparecida! Viva Aparecida!*" The refrain rolls through the basilica like thunder, filling the air. A priest lifts the small black statue of Our Lady of Aparecida high in the air, turning from side to side for all to see.

It is October 12, the Feast of Aparecida, Brazil's Patron. Today is the culmination of nine days of prayer, rosaries, and masses in honor of Aparecida. Hundreds of buses from all over Brazil sit in the oversize parking lots outside. For many, the open baggage compartments of the buses provide their only shelter. For some, this is a pilgrimage made every year; for others, like myself, it is the first time. I meet no other North American in the crowds over the days I spend here at the Canisian Sister's Retreat House near the shrine. I think of Durga's nine-day October feast going on in Nepal and India. The Great Mothers.

An enormous white banner hangs across one of the four naves that open onto the main octagonal altar. The Portuguese words emblazoned high in the air across the western nave in bold black letters are *Aparecida Mae dos Excluidos do Brasil,* "Aparecida Mother of the Excluded of Brazil." Archbishop Dom Aloysius Lorscheider tells me that all who have been marginalized by conventional society are upheld and revered in the figure of this Virgin—the poor, the broken, and the dark. She is their champion. She is black because she is the Mother of All.

This Dark One who champions all that is left out also symbolizes what must be included now. Standing in this basilica amid the shouts for Aparecida, I think of the statue in Benares that I was told was Kali, that set me off on the path to find the Black Madonna. I find the Dark Mother in culture after culture. She weaves a bond that reaches beyond cultures, across time, that gives us back our history with one another. She provides a way across cultures, a bridge. She gives us back not only the connection between the sacred and the world of nature, the body, but she gives us the ground of being, the world-body in which we live with all creatures. She gives us earth, water, air, and fire. Creation. Then goes beyond. Helps us cross over. Is the other side, the river and the shore.

Whoever this Dark One is, whether she appears as Virgin, Mother, Crone, or Queen, she is found underlying tradition after tradition: The Aztec Goddess Tonantsin, at whose site Our Lady of Guadalupe, the

Patron of All the Americas, appeared in Mexico; La Pachamama, the source of all life, beloved by the people of the Andes; Maria Lionza, the mountain goddess of Venezuela; the Egyptian-African Goddess Isis, whose worship spread throughout Europe up until the second and third centuries C.E.; the Hindu Kali, carried from India by the Gypsies on their migrations; the Orishas, brought from Africa to Brazil—she is the ground, she is both the earth itself and the root below. She gives us our depth, the darkness we need to grow. The taller the tree, the deeper the root system. She is also the Tree of Life, this little dark one, *la morenita*, our mother. I too, a white woman, can claim her, the ancient Earth Mother of Old Europe, the indigenous black Caucasian goddess of regeneration and fertility of whom I was told, the Earth Mother who was worshipped in pre-Indo-European Europe when the color black symbolized life and white meant death. We need only examine our own tradition, look beneath; she has been there all along, right under our feet.[6]

Venerated for centuries in great cathedrals around the globe, the Black Madonnas have long been proclaimed to be especially powerful miracle workers and healers. Yet few have commented on the darkness of her face. Some say it was because she survived fires that destroyed all but her, that she was darkened by candle smoke. Could it not be, as I have written before, that she is dark because she enters lives on fire, because she has absorbed so much suffering?

Some say that she is black for no reason, that her darkness means nothing. Others say she is a symbol, an archetype, psyche's shadow. I say she is all these things and also that she is a black woman, a woman of color, a brown woman, a red woman, and more. She is not white. She is more, she includes all colors. She is dark because we come in so many colors, hues, and shades, and none is to be left out.

Like a river, her darkness comes from numerous sources, a multiplicity of streams. She surfaces in European and Near Eastern sites where black meteorite stones fell out of the sky and were then venerated. She rises by healing waters, streams, rivers, and deltas. In some

---

6 See Mary Judith Ress's essay, "After Five Centuries of Mixing, Who Are We? Walking with Our Dark Grandmother's Feet," in Rosemary Radford Ruether, ed., *Women Healing the Earth: Third World Women on Ecology, Feminism, and Religion* (Maryknoll, NY: Orbis Books, 1996) pp. 51–61.

places she is associated with storms, lightning, and thunder. Her waters are fed by streams of a tradition in which black symbolized Wisdom; the Womb of God; the world of medieval mystics; the Womb of Enlightenment from the East, from Africa; the Root; Wisdom Herself. She is rising to remind us that what we call darkness is invisible light—that 90 percent of what is, is invisible. That darkness matters, is to be valued, treasured.[7]

The image of the Black Madonna, the Dark Mother, is arising in the human psyche now because we need her. Images of the sacred are vessels, containers. They function as portals, doorways, porous membranes through which the unseen world can pour. What we need now is an awareness of the indivisibility of our relationship with each other—peoples of all races, nationalities, ethnicities, and classes—and with the Earth and all her creatures. We suckle and feed upon her, this planet we share. We are completely dependent upon our relationships. We are dying because we leave out our relatedness—with the Earth and with one another.

The shouts for Aparecida reach a new crescendo. The priest is taking her from the altar and elevating her again for the crowd to see, this little Dark One, this Black Mary. Suddenly I remember Gabriel and his answer to Mary when she asked him how she could conceive a child: "The Holy Spirit will come upon you, and the power of the Most High will cover you with its shadow. And so the child will be holy and will be called Son of God," he told her (Luke 1: 35).

The Black Madonna is also Mary at the moment of conception, impregnation, when she was shadowed by God. It was God's shadow that made the child holy, His darkness. This is what it looks like to be covered by God.

The crowd goes wild as the priest holds Aparecida aloft, turning slowly in all four directions, then finally plunges down the red carpeted steps for the long walk to the end of the eastern nave of the basilica. The priest slowly makes his way down the long aisle with the Virgin, holding her up for people to see and touch. The glare of

---

[7] See China Galland, *Longing for Darkness: Tara and the Black Madonna* (New York: Viking/Penguin, 1990/1991) for a fuller discussion of this subject.

television lights is blinding; he makes his way patiently, pale and per-
spiring.

The faithful strain against heavy velvet ropes, their hands out-
stretched to touch, if they are lucky, the statue as it passes by. If not,
they seem equally happy to receive her graces from a distance. People
hold up babies, rosaries, little statues of Aparecida, bottles of holy
water, slips of paper with thanks or requests for miracles. Whatever
they have brought, they wave high in the air for Aparecida to bless.
The priest turns when he reaches the end of the red carpet and slowly
makes his way back up the aisle to return her to the altar.

Is there an upstart in the crowd? A young woman in cream-
colored pants and top with a pale purple scarf around her neck follows
the priest to the altar, takes the microphone, and begins to walk
around, speaking passionately to the enormous crowds on all four
sides of the altar. She speaks with her whole body, pacing back and
forth across the altar, of the "Excluded" to whom Aparecida is the
Mother. And as she speaks, an old, dark woman wearing a gray skirt,
black slippers, and a scarf over her head begins the long walk down
the aisle to join her on the altar. Just behind the old woman, thirty feet
or so, is a slender, attractive, well-made-up woman in skin-tight black
pants, with a bright red, sequined, body-hugging top and black, spiky
high heels. Behind her is a tall young woman in a blue jumper, at least
eight months pregnant, holding her stomach. I don't know why they
are doing this. Next, in this surprising procession, is a man in the
striped suit of a convict, followed by a man in a hospital gown, holding up a bottle of IV fluid for the tube that runs into his arm. As they
walk slowly single-file down the nave of the basilica to the altar, they
stop every few steps to hold up their hands and cross their wrists as
though they are in chains.

Once they reach the altar, they climb up the steps and turn away
from one another, each finding a place to stand alone with their backs
to one another on the octagonal altar, creating a vivid tableau of the
Excluded, the forgotten and the rejected. The convict comes forward
as the woman in the purple scarf narrates. She tells us that he is a man
trying to start his life over, that he is unable to find work, that no one
will give him a chance. The woman in red now steps forward. She represents the women and girls who are forced into prostitution to merely
survive. Next the hospital patient, who represents the people ravaged

by AIDS whom no one will touch or acknowledge. All the members of the tableau move away from him with gestures of fear of contagion. The pregnant woman represents the young mothers with babies, left to fend for themselves, abandoned by society. The old woman stands for the elderly who are left out and ignored, discarded. I am spellbound. This is a service such as I've never seen. The entire basilica of seventy thousand people is hushed, the truth of what is being depicted on the altar so fully recognized.

A young man in a white robe, representing Christ, then approaches and embraces each person in a simple liturgical dance. He draws the Excluded around him into a circle and gives the old woman the statue of Aparecida. The mood of the tableau shifts dramatically. The sorrow of the Excluded is suddenly transformed. The old woman holding the Madonna becomes the center of the circle. She turns and turns, radiant and laughing, on the altar, holding the Black Madonna high in the air as Christ and the circle of the Excluded move counter-clockwise, dancing, around her. The congregation explodes in applause.

It is fitting that it is the old woman who holds the Madonna aloft. The wisdom of her devotion shines in her face as she dances before thousands and thousands of people. She is a sister to Indramaya, the old woman who danced at the Devi's in Kathmandu last October. My heart leaps now, as it did when Indramaya danced, leaps at the sight of this old woman, encircled by a love that excludes no one. She turns and dips, and waves the Virgin. "*Viva Aparecida!*" we all shout, rising to our feet, hands in the air, flags waving, shouting louder and louder, "*Viva Aparecida! Viva ApareciiiiiiiiiiidAAA!*"

I think of the women I've seen in churches around the world, pray-ing before the altar of the Madonna. Many times there might be no one in the church but the old women. They care for the altar, bring the fresh flowers, trim the candles, embroider the vestments and the altar cloth. As I watch this old woman dancing, it occurs to me that these women have been doing something important for everyone. Through their prayers and devotion, through their practice of the Rosary— telling the story of Mary's life with Jesus, over and over—they have been keeping Mary alive, they have been honoring her. Wisdom itself. They have been upholding the feminine face of God.

Women uphold the feminine face of God.

Yet, before the day's celebration comes to an end outside with singing and dancing, the priests are exhorting people to "be more like Mary . . . be obedient, reasonable, serene." Above all obedient. Once again, I see how the devotion to Mary can be full of ambiguity and used by the Church to control people, especially women.

Does anyone praise Mary for her fierce side? It exists. Consider the Mary who praised God for bringing down the mighty, the Mary of liberation, the Mary who agreed to bear a child under circumstances which she could not explain, for which she could have been stoned or ostracized, the Mary who was a refugee, who rose in the night, took up her child to flee to Egypt with only Joseph and his dream. Consider the Mary who entered the bastion of the temple, the one who spoke publicly, who chided her son, held him accountable. The Mary who raised a rabble-rouser. The Mary who watched her son be beaten, humiliated, nailed to the cross; who watched him die and who kept standing; who bore witness, powerful witness; who withstood the pain and then kept going. The Mary who went on, some say, to lead the Apostles. This is a woman of towering strength. Mary as the Black Madonna, the Dark One, carries this earthy, fiery energy.

Now I feel ready to go to Argentina, to Laura Bonaparte and the Mothers of the Disappeared, to the Madres de la Plaza de Mayo Linea Fundadora. Seeing the old woman dancing touches something in me, taps an energy. Now I'm more eager than ever to be with women who embody this energy in the world.

The old woman dancing on the center of the altar, holding up the Black Madonna, is prophetic and victorious.

The Underground Stream

Edward Bilous

Composer and educator, Edward Bilous is the chairman of the Literature and Materials of Music Department and founding director of the Music Technology Center at the Juilliard School. He is also the cofounder and director of *Beyond The Machine, A Festival of Electronic and Interactive Music* in New York. Bilous is a nationally-recognized expert in the field of arts education and has conducted classes and seminars at the Lincoln Center Institute, The Tanglewood Institute, The Philadelphia Orchestra, Teachers College–Columbia University, The Leonard Bernstein Center for Arts and Education, Chamber Music America, Bowling Green University, The State University of New York in Albany and The Center for Creativity, Zermatt, Switzerland. Among his recent compositions are, *Portraits of Grief*, a tribute to the victims of the September 11th, 2001 tragedy commissioned by *The New York Times*, *Chaconne for String Orchestra* recorded by the Prague Film Orchestra for the Academy Award-nominated documentary *Scottsboro* and *Frame of Reference* written for frame drum master Glen Velez.

Coinciding with the publication of this book, Ed Bilous' *The Underground Stream* is the first of a planned series of musical works called *Archetypes*. It explores an archetype that has been at the core of human imagination since prehistory. Using texts and images culled from both ancient and modern sources, *The Underground Stream* reveals a hidden link between the Gnostic traditions of the Western world, including Judaism, Christianity and Islam.

The Underground Stream is a cantata for female soloists with chorus and an ensemble of classical, folk, and electronic instruments. The texts are sung in several languages, including Arabic, Aramaic, Catalan, Farsi, Hebrew, Ladino, Latin, and Provencal. Although not required for performance, the work can support a sensitive and informed theatrical staging or choreographic interpretation.

Prelude

There is a psychological and spiritual dimension to our world that cannot be understood through reason alone, but needs to be experienced directly through feelings, dreams, and intuitions. This larger reality is woven through our lives like the subtext of a great play. Once we become attentive to it, even the simplest of acts resonates with a greater sense of purpose and the smallest object becomes a metaphor for the world.

Four years ago, I had my first conscious encounter with the image of a Black Madonna. I immediately recognized her as a metaphor for psychological and spiritual energies that had motivated a great deal of my work both as an artist and a teacher. Eventually, I came to realize these forces have been familiar to me since earliest childhood. This essay is a brief history of my connection to this ancient archetype and how she ultimately became the focus of a musical composition, *The Underground Stream*.

Beginnings

The Watchung Reservation is a small forest in central New Jersey named after a tribe of Native Americans vanquished by European settlers more than two and a half centuries ago. Tombstones marking the graves of Revolutionary War heroes are scattered about the forest like old apple trees in an abandoned orchard. Stone walls that once served to protect colonial farms from the dangers of the forest now serve as highly-valued lawn ornaments in a continuum of suburban development stretching from New York to Pennsylvania.

I grew up in a small house on the edge of the reservation in a little town ambitiously called Mountainside, which is situated on the first hill of any significance west of New York City. Not far from my house was a watchtower built by the local fire department during the Great Depression. On clear days, my friends and I would climb to the top of the rickety tower to monitor the progress on construction of the World Trade Center 50 miles away. "How much bigger could they possibly get?" we wondered as the two towers slowly pierced the eastern sky. Years later, while working as a tour guide in New York, I would find myself on the observation deck of the World Trade Center scanning the western horizon, looking for the little fire tower in Mountainside.

My favorite spot in the forest was a small spring only a few feet wide and, due to its murky bottom, of indeterminable depth. The spring was a constant source of attraction for me. I would often sit on a nearby log and study the water as it trickled up from the dark earth and flowed out over mossy rocks and rotting leaves. Many times, I reached my hand down into the cold mud searching for an opening that I was certain would lead to a great cave or underground passage filled with treasures from precolonial times. Although I never found the cave or any secret treasures, I always believed that they lay hidden somewhere under the forest floor.

I was not the only one interested in the small spring. The trees surrounding it were filled with birds of every sort. Footprints of a red fox and raccoon could be found in the mud, and trappers, hoping to snare them, left instruments of torture and death chained to a nearby tree. Every time I visited the spring, I pulled the traps and threw them in the bramble of thickets until eventually the trappers gave up and never returned.

Despite my young age, it was clear to me this small spring was a magical place, a place of natural beauty and power. It was there I first considered the forest and all the life it contained as an intricate web in which everything seemed to be connected to everything else. I longed to be part of that magical community, and at times I would imagine I could understand the secret language of the birds and the wind. Yet, however hard I tried, I knew I could never be more than a visitor to this place. More than once I found myself overcome with fear and would run as fast as I could to the security of home, where my mother would be working in the kitchen.

Many years later, after I had grown and my family had left New Jersey, I returned to the wooded hillside where I lived as a boy. Much of the forest near my home had been eviscerated by a superhighway designed to save minutes of valuable commuting time for workers heading to Manhattan. Wetlands were paved over, and the cold water, which for millennia flowed up from the dark, muddy spring, now dripped out of the sides of rock cliffs, carved by giant excavating equipment. I looked at the area that was once home to my sacred spring and wondered whether the men operating the earth-moving machinery had discovered any secret treasure or the entrance to an underground cave.

Images from childhood are powerful because they are metaphors for our first encounters with the primary forces of life. Like ancient icons kept in the basement of a museum, they are stored deep in our memory. With time, this gallery of images evolves to form the vocabulary of a symbolic language our unconscious uses to speak with us. It is a language we first hear in our dreams and visions and eventually come to understand through feeling and intuition. It is this language of images and metaphors that gives our life a sense of continuity and of communion with our ancestors.

The experiences I had in my childhood at the little spring were a reenactment of experiences our ancestors had during the childhood of mankind. To ancient man, images of darkness resonated with profound meaning. For just as the sun is born of the night, so, too, does life flow from the dark earth. Darkness represents the beginning and the end of the cycle of creation, the incomprehensible source of all life, and the inevitability of death.

As the mysteries of the human genome are gradually revealed, we have come to learn the original "Mitochondrial" Eve, biological mother of all humanity, was a dark-skinned woman from Africa. We have also come to understand that the first manifestation of the Divine was not as a God, but as a Goddess, the Great Mother Earth, and she, too, was black. Black Madonnas are recent manifestations of the Great Mother, *Anima Mundi*, and as such, are connected to primal forces from our collective past. Many of the most venerated were, according to legend, not carved by artists, but found in the hollow of an old tree, in a cave, or near a spring deep in the forest.

The association between darkness and divinity evolved for thousands of years and eventually came to represent far more than fertility and the power of creation. To the descendants of Abraham it became a metaphor for the incomprehensible, unknowable face of God. The story of creation from The Old Testament tells us that before there was light, God existed in darkness. Thousands of years later, the Sephardic Jews of Andalusia would reaffirm God's connection to darkness in one of the most elegant metaphors for Divine Manifestation ever created, the "Tree of Life," from the sacred Kabbalah. The Tree of Life is a geometrical design consisting of 10 Sefiroth, or Emanations, that represent the path through which God's creative energy flows as it descends from a plane of cosmic perfection to the earthly realm. Suspended above the Tree of Life are three veils where light was born, *Ain, Ain Sof*, and *Ain Sof Aur*. Beyond that we find God's original face, and again, it exists in incomprehensible darkness.

While traveling the vast expanse of the Sahara Desert, early followers of the Prophet Mohammed also found a connection between

God and darkness. For in their attempt to illuminate the black of night with nothing but a campfire, they saw a metaphor for the struggle to understand God's omnipresence with only the light of reason to guide them. Similar analogies can be found in Christianity as well. St. John of the Cross spoke of the "Dark Night of the Soul" as the last step of a mystic's journey before achieving union with God, and the 14th-century mystic William Johnson referred to "Divine Darkness" and the "Cloud of Unknowing."

All human beings have an innate attraction to darkness. Not the black evil of a Hollywood horror story, but the darkness that is home to our unexpressed longings and desires. Darkness is the most direct metaphor for what we have not yet dared to think or what we are afraid to feel. It is the color the soul uses to paint our unconscious yearnings. Because much of what we learn through intuition and feeling may conflict with the teachings of religion and the values of our society, a tradition of fear prohibits us from exploring the shadows of our unconscious. Indeed, many religions have made darkness a synonym for evil in a naive attempt to subdue human imagination and silence our quest for self-understanding and truth. History is filled with an entire genealogy of demons created by man to serve as soldiers in God's army. As human consciousness has unfolded, we have come to understand evil is not an independent malevolent force, but rather a concept we created to hide our fears, hatred, prejudices, and misunderstandings.

It is important to note that many of the most well-known symbols of malevolence, including the night, the moon, and the darkness of the forest, as well as our sensual and erotic yearnings, were originally associated with the Mother Goddess. Indeed, Nature Herself was considered a consort of the devil, and women in general were known keepers of diabolical powers. The association of the feminine with evil still continues today in many parts of the world. Even after the demise of the Taliban regime in Afghanistan, a teenage girl, who became pregnant after being raped by her brother-in-law, was charged with tempting the man into committing acts of infidelity. The tribal court found her guilty and sentenced her to death by stoning. In another, similarly horrible incident, a young man made the fateful mistake of publicly declaring his love for a woman of a higher social class. In punishment for the insult he brought on the girl's family, the tribal court condemned the man's fourteen-year-old sister to violation by the entire council of tribal elders. The shame of the loss of the young girl's virginity would have made her ineligible for marriage and caused a permanent stain on the family name. Fortunately, thanks to broad international appeal, both women were spared their punishments.

How tragic it is that the Feminine Divine has become a source of so much fear. We can only imagine how different our history would be if the sun and the moon were allowed equal reign over our hearts and minds, and the Great Mother shared the throne with God the Father. No single image speaks of this epic loss more eloquently than the Black Madonna.

Becoming an Artist

I left home at the age of 18 and moved to New York to study music and become a composer. I paid my rent by working in the gift shop at the Cathedral of St. John the Divine, selling laminated pictures of Jesus and alabaster statues of the Virgin. At the time, I had not yet developed an interest in religious art, otherwise I might have paid more attention to the reproduction of the Black Madonna of Czestochowa that hung just off the nave of the cathedral. A replica of the Black Madonna of Montserrat stands in a similar location in the Church of St. Ignatius Loyola on Park Avenue, where the funeral for Jacqueline Onassis Kennedy was held and where Sir Paul McCartney, composer of "Let It Be," recently performed.

One summer, an anthropology professor of mine invited me to the Museum of Natural History to see an exhibition of prehistoric art that she thought I would be interested in. The exhibition featured a wonderful collection of artifacts, including a small, rotund fertility goddess and replicas of the paintings found on the cave walls at Lascaux.

At the far end of the exhibition hall was a small glass case, which, to my astonishment, contained a wooden flute and drum dating back thousands of years before the pyramids were built and before words were first written. What an extraordinary revelation it was for me to learn that in a time when every human effort was part of the struggle for survival, people felt the need to make music! For the first time in my life, I had a sense of the profound role the arts play in our lives and in the evolution of consciousness.

The arts emerged from the ancient wellspring of feeling and emotion and were among the first concrete manifestations of human imagination. By their very nature, the arts are children of the Great Mother. Through them, we reenact the miracle of creation and participate in the mystery of the sacred life cycle. The making of art begins when we are attentive to the thoughts and feelings that rise up from the darkness of our unconscious. By nurturing those feelings, we allow them to grow and unfold. In turn, they cultivate our imaginations and deepen our understanding of ourselves and of the world we live in.

The arts are the ancient voice of the human soul. We know from the study of egalitarian cultures around the world that shamans and healers are often singers and dancers as well. Their ability to "see" beyond the ordinary to the extraordinary is enhanced through sounds, images, and movement. In fact, their wisdom is often expressed in the form of a sacred song or dance. Throughout history, artists have described the process of making art as *participating* in a greater reality. Composers from Bach to Stravinsky thought of themselves not solely as creators, but as agents of God's will.

Because they have no fixed meaning, the arts must be experienced directly in order to be understood. Like the luminous veil that crowns the Tree of Life, the arts form a bridge between the light of the known and the darkness not yet known. Creating and encountering works of art is a dynamic and interactive process that is in a constant state of flux. Artists have often noted that during the process of creation their material has as much effect on them as they have on it. Likewise, the perceiver of a work of art seems to constantly re-create the object, just as the object seems to change the way the perceiver *sees*. Einstein clearly understood the dynamic relationship between the creator and the created when he said, "what we observe is not nature, but nature exposed to our method of questioning."

In the last century we witnessed the phenomenal rise of mass media, and with it, the creation of the entertainment industry and commercial art. The entertainment industry has had a profound effect on our culture. Like many industries, the criterion for success is less dependent on the quality of the products made than the quantity of products sold. In order to reach the widest possible audience, commercial art must play to our most basic drives, not on our loftiest ideals. The tragic result is that depth of feeling is often sacrificed for immediacy of sensation; self-understanding becomes confused with self-interest, and pornography is mistaken for passion. Gradually, our appreciation of the transformative power that a great work of art can have on our lives is being lowered, and in the process, we are denying ourselves one of life's deepest pleasures.

The powerful influence of mass media has also affected the quality of our home life and educational system. In the many years I spent working in arts education I've spoken with scores of teachers who lamented about being required to adopt curriculums that are easily evaluated on standardized tests, but do not encourage imagination or creativity, nor do they cultivate a student's inner life. This tendency is reinforced at home where students spend hours passively watching TV or playing electronic games. But television does not require that we participate—only that we observe—and, while some skill is needed to play electronic games, imagination is not. Mass media has dulled our sensitivity to the sound of our inner voice and the creative needs of our imagination. Indeed, television has become the modern-day Medusa, turning the hearts and minds of those who watch her into stone.

In order to reverse the steady decline in our educational system, we must adopt curricula that integrate traditional academic studies with the kind of non-linear, creative work regularly done by artists. For every learning experience is a creative act requiring imagination and nothing encourages the use of imagination better than the making and participating in a work of art. An encounter with a great work of art thrusts us out of the constraints of linear modes of thinking into the realm of possibilities. It forces the light of the conscious mind to come into contact with the potentials hidden in the darkness of the unconscious.

First Encounter

My first conscious encounter with a Black Madonna occurred while I was researching the connections between Gnostic traditions of Judaism, Christianity, and Islam for a choral work I wanted to compose. I felt particularly drawn to the part of Europe extending from Provence to Granada where, for several centuries, followers of these great faiths coexisted in relative peace and shared cultural and religious ideas and values. That area nurtured the creation of the

Kabbalah, alchemy, the tarot, the troubadour movement, and several monastic orders, including the enigmatic Knights Templar.

While scanning through a collection of images of sacred art, I came upon a photograph of the Black Madonna of Montserrat or "La Morenita" as she is affectionately referred to in Barcelona. I was deeply moved by the small, black statue, yet, at the same time, I found her profoundly disturbing. She did not look at all like the tragic figure whose quiet suffering served as a model for women for centuries. Nor did she comply with the traditional ideals of feminine beauty I was so accustomed to seeing in Marian art. Instead, this statue portrays a figure who is powerful and wise and whose commanding presence demands the full attention of her followers. She has the kind of regal majesty that places her on the same plane as her male counterparts. She is not merely Theotokos, Mother of God, she is God.

Shortly after my discovery, I was traveling in Northern California and had brought with me a copy of Fred Gustafson's book, *The Black Madonna*, for holiday reading. I had become deeply interested in the mysterious icon and spent every minute of my free time learning as much about Her as I could. On the final day of my trip, I boarded a shuttle bus to the San Francisco Airport, the Gustafson book in hand. In a remarkable moment of synchronicity, I turned to a photograph of a statue of a Black Madonna in the back of the book just as the bus entered the gates to the Airport (see Plate 1). The caption under the photograph read, "Peace, a sculpture by Beniamino Bufano at the San Francisco Airport."

My exploration of the myth of the Black Madonna took an unexpected turn when I received an invitation to compose the score to *Scottsboro*, a documentary about the famous trial of the same name. Nominated for an Academy Award in 2001, the film tells the story of nine black teenagers wrongly convicted of raping two white women in Alabama in 1931. I was in Los Angeles for the awards ceremony, but privately I was looking forward to the day when I could return home and begin work on what would become *The Underground Stream*. One day, while walking down one of Hollywood's busy avenues, my mind particularly clouded by the prime-time energy that fills the town, I passed a woman organizing some objects for display in the window of an antique shop. As if some magnetic force had taken hold of my free will, I turned and entered the store. To my amazement, standing on a table, ready to be tagged "For Sale—20% Off," was a small wooden statue of Mary with child. By now, her noble stance and imposing gaze had become very familiar to me. With the exception of a few patches on her face where the original color had been worn off, this Madonna was black. I realized at that moment that I did not choose the Black Madonna as the focus of a musical work, she chose me.

The woman in the antique shop told me that she bought the statue at an auction in the South of France, and that it was carved in the late 15th or early 16th century. Although she realized I was very interested in it (and thus sensed a possible sale), she also knew that a worm-eaten, gritty little statue of an aquiline-featured woman with child in tow would not easily find a home in the Hollywood Hills. Some time later, the Madonna and I left the shop together for her new home in the study in my house in Litchfield, Connecticut. Litchfield is also home to the "Shrine of Our Lady of Lourdes," a replica of the famous Grotto in France where the Virgin Mary appeared to Bernadette Soubirous, later canonized St. Bernadette. Bernadette is said to have discovered a magical spring emanating from the place where the Virgin stood.

Several weeks later, in April 2001, Daniel Druckman, percussionist and son of the great American composer Jacob Druckman, asked if I had any works that featured percussion and electronics for a concert he was conducting at the Juilliard School in October. I told him I was developing a work that utilized the forces he was looking for. He asked me if I could finish part of it for a premier in October. I agreed.

An Archetype Set to Music

The abstract nature of the myth of the Black Madonna compelled me to choose the cantata form over other possible musical structures for this work. Unlike opera, a cantata does not require a libretto with a dramatic through-line. It is, instead, a setting of poetic texts for singers, often with chorus, and instruments, that expresses a common theme or subject. The various aspects of the myth of the Black Madonna I wanted to explore were:

I. The Great Mother

II. The Virgin

III. The Rose

IV. Queen of the Heavens, Star of the Sea

V. Mother of Sorrows

VI. The Wanderers

VII. The Underground Stream

The seven themes represent different aspects of the mythology and symbolism of the Black Madonna. The texts are culled from pagan, Judaic, Christian, and Islamic sources and are intended to be sung in the original languages including Arabic, Aramaic, Catalan, Farsi, Hebrew, Ladino, Latin, and Provencal.

The text I chose to set for the Juilliard premier is titled "The Place Light Was Born." It is a meditation on the theme of ecstatic love represented by the young lovers in The Song of Songs of the Old Testament, La Dame of the medieval troubadours, and The Beloved of Sufi mystics. Ecstatic love is used as a metaphor for mystical union with God in all three traditions and is often associated with images of darkness.

The traditions of medieval Persia allowed poets and mystics to use feminine and sometimes erotic imagery when referring to the mystical state of union with God. The troubadours of medieval Europe, however, were under the watchful eye of the Roman Church. Any reference to a feminine aspect of God was strictly forbidden. Likewise, sex was generally considered a sinful act and not a path to spiritual illumination. Poets of medieval Europe had to develop a symbolic language with which to express these ideas. The Black Madonna was their inspiration.

Often credited with starting the troubadour movement, St. Bernard was deeply devoted to Notre Dame. Indeed, his work marks the beginning of a great reawakening to the Feminine Divine in Europe. It is believed that Bernard was familiar with the writings of Sufi mystics and that his devotion to Our Lady was influenced by the passionate imagery of The Beloved. Bernard wrote over 280 sermons on the epic love poem from the Old Testament, the Song of Songs, which begins with the well-known phrase, "I am black but comely." Legend has it he was weaned by a statue of the Black Madonna after his birth mother abandoned him.

I assembled the text for this piece from writings of various Sufi mystics, with the help of a Persian artist and friend of mine. I decided to set the text with chant-like melodies sung by three women and accompanied by an ensemble of 18 musicians performing complex rhythmic patterns similar to those played by drummers of the Mediterranean and North Africa. Both the instrumentation and the style of playing reflect my interest in nonclassical and world music.

In this movement, darkness is a metaphor for the unknowable face of God that existed before Creation, hence the title, "The Place Light Was Born." It also represents the sensual side of human spirituality, long ago repressed in the West, but not forgotten.

THE PLACE LIGHT WAS BORN

You come to me like a dream,
a celestial stream from beyond the stars.

Your unimaginable beauty pours down
through the black emptiness of space,
flowing from the place light was born.

You come to me like the moon
casting love's luminous glow across the garden.

You caress the world like a gentle breeze
filling the night with longing,
awakening ancient memories of universal love.

It is for your love that the night was made,
devouring the naïve certainty of the day.

It is for your love that the stars were made,
bringing visions of peace from the place light was born.

Oh my Beloved! You are the voice of eternal love.
Through you the sun and the moon become one
and the ordinary is once again made sacred.

The Day The World Changed

By September 10, 2001, I was nearly finished composing "The Place Light Was Born." I needed to write only a few measures before I could send the score to my copyist so parts for the musicians could be extracted. Then, on the morning of the 11th, the world changed. For the first time in its history, New York came to a complete stop. Offices, schools, and restaurants were all closed. Meetings and events were cancelled and people fled the city by the thousands. Police officers with high-powered weapons patrolled the streets while a squadron of F-16s streaked back and forth across the sky, and a battleship moved into New York Harbor. By nightfall, the city was immobilized with fear, pain, anger, and confusion.

My studio is three doors down from the main office of the New York City Fire Department and three blocks away from the Armory where the families of people who worked in the World Trade Center had gathered. For days after the attack, I sat looking out my window at the smoke billowing up on the horizon where the two towers once stood. Police sharpshooters were poised on nearby rooftops, sirens screamed day and night, and helicopters raced by in an unending frenzy. The storefronts along the street were covered with pictures of loved ones missing since the disaster, while family members, with candles in hand, kept quiet vigil.

Several days after the 11th, I returned to my work. However, a continuous stream of horrifying images kept running through my mind, and I could not finish the last few measures. I left my studio and went to a local bar to spend some time with other New Yorkers who, for a few short weeks, would be my brothers and sisters.

I sat next to a young woman who was alone, quietly staring at her drink. We began our conversation the way all conversations began at that time, without smiles or hellos, but with a hollow gaze followed by something like, "Unbelievable, isn't it?" or, "Did you know anyone who was there?" After a long pause, she told me her fiancé died in the first tower. "The moment I saw the giant structure collapse," she said, "I knew that he was dead." Her fiancé's name was Freddie. I told her how deeply sorry I was, that I could not image how much pain she was in. "It is all so unbelievable," I said. "What is unbelievable" she replied, "is that my brother was in the other tower when it fell."

238   THE MOONLIT PATH

The alienation and mistrust that fueled the events of September 11th would not have been possible if Jews, Christians, and Muslims saw themselves not as inheritors of the earth, but as children of it, and, as such, brothers and sisters. If we are ever to achieve the peace we dream of, we must regain the sense our ancestors had of the interconnectedness of all things. They believed all life was sacred and worthy of their deepest respect. Until the religions of the world can, once again, make room for the Great Mother at the altar, it will be left to mystics, visionaries, and artists to remind us of the sacredness of life we so easily destroy.

I returned to my office that night, and using the three letters of Freddie's name that corresponded to musical tones F, E, and D, I finished my work. I stopped by the bar the next day and gave the bartender a copy of the page with Freddie's abbreviated name spelled out in notes. "If you ever see her again" I said, "give her this page and tell her I will never forget. "The Place Light Was Born" premiered at the Juilliard School on October 9, 2001.

A few months later, I received a call from New York Times Television, inviting me to compose the musical score to *Portraits of Grief*, a special program dedicated to the memory of the people who died on September 11th. The program is based on the series of the same name that ran in the *Times* for several months after 9/11. The producers of the show told me about a young woman they heard of who lost her fiancé in one of the towers and her brother in the other. They tried to locate her to see if she would agree to share her story on the program. Despite all their efforts, they could not find her.

I returned to the bar almost a year later and found the same fellow working there. He remembered me and said that the young lady I spoke with did return once. He gave her the page of the score I left with him and told her what I said. She thanked him for the message and said that she was certain that Freddie enjoyed the performance.

Some Final Thoughts

Direct contact with archetypal energies can signal dramatic changes in our lives. They bring us face to face with the primary forces of life and demand we become attentive, if only for a moment, to our inner voice. Through my exploration of the myth of the Black Madonna, I've gained an understanding of the powerful effect these forces have on the structure of consciousness. I've also discovered important themes that are woven through the fabric of my life and have learned that on a very deep level, my work as an artist and a teacher are expressions of those same forces.

In *The Undiscovered Self,* Jung wrote, "We are living in what the Greeks called Kairos—the right time—for a 'metamorphosis of the gods.'"[1] We see this transformation taking place today as people of all faiths become sensitive to powerful archetypal energies buried long ago by fear and misunderstanding. They are demanding that religious and political leaders address the spiritual imbalance that permeates our world and poisons our planet. Although this increase in sensitivity and awareness may herald the beginning of a new age in human understanding, much of the world is still filled with mistrust and alienation.

As I write this essay, battle lines are being drawn in the same sand where prophets once walked and armies, divided not by geography but by mythology, prepare for holy war. Yet, as violence and misunderstanding spread, images of the Black Madonna abound and people of all faiths are embracing her with renewed passion and meaning. Indeed, one need only review *The New York Times* in recent years to see that She seems to be everywhere.

She is in the Armenian section of the Church of the Nativity in Jerusalem where a Palestinian woman, who is also a Muslim, reaches up to touch an image of the Virgin Mary. She thanks the Black Madonna for saving her son's life during a recent military siege and asks her to protect him again as he has been exiled from his homeland. *Mirium,* Arabic for Mary, is a revered figure in Islam and the only woman to whom an entire chapter of the Koran is dedicated.

She is on the coast of the Black Sea where a man, grieving the loss of his daughter during an act of political violence, cries out "no man born of a mother could do such a thing." Near by, on the steps of a Byzantine Church, an old woman is selling icons of a Black Virgin.

She is in the Vatican where the pope has convened an emergency conference of American cardinals to discuss the epidemic of pedophilia that plagues the Roman Catholic Church. The pope prays to an image

---

[1] C. G. Jung, *The Undiscovered Self,* R. F. C. Hull, trans. (New York: Little, Brown, 1961), p. 123.

of the Black Madonna of Czestochowa, patron saint of Poland, and asks her help in saving his scandal-ridden church.

She is in India, where scores of Hindu mothers have gathered to pray to the Great Goddess and grieve the loss of their children killed in terrorist attacks by Muslim separatists.

She is in Moscow, where a public outcry has demanded that the word "Fatherland" be removed from the national anthem and replaced with the ancient phrase "Mother Russia." Communist ideologues adopted the term "Fatherland" as a symbol of strength. From the earliest time in European history however, the maternally-oriented Slavs used the term "motherland" to refer to their home while Germanic tribes preferred "fatherland." The presence of the Great Mother is still felt in the mysteries and rituals of the Eastern Orthodox Church.

When I was 14, I traveled with my mother to her native Poland to meet relatives she had not seen since the outbreak of WWII 30 years earlier. The reunion was a bittersweet one, for like those of so many people of her generation, her life was filled with images of inhumanity and indescribable horror. Her first husband was murdered in front of her eyes by a Nazi soldier and her five-year-old son was crushed to death by the sliding doors of a crowded train while in route to a refugee camp. Everywhere we went, she was reminded of the horrible fate that befell so many of her friends and relatives. Of all the places we visited, perhaps none was more important to her then the shrine of the Black Madonna of Czestochowa. While I have little memory of the icon, I do remember how important that visit was to my mother and the rest of her family.

Despite the immensity of her grief and the unending sense of loss, she managed to live her life with great faith and dignity. Her unyielding devotion and depth of feeling have had a profound effect on my life and are a never-ending source of inspiration for my work. This essay is dedicated to her.

The Spiritual Power of Matter

Pierre Teilhard de Chardin

Pierre Teilhard de Chardin, S. J., the scientist-priest, held positions as professor of geology at the Catholic Institute in Paris, director of the National Geologic Survey of China, and director of the National Research Center of France. He lived in China for many years where he played a major role in the discovery of Peking man. He is the author of a number of books including, *The Phenomenon of Man* (Harper & Row, 1964), *The Divine Milieu* (Harper & Row, 1960), and *The Future of Man* (Harper Perennial, 1976). He worked under the auspices of the Wenner-Gren Foundation in New York until his death in 1955. His work continues to be highly respected in both scientific and religious circles.

The following is excerpted from "The Spiritual Power of Matter" in *Hymn of the Universe* by Pierre Teilhard de Chardin (Harper, 1965). Special recognition is given to Georges Borchardt, Inc. for permission to quote from this chapter.

The man was walking in the desert, followed by his companion, when the Thing swooped down on him. . . .

And then the man perceived that the little pale cloud of vapour was but the center of an infinitely greater reality moving towards them without restriction, formless, boundless.

What was advancing towards them was the *moving heart of an immeasurable pervasive subtlety.*

The man fell prostrate to the ground; and hiding his face in his hands he waited.

A great silence fell around him.

Then, suddenly, a breath of scorching air passed across his forehead, broke through the barrier of his closed eyelids, and penetrated his soul. The man felt that he was ceasing to be merely himself; an irresistible rapture took possession of him as though all the sap of all living things, flowing at one and the same moment into the too narrow confines of his heart, was mightily refashioning the enfeebled fibres of his being. And at the same time the anguish of some superhuman peril oppressed him, a confused feeling that the force which had swept down upon him was equivocal, turbid, the combined essence of all evil and all goodness.

The hurricane was within himself.

And now, in the very depths of the being it had invaded, the tempest of life, infinitely gentle, infinitely brutal, was murmuring to the one secret point in the soul which it had not altogether demolished:

"You called me: here I am. Driven by the Spirit far from humanity's caravan routes, you dared to venture into the untouched wilderness; grown weary of abstractions, of attenuations, of the wordiness of social life, you wanted to pit yourself against Reality entire and untamed.

"You had need of me in order to grow; and I was waiting for you in order to be made holy.

"Always you have, without knowing it, desired me; and always I have been drawing you to me.

"And now I am established on you for life, or for death. You can never go back, never return to commonplace gratifications or untroubled worship. He who has once seen me can never forget me: he must either damn himself with me or save me with himself.

"Are you coming?"

"O you who are divine and mighty, what is your name? Speak."

"I am the fire that consumes and the water that over-throws; I am the love that initiates and the truth that passes away. All that compels acceptance and all that brings renewal; all that breaks apart and all that binds together; power, experiment, progress—matter: all this am I.

"Because in my violence I sometimes slay my lovers; because he who touches me never knows what power he is unleashing, wise men fear me and curse me. They speak of me with scorn, calling me beggar-woman or witch or harlot; but their words are at variance with life, and the pharisees who condemn me, waste away in the outlook to which they confine themselves; they die of inanition and their disciples desert them because I am the essence of all that is tangible, and men cannot do without me.

"You who have grasped that the world—the world beloved of God—has, even more than individuals, a soul to be redeemed, lay your whole being wide open to my inspiration, and receive the spirit of the earth which is to be saved.

"The supreme key to the enigma, the dazzling utterance which is inscribed on my brow and which henceforth will burn into your eyes even though you close them is this: *Nothing is precious save what is yourself in others and others in yourself.* In heaven, all things are but one. In heaven all is one.

"Come, do you not feel my breath uprooting you and carrying you away? Up, man of God, and make haste. For according to the way a man surrenders himself to it, the whirlwind will either drag him down into the darkness of its depths or lift him up into the blue skies. Your salvation and mine hang on this first moment."

"O you who are matter: my heart, as you see, is trembling. Since it is you, tell me: what would you have me do?"

"Take up your arms, O Israel, and do battle boldly against me."

The wind, having at first penetrated and pervaded him stealthily, like a philter, had now become aggressive, hostile.

From within its coils it exhaled now the acrid stench of battle.

The musky smell of forests, the feverish atmosphere of cities, the sinister, heady scent that rises up from nations locked in battle: all this writhed within its folds, a vapour gathered from the four corners of the earth.

The man, still prostrate, suddenly started, as though his flesh had felt the spur: he leapt to his feet and stood erect, facing the storm.

It was the soul of his entire race that had shuddered within him: an obscure memory of a first sudden awakening in the midst of beasts stronger, better-armed than he; a sad echo of the long struggle to tame the corn and to master the fire; a rancorous dread of the maleficent forces of nature, a lust for knowledge and possession. . . .

A moment ago, in the sweetness of the first contact, he had instinctively longed to lose himself in the warm wind which enfolded him.

Now, this wave of bliss in which he had all but melted away was changed into a ruthless determination towards increased being. . . .

He dug his feet into the ground, and began his battle.

He fought first of all in order not be to swept away; but then he began to fight for the joy of fighting, the joy of feeling his own strength. . . .

In a reciprocal awakening of their opposed powers, he stirred up his utmost strength to achieve the mastery over it, while it revealed all its treasures in order to surrender them to him.

"Son of earth, steep yourself in the sea of matter, bathe in its fiery waters, for it is the source of your life and your youthfulness.

"You thought you could do without it because the power of thought has been kindled in you? You hoped that the more thoroughly you rejected the tangible, the closer you would be to spirit: that you would be more divine if you lived in the world of pure thought, or at least more angelic if you fled the corporeal? Well, you were like to have perished of hunger.

"You must have oil for your limbs, blood for your veins, water for your soul, the world of reality for your intellect: do you not see that the very law of your own nature makes these a necessity for you?

"Never, if you work to live and to grow, never will you be able to say to matter, 'I have seen enough of you; I have surveyed your mysteries and have taken from them enough food for my thought to last me for ever.' I tell you: even though like the Sage of sages, you carried in your memory the image of all the beings that people the earth or swim in the seas, still all that knowledge would be as nothing for your soul, for all abstract knowledge is only a faded reality: this is because to understand the world knowledge is not enough, you must see it, touch it, live in its presence and drink the vital heat of existence in the very heart of reality.

"Never say, then, as some say: 'The kingdom of matter is worn out, matter is dead': till the very end of time matter will always remain young, exuberant, sparkling, new-born for those who are willing.

"Never say, 'Matter is accursed, matter is evil': for there has come one who said, 'You will drink poisonous draughts and they shall not harm you,' and again, 'Life shall spring forth out of death,' and then finally, the words which spell my definitive liberation, 'This is my body'. . . .

"Oh, the beauty of spirit as it rises up adorned with all the riches of the earth!

"Son of man, bathe yourself in the ocean of matter; plunge into it where it is deepest and most violent; struggle in its currents and drink of its waters. For it cradled you long ago in your preconscious existence; and it is that ocean that will raise you up to God". . . .

The Stroke—
Discovering the Feminine

Father Bede Griffiths

Fr. Bede Griffiths, S. J., was a Benedictine monk who spent the last 37 years of his life in an ashram in India, welcoming people of all religions. He is the author of several books including *The Golden String* (1992), *The Marriage of East and West: A Sequel to the Golden String* (1992), *The Other Half of My Soul: Bede Griffiths and the Hindu-Christian Dialogue* with Beatrice Bruteau (1996), *The Cosmic Revelation* (1994), and *The New Creation in Christ* (1994). He died in India in 1993. The following comprises excerpts from the chapter of the same title in *A Human Search: Bede Griffiths Reflects on His Life* edited by John Swindells (Liguori, MO: Triumph Books, 1997), reprinted here with the kind permission of Triumph Books.

On January 25, 1990, I was sitting meditating, as I usually do at six o'clock, on the verandah of my hut; and suddenly, without any warning, a terrific force came and hit me on the head. It seemed like a sort of sledgehammer. Everything seemed like a television screen before the picture is focused. Just everything was like this. Then this force seemed to be dragging me out of the chair. It was coming from the left and pulling me out of my chair. It came suddenly, absolutely unexpected, without any warning. It was very scary, really. I managed to crawl onto the bed. I think I was breathing very heavily. Christudas came about an hour afterward. I lost count of time. He found me there, and then the news went around.

For the next week, I'm told, I didn't speak at all. I can't recall anything in detail. I don't know what happened during that week. There was a period of blankness. Then I began to come around. I woke up one night at about one o'clock, and I thought I was going to die. Everybody thought I was going to die. I decided to prepare for death, so I said the prayers, the normal prayers, and invoked the angels and so on, and waited for death. Nothing happened. Then, after an hour or two, Christudas came along and massaged me, and I began to get back to normal.

I had some breakfast, and then I felt sort of restless, disturbed, not knowing quite what was happening. The inspiration came suddenly again to surrender to the Mother. It was quite unexpected: "Surrender to the Mother." And so somehow I made a surrender to the Mother. Then I had an experience of overwhelming love. Waves of love sort of flowed into me. Judy Walter, my great friend, was watching. Friends were watching beside me all the time. I called out to her, "I'm being overwhelmed by love."

It was an extraordinary experience. Psychologically, I think, it was the breakthrough to the feminine. I was very masculine and patriarchal and had been developing the *animus*, the left brain, all this time. Now the right brain—the feminine, the phonic power, the earth power—came and hit me. It opened up the whole dimension of the feminine, of the earth, and so on. When I thought of surrendering to the Mother, it was certainly Mary, because I often say the "Hail Mary," but also it was more the Black Madonna that came into my mind. The mother who is mother of the earth as well as the heavens— Mother Nature, as a whole. I also thought of my own mother, and motherhood in general.

This was really the opening of a totally new dimension to me. I can see how growing up in a patriarchal society, and living all this time so much from the intellect, this [other] side had been suppressed. Now it simply came up like this. It was very violent at first, like something that hits you on the head; but then it is extremely loving. It comes and embraces you. So this was a wonderful experience, and it's gone on ever since.

What I understood this to mean, after a time, was that the left brain and the whole rational system had been knocked down, and the right brain and the intuitive understanding, the sympathetic mind, had been opened up. The left brain keeps going all the time, but the right brain is always in control. I got this sense of *advaita*, nonduality. The divisions between things broke away, and everything was flowing into everything else.

Today I still see the divisions, but I feel differently about people and things: It's all one, in a sense. And I have never lost the sense that all the diversities are contained in the one. This has become more and more my understanding.

Advaita does not mean "one" in the sense of eliminating all differences. The differences are present in the one in a mysterious way. They are not separated anymore, and yet they are there. To me, this is extremely important. When we go to a deeper level of consciousness, we should not lose the diversity of things and their individuality. On the contrary, the diversity, the multiplicity, is taken up into the unity. It cannot be put into words properly, and it cannot be explained rationally. It is simply an experience of *advaita*. The more one reads from the Hindu or the Buddhist or the Taoist or the Christian mystics, the more one realizes that this nonduality has been the great discovery beyond the rational mind with all its dualities of good and evil, light and darkness, black and white, conscious and unconscious, male and female. All these divisions are there, but they are contained in a unity. That is the important thing. . . .

The chaos is in God. Creation is chaos. From out of the depths of the Divine Mystery, the whole of creation comes forth, and it's not simply the intelligible world, as Plato and others would have thought. God is not simply in the light, in the intelligible world, in the rational order. God is in the darkness, in the womb, in the Mother, in the chaos from which the order comes. So the chaos is in God, we could say, and that is why discovering the darkness is so important. We tend to reject it as evil and as negative and so on, but the darkness is the womb of life. Yet we are always trying to discover how to relate the opposites. You cannot dismiss one or the other. You have to be open to the *coincidencia oppositorum*, the coincidence of opposites. That is the secret.

There is always order in chaos. And the more one discovers the order—the *rita*, the rhythm of the universe—the more one discovers that it is the chaos which is behind it all. And so we try to bring the chaos and the order together. This does not mean eliminating the chaos. We see this in the movement in science today. Behind all the order is chaotic movement that cannot be described or visualized or even mathematically examined. It is something really beyond the human mind, and yet the whole order of the universe is coming out of that chaos. I think that enlightenment is the union of this divine reality with the chaos of life, of nature, of matter, of the world. One is trying always to relate to the physical universe and all the confusions of life. The two are not something to be dismissed, but are integral to the whole state of understanding. . . .

Bibliography

Baigent, Michael, Richard Leigh, and Henry Lincoln. *Holy Blood, Holy Grail*. New York: Dell, 1983.

Baltazar, Eulalio R. *The Dark Center: A Process Theology of Blackness*. New York: Paulist, 1973.

Barber, Benjamin. *Jihad Verses McWorld: How Globalism and Tribalism Are Reshaping Our World*. New York: Ballantine, 1996.

Bedi, Anjula. *Gods and Goddesses of India*. Mumbai: Eeshwar/Business Publications Inc., 1998.

Bernstein, Jerome S. *Power and Politics: The Psychology of Soviet-American Partnership*. Boston: Shambhala, 1989.

Berry, Thomas. *The Dream of the Earth*. San Francisco: Sierra Club Books, 1990.

———. *The Great Work*. New York: Bell Tower, 1999.

Birnbaum, Lucia Chiavola. *Dark Mother: African Origins and Godmothers*. New York: Authors Choice Books, 2001.

Blackmur, R. P. *Henry Adams*. New York: Harcourt Brace Jovanovich, 1980.

Bonhoeffer, Dietrich. *Letters and Papers from Prison*. New York: Macmillan, 1981.

Boswell, John. *Christianity, Tolerance, and Homosexuality*. Chicago: University of Chicago Press, 1980.

Bower, Bruce. "Inside Violent Worlds: Political Conflict and Terror Look Different Up Close and Local." *Science News* 158, no. 6, August 5, 2000: 88-90.

Brandenburg, Jim. *Chased by the Light*. Chanhassen, MN: NorthWord Press, 1998.

Butoh. http://www.artandculture.com/cgi-bin/WebObjects/ACLive.woa/wa/ movement?id=891

Chenu, M. D. *Nature, Man and Society in the Twelfth Century*. Chicago: University of Chicago Press, 1957.

Chödron, Pema. *When Things Fall Apart: Heart Advice for Difficult Times.* Boston & London: Shambhala, 1997.

Craine, Renata. *Hildegard of Bingen: Prophet of the Cosmic Christ.* New York: Crossword Publishing, 1957.

Cross, T. P. and C. H. Slover. *Ancient Irish Tales.* New York: Henry Holt, 1936.

D'Arbois de Jubainville, H. D. *The Irish Mythological Cycle and Celtic Mythology.* R. I. Best, trans., 1903. New York: Lemma Publishing, 1970.

Deep Sea, Deep Secrets, www.discovery.com, September 1998.

De la Huerta, Christian. *Coming Out Spirituality: The Next Step.* New York: Jeremy Tarcher, 1999.

Diagnostic and Statistical Manual of Mental Disorders, 4th Edition. Washington, DC: American Psychiatric Association, 1994.

Eckel, Mike. "Fury and Fame Swallow Janet McKenzie and Her Painting." South Burlington, VT: *The Bennington Banner*/Associated Press, April 29, 2000.

England: Jason Aaronson, 1986.

Edinger, Edward F. *Anatomy of the Psyche: Alchemical Symbolism in Psychotherapy.* LaSalle, IL: Open Court Publishing, 1985.

Eigen, Michael. *The Psychotic Core.* Northvale, NJ and London, Euripides. *Medea and Other Plays.* London: Penguin Books, 1963.

Fox, Matthew. *Meditations with Meister Eckhart.* Santa Fe: Bear & Co., 1982.

————. *Passion for Creation: The Earth-Honoring Spirituality of Meister Eckhart.* Rochester, VT: Inner Traditions, 2000.

————. *The Reinvention of Work.* San Francisco: HarperSanFrancisco, 1995.

————. *Sins of the Spirit, Blessings of the Flesh.* New York: Harmony, 1999.

Freud, Sigmund. *Standard Edition of the Complete Psychology of Sigmund Freud.* London: Hogarth Press, 1953-1974.

Gablik, Suzi. *The Reenchantment of Art.* New York: Thames and Hudson, 1991.

Galland, China. *Longing for Darkness: Tara and the Black Madonna.* New York: Viking/Penguin, 1990/1991.

Gantz, Jeffrey. *Early Irish Myths and Sagas.* London and New York: Penguin Books, 1981.

Gebara, Ivone and Maria Clara Bingemer. *Mary: Mother of God, Mother of the Poor.* Maryknoll, NY: Orbis Books, 1989.

Ghiselin, Brewster, ed. *The Creative Process.* New York: Mentor Books, 1952.

Gimbutas, Marija. *The Language of the Goddess.* San Francisco: Harper and Row, 1989.

Gray, Elizabeth A. *Cath Maige Tuired: The Second Battle of Mag Tuired.* London: Irish Texts Society, 1982.

Grinberg, Leon, Dario Sor, and E. Tabak de Bianchedi. *Introduction to the Work of Bion.* New York: Jason Aaronson, 1977.

Gustafson, Fred. *The Black Madonna.* Boston: Sigo Press, 1990.

Gwynn, Edward. *The Metrical Dindsenchas,* vol. 2, 1903. Dublin: Institute for Advanced Studies, 1941.

Hacker, Carol "AMHCA Helps the Healing of Desert Storm." *The Advocate* 14, no. 7, March, 1991.

———. "AMHCA Responds to the Traumas of Desert Storm." *The Advocate* 14, no. 6, February, 1991.

Harvey, Andrew. *The Return of the Mother.* Berkeley, CA: Frog, Ltd. 1995.

———. *The Way of Passion: A Celebration of Rumi.* Berkeley: Frog, Ltd., 1994.

Herzog, Edgar. *Psyche and Death.* New York: G. P. Putnam and Sons, 1966.

Hill, Gareth. *The Masculine and the Feminine: The Natural Flow of Opposites in the Psyche.* Boston: Shambhala, 1995.

Ierodiakonou, C. S. "The Effect of the Threat of War on Neurotic Patients in Psychotherapy." *American Journal of Psychotherapy* 24, no. 4, October, 1970: 643 *ff.*

Jung, C. G. *The Archetypes and the Collective Unconscious. The Collected Works of C. G. Jung,* vol. 9i. Michael Fordham, ed. R. F. C. Hull, trans. Bollingen Series XX. Princeton: Princeton University Press, 1969.

———. *Letters I: 1906-1950.* Gerhard Adler, Aniela Jaffé, eds. R.F.C. Hull, trans. Princeton: Princeton University Press, 1973.

———. *Mysterium Coniunctionis. The Collected Works of C. G. Jung,* vol. 14. R. F. C. Hull, trans. Bollingen Series XX. Princeton: Princeton University Press, 1970.

———. "A Psychological Approach to the Dogma of the Trinity,"

(1942/48). In *Psychology and Religion: West and East. The Collected Works of C. G. Jung,* vol. II, Bollingen Series XX. Princeton: Princeton University Press, 1958/1969.

———. *Psychology and Alchemy. The Collected Works of C. G. Jung.* vol. 12, R. F. C. Hull, trans. Bollingen Series XX. Princeton: Princeton University Press, 1968.

———. *Psychology and Religion: West and East. The Collected Works of C. G. Jung,* vol. 11. R. F. C. Hull, trans. Bollingen Series XX. New York: Pantheon Books, 1963.

———. *The Symbolic Life. The Collected Works of C. G. Jung,* vol. 18. William McGuire, ed., R. F. C. Hull, trans. Bollingen Series XX. Princeton: Princeton University Press, 1977.

———. *Two Essays in Analytical Psychology. The Collected Works of C. G. Jung,* vol. 7. R. F. C. Hull, trans. Bollingen Series XX. Princeton: Princeton University Press, 1972.

Kalsched, Donald. *The Inner World of Trauma: Archetypal Defenses of the Personal Spirit.* London and New York: Routledge, 1996.

Keen, Sam. *Faces of the Enemy: Reflections of the Hostile Imagination.* San Francisco: Harper & Row, 1986.

Kinsella, Thomas, ed. *The Tain.* Translated from the Irish epic *Tain Bo Cuailnge.* London: Oxford University Press/Dublin: The Dolmen Press, 1970.

Kinsley, David. *Hindu Goddesses, Visions of the Divine Feminine in the Hindu Religious Tradition.* Berkeley: University of California Press, 1986.

Koltov, Barbara Black. *The Book of Lilith.* Berwick, ME: Nicolas-Hays, 1986.

Macy, Joanna. "Interview." *New Age Journal,* January/February, 1991: 36.

Masson, J. *The Assault on Truth: Freud's Suppression of the Seduction Theory.* New York: Farrar, Straus & Giroux, 1984.

McKinney-Johnson, Eloise. "Egypt's Isis: The Original Black Madonna." *Journal of African Civilizations,* April, 1984, p. 66.

Neruda, Pablo. *Fully Empowered.* Alastair Reid, trans. New York: Farrar, Straus and Giroux, 1967.

Neumann, Erich. "Fear of the Feminine." *Quadrant* 19, no. 1, 1986: 28.

———. *The Great Mother: An Analysis of the Archetype.* Princeton: Princeton University Press, 1955.

———. "The Psyche and the Transformation of the Reality Planes." *Spring,* 1956: 81–111.

Norris, Kathleen. *Little Girls in Church*. Pittsburgh: University of Pittsburgh Press, 1995.

Ogden, Thomas H. *The Primitive Edge of Experience*. Northvale, NJ: Jason Aaronson, 1989.

Osmond, Humphrey, Miriam Siegler, and Richard Smoke. "Typology Revisited: A New Perspective." *Psychological Perspectives* (Fall 1977): 206–219.

Patai, Raphael. *The Hebrew Goddess*. Detroit: Wayne State University Press, 1967.

Pereira, Filomena Maria. *Lilith: The Edge of Forever*. Irving, TX: Ide House, 1998.

Perera, Sylvia B. "Ritual Integration of Aggression in Psychotherapy." Murray Stein and Nathan Schwartz-Salant, eds. *The Borderline Personality in Analysis*. Wilmette, IL: Chiron, 1988.

Racker, Heinrich. *Transference and Countertransference*. New York: International Universities Press, 1968.

Ress, Mary Judith. "After Five Centuries of Mixing, Who Are We? Walking with Our Dark Grandmother's Feet." Rosemary Radford Ruether, ed., *Women Healing the Earth: Third World Women on Ecology, Feminism, and Religion*. Maryknoll, NY: Orbis Books, 1996.

Rosen, David H. *Transforming Depression: Healing the Soul through Creativity*. Berwick, ME: Nicolas-Hays, 2002.

Ross, Anne. *Pagan Celtic Britain: Studies in Iconography and Tradition*. London: Routledge and Kegan Paul, 1967.

Sardello, Robert. "Soul Tasks of the Coming Age." *Common Boundary* (November/December 1992): 42.

Sjoestedt, Marie-Louise. *Gods and Heroes of the Celts*. Berkeley: Turtle Island Foundation, 1982.

Starbird, Margaret. *The Woman with the Alabaster Jar*. Rochester, VT: Bear & Company, 1993.

Stevens, Anthony. *The Roots of War: A Jungian Perspective*. New York: Paragon House, 1989.

Stewart, Louis H. "Work in Progress. Affect and Archetype: A Contribution to a Comprehensive Theory of the Structure of the Psyche." Murray Stein and Nathan Schwartz-Salant, eds. *The Body in Analysis*. Wilmette, IL: Chiron, 1986.

Swimme, Brian. *The Hidden Heart of the Cosmos*. Maryknoll, NY: Orbis Books, 1996.

Swimme, Brian and Thomas Berry. *The Universe Story.* San Francisco: HarperSanFrancisco, 1992.

Swindells, John, ed. *A Human Search: Bede Griffiths Reflects on His Life.* Liguori, MO: Triumph Books, 1997.

Teilhard de Chardin, Pierre. *Hymn of the Universe.* New York: Harper and Row, 1965.

"Universal Prayer: Confession of Sins and Asking Forgiveness." http://www.vatican.va/news_services/liturgy/documents/ns_lit_doc_20000312_prayer-day-pardon_en.html

Von Franz, Marie-Louise. *The Cat: A Tale of Feminine Redemption.* Toronto: Inner City Books, 1999.

———. *Creation Myths.* Boston & London: Shambhala, 1995.

Wagner, Rojean. "The Effects of War." *The Psychiatric Times* 8, no. 3, March, 1991.

Walker, Barbara G. *The Women's Encyclopedia of Myths and Secrets.* San Francisco: Harper and Row, 1983.

Winnicott, Donald W. *The Maturational Processes and the Facilitating Environment: Studies in the Theory of Emotional Development.* New York: International Universities Press, 1965.

Wolkestein, Diane and Samuel Noah Kramer. *Innana: Queen of Heaven and Earth; Her Stories and Hymns for Sumer.* New York: Harper and Row Publishers, 1983.

Woodman, Marion. *Addiction to Perfection: The Still Unravished Bride.* Toronto: Inner City Books, 1982.

———. *The Pregnant Virgin: A Process of Psychological Transformation.* Toronto: Inner City Books, 1988.

Woodruff, Sue. *Meditations with Mechtild of Magdeburg.* Sante Fe: Bear & Co., 1982.

www.saintmeinrad.edu/friends/history.html

Zimmer, Heinrich. *Myths and Symbols in Indian Art and Civilization.* Bollingen Series VI. Joseph Campbell, ed. New York: Pantheon Books, 1946.

Zohar. Translated by Harry Sperling and Maurice Simon. London: The Soncino Press, 1984.

Index